Illuminating the Shadow

Also by the Same Author...

The Healer Within

The Keys to the Temple

Working With Earth Energies

Develop Your Intuition and Psychic Power

The Frog Prince (Poem)

Healing Your Ancestral Patterns

Illuminating the Shadow

Transmuting the Dark Side of the Psyche

David Furlong

Copyright © 2016 David Furlong

The moral right of the author has been asserted.

Apart from any fair dealing for the purposes of research or private study, or criticism or review, as permitted under the Copyright, Designs and Patents Act 1988, this publication may only be reproduced, stored or transmitted, in any form or by any means, with the prior permission in writing of the publishers, or in the case of reprographic reproduction in accordance with the terms of licences issued by the Copyright Licensing Agency. Enquiries concerning reproduction outside those terms should be sent to the publishers.

Atlanta Books
Myrtles, Como Road,
Malvern, Worcestershire, WR14 2TH
www.atlanta-association.com

ISBN 978 0955979 569

British Library Cataloguing in Publication Data.
A catalogue record for this book is available from the British Library.

Typeset in 11pt Aldine401 BT by Troubador Publishing Ltd, Leicester, UK
Printed and bound by CPI Group (UK) Ltd, Croydon, CR0 4YY

MIX
Paper from responsible sources
FSC® C013604

To Frida

Acknowledgements

I wish to thank all those who have helped to formulate the ideas contained within this book and in particular the colleagues who have worked with me in the exploration of the *shadow*. In this context I particularly wish to thank Frida Siton, Kathryn Logan, Lily Furlong, Fay Rodrigues and Ced Jackson for their comments and contributions. I also wish to thank Dr Terence Palmer for the Foreword and for making many valuable and supportive comments on the original manuscript. Grateful thanks go to my editor Jane Struthers for checking and editing the final manuscript and making valuable contributions along the way.

I acknowledge the valuable contributions into this field by Jeremiah Abrams, Deepak Chopra, Debbie Ford, Robert A Johnson, Marianne Williamson, Tom Zinser and Connie Zweig.

Finally, I wish to express my gratitude to Dr Carl Jung for his insights and pioneering work in the understanding of the *shadow*.

Acknowledgment and thanks are given to the Findhorn Foundation for permission to the use the text from R. Ogilvie Crombie quoted from pp.113-115, Chapter 4 'ROC', from *The Findhorn Garden Story* © The Findhorn Foundation, 1976; 4th edition published by Findhorn Press in 2008.

The front cover illustration is based on two statues by Jacob Epstein (1880-1959). The statue of St Michael can be found on the east wall of Coventry Cathedral. The statue of Lucifer is held in the Birmingham Museum and Art Gallery and is reproduced here with their permission.

Contents

Acknowledgements	vi
Foreword by Dr Terence Palmer	ix
Introduction	xiii

SECTION 1 – Illuminating the Shadow

Chapter 1 – What is the Shadow?	3
Chapter 2 – The Shadow in Films, TV and Video Games	21
Chapter 3 – The Shadow in Literature and Drama	38
Chapter 4 – The Shadow in Mythology	55
Chapter 5 – The Shadow in Metaphor and Fairy Tale	84

SECTION 2 – The Shadow's Manifestation

Chapter 6 – The Cosmic Shadow	107
Chapter 7 – The Personal Shadow	133
Chapter 8 – The Collective Shadow	159

SECTION 3 – Transmuting and Healing the Dark Side of the Psyche

Chapter 9 – The Higher-Self and the Shadow	195
Chapter 10 – Sub-Personalities, Archetypes and the Shadow	225
Chapter 11 – Soul Wounds and the Shadow	249
Chapter 12 – Into the Light	276
Conclusion	288

References and Bibliography	292
Useful Addresses	313
Index	315

Foreword

Whenever I read something that shines a light, cutting through the darkness of ignorance, I am reminded of the little boy in Hans Christian Andersen's folk tale of *The Emperor's New Clothes*. When everyone else was extolling the magnificence of the Emperor's new clothes, one little boy in the crowd could see through the false belief, planted in the collective mind of the crowd, and he could see that the Emperor was, in reality, naked. The trick played by the designers of the Emperor's new clothes was the *suggestion* that only the wise could appreciate them and those who couldn't were stupid. No one wants to be seen as stupid or lacking vision of what is real, so a false sense of reality is created from the need to be accepted by social consensus. Hans Christian Andersen was an insightful and creative storyteller and this particular story illustrates, in an amusing way, how society (that is, a very large group of people) can be misled by false suggestions and hidden agendas.

Modern science *suggests* to us that the only reality is the three-dimensional physical universe, quite simply because that is all that material science can see, weigh and measure. Popular television documentaries fronted by charismatic presenters such as Brian Cox, Richard Dawkins and Robert Winston reinforce this world view and anything that does not fit with the prevailing mechanistic perspective is rejected, denied or even ridiculed. But the day-to-day experiences of ordinary people, as they go about their business, dictate that the material world is not all there is, and that the physical sciences cannot accommodate or explain a very wide range of such experiences. This has created the demand for an expansion in scientific enquiry that includes the 'transpersonal' of subjective experience. Research into the nature of consciousness and what has become known as 'psi', which was started in the late nineteenth century under the name of 'psychical' phenomena, is now becoming fashionable. Twentieth-century discoveries in the field of quantum mechanics, coupled with the development of research methods in neuro-imaging, mean that science now has an 'expanded natural' framework for investigating phenomena that the physical sciences were previously unable to accommodate or explain.

David Furlong's book, *Illuminating the Shadow*, is one of those books that shines a light through false perceptions and the rigid ideology of the physical sciences, and shouts loudly, 'Look, the Emperor has no clothes.' The true value of this book, in my own humble opinion, is that it shouts very loudly about the concept of 'denial' at the subconscious levels of the individual and the wider collective of society and the physical sciences in particular. David takes us by the hand and, with careful, logical deduction that is grounded in practical experience, leads us through the darkness of ignorance and false beliefs into the realms of the *shadow* of human consciousness, and teaches us how to recognize and deal with it in pragmatic and effective ways.

The world is experiencing a series of crises, including the expansion of violent fundamentalism in Africa and the Middle East, and the excruciating agony of refugees fleeing war, economic deprivation and ethnic persecution. Desperate people with families are drowning in the Mediterranean as they try to breach the political defences of Fortress Europe and in the east there is a new wave of 'Boat People' adrift on the open sea while eastern countries refuse to accommodate them. 'Where is humanity?' we may rightly ask. Closer to home, in the UK the number of families needing help from food banks is increasing as more families are being made homeless by an economic system that rewards exploitation and punishes the needy. The UK's NHS is suffering pressure from increased costs, increased demand for its services from an ageing and ever-expanding population, and increased stress and sickness within its own ranks. There is a huge elephant in the room of the NHS – it doesn't know how to deal with the stress it creates for itself and it doesn't know how to treat its patients who have any kind of mental or emotional sickness. During the 2015 General Election all political parties promised more money for mental health services, but no one knows where the money is going to come from. Furthermore, if more money were to be made available for the treatment of mental illness, it would without doubt be lost in a black hole of purchasing more drugs and training more doctors to administer them. A fundamental truth is that to continue to do the same thing will always produce the same results. Therefore, if you want a different outcome you have to apply a different solution. Failure to recognize this simple truth is another form of denial. This is delusional thinking, and when a government (irrespective of political orientation) acts in this way it is delusional thinking on a grand scale that will continue to have disastrous consequences.

David Furlong's book is intended as a self-help manual for those with the intelligence to recognize that there is a problem to be solved, whether they are sufferer themselves or therapists with the agenda of helping others. It is a great shame that the work of self-help manuals and self-motivated therapists is not integrated into mainstream medicine. It is my own firm belief that this book ought to be at the top of the 'essential reading' list of all students of psychiatry and clinical psychology. But much more than that, the lessons that David Furlong is teaching in this book should be used as a standard in therapeutic technique for solving a range of mental and emotional problems that mainstream medicine has been unable to treat with any degree of efficacy to date. The time has come for mental health services to change the way they go about their business and aim for better outcomes at lower costs, for the benefit of individuals who need help and an NHS that needs help too. May this book be a significant contribution to a change in direction for mental health services in western medical practice.

Terence Palmer PhD
Author of *The Science of Spirit Possession*

Introduction

The beginnings and ends of shadow lie between the light and darkness and may be infinitely diminished and infinitely increased. Shadow is the means by which bodies display their form. The forms of bodies could not be understood in detail but for shadow.

Leonardo da Vinci

Science tells us that 95 per cent of the universe is composed of dark matter of which we know practically nothing. We all have a 'dark side', which Swiss psychologist Carl Jung called the *shadow*. Fortunately for us, while the majority of people have given little thought to this aspect of their psyche, its manifestation can be detected through a number of simple methods and therefore it need not remain hidden, like the dark matter of the universe. This book sets out to promote this fascinating and little understood aspect of our being, showing that its realization can profoundly change our lives when brought into the light of conscious awareness.

Your *shadow* self holds two primary components. The first is those aspects of your psyche that are either unacknowledged or not yet manifested within you; in other words, everything that is part of your optimum potential within this lifetime that has not yet been realized. All that you wish for yourself is part of your positive *shadow*. It forms your inspiration and ambition for all that you hold in store for yourself in your current life. It contains the spur that leads to greatness; to discovering who and what you truly are and, from there, finding a sense of balance and fulfilment. That to which we aspire, that of which we dream, sits within our *shadow* self, until that moment when those aspirations have been fully realized. Their accomplishment allows us to bathe in the recognition of what can be achieved by the human spirit. It is a step on the path towards wholeness, through a process that Carl Jung called 'individuation'.

What is interesting about this paradigm is the suggestion that this is a never-ending process. For as much as you become, so the greater is your potential to become. As we shall see, this book challenges the concept that your consciousness is extinguished at death and posits the idea that this process of growing and becoming is eternal.

The second element of the shadow consists of those parts of your being that have been repressed or rejected. The components of the repressed *shadow* generally sit within the subconscious self, leaking out to influence and manipulate our lives in many different ways. Until healed, we can never escape their influence. In some people, the negative shadow can be made manifest in a range of malign and evil acts that are part of the criminal fraternity. Paradoxically, the *shadow*, when explored, and its elements understood and mastered, provides a golden seam of insight and self-knowledge of inestimable value.

For shadows to exist there must be light. Jung suggested this light is the light of conscious awareness. This book takes this concept one stage further and suggests a greater light can be accessed – the light of our soul or spiritual self. In other words, the light that comes from a higher-dimensional aspect of our consciousness. As we shall see, this element is all-important when trying to understand the underlying patterns that cause us to be who and what we are. It provides profound insights into the traumas and blockages within the self, whether these stem from this current life or possibly from a previous experience. It can also give insight into the expression of the negative *shadow* that manifests through what we might consider as acts of evil. It contains the overview of all that we have ever been, both physically and spiritually.

Accessing a Higher Dimension of the Self

From many years working as a therapist, helping clients come to terms with their own personal *shadows*, I have come to appreciate the significance and power of this higher aspect of the psyche to illuminate and heal that which has been repressed, buried or rejected. We all have a magnificent source of understanding within us if we can but open up to its full expression. The *shadows* within the self fly before this greater luminance as its searchlight beams seek out those hidden elements that need to be understood, accepted and healed. This book will show in simple ways how this profound part of our being can be accessed, and its wisdom drawn upon, to assist all aspects of our life.

As already stated, our *shadow* contains two distinct elements, which are sometimes termed the 'positive' and 'negative' *shadows*. The positive *shadow* retains our full potential as a human being; all that we might consciously aspire to within our lives, and probably a great deal more, for how many of us truly achieve our full potential? The negative *shadow* holds that which causes us pain. This is why dealing with its elements can be very challenging. The pain inevitably stems from two distinct sources – our *fear* and our *self-loathing*; these are the elements of our nature or psyche that we tend to ignore, avoid or reject. When this happens, these repressed parts are then projected out onto those around us.

The Projected Shadow

Pause for a moment and consider your friends, workmates and family members. Amongst them, who do you get on with and who causes you some form of distress, aggravation or irritation? Those who fall into the latter category will inevitably hold some part of your negative *shadow*, for that which we dislike in others reflects that which we dislike in ourselves. On the other hand, what we admire or extol in others can also reflect that which we honour and aspire to as individuals, for all elements at this level contain a dynamic that seeks balance or homeostasis.

The Balance of Opposites

To understand this principle we need to comprehend how opposites flow through everything. The computer, which I am using to type this document, with all its amazing complexity, is based upon the principle of whether a circuit is 'on' or 'off'. This essentially simple concept, and its flow through life, has taxed the minds of philosophers and scientists through the ages. The insights that stem from this fundamental law have probably found their highest level of elucidation within the ancient Chinese philosophy of Taoism, the origin of the concept of yin and yang. The Tao Te Ching (the Way and its Power) tells how the universe and everything in it works in a flux of balance between dark and light, positive and negative, yin and yang, at every level from the individual through to the entire cosmos. To the Chinese sages, all life, everything that exists, was held together by the weaving of these two fundamental principles. At a human level, we can see this expression in whether we are male or female. This gender manifestation has its inner counterpoint in what Jung called the 'anima' and the 'animus'. In other words, a feminine constituent or anima exists within every man and a masculine constituent or animus within every woman. What does this mean in practice? By learning to understand and balance the corresponding polarities within the self, we can begin to find wholeness. This, in turn, can lead to a sense of peace, happiness and fulfilment. The challenge is how to balance these dualistic elements of the psyche.

Polarity elements can regularly be evidenced in conversation. By listening to what people say about themselves, or by considering what you say about yourself, you can witness this dynamic in action. For as soon as I make any statement about myself, the opposite potentially sits within my *shadow*. If I affirm that I am an honest upright citizen, I need to acknowledge the potential dishonest liar within me. If I do not, and I reject this potential, then someone, somewhere, will carry this dynamic for me. One can almost guarantee that when a politician states 'I will not resign', he or she will be gone within a few days. You can also be sure that the friend or acquaintance who is always complaining about a particular theme or a person's behaviour, is highlighting some part of themselves, which they are unable to acknowledge or own. Periodically, we are all caught in this process, for this is how we learn to discern our own *shadows*, by seeing them projected onto the screen of other people's lives and seeing others reflect these patterns back to us. As the saying goes, 'We see things not as they are, but as we are', which is otherwise known as 'mirroring' or 'projection'.

If you think about what specifically upsets you about your friends, colleagues or acquaintances, you can be certain that those are the same aspects which you reject or deny within yourself. As soon as you have a negative emotional reaction or charge, in any situation or circumstance, you know that your *shadow* is being triggered. Many of my clients have struggled with this simple idea. The individual who finds it hard to express or acknowledge their anger will inevitably find himself or herself surrounded by angry people; their *shadow* seeps out to affect or infect others. For we are drawn, inexorably, like moths to the flame, to those who express the elements we deny within ourselves. The magnetic attraction in these situations can be all-powerful. It is only by switching the current and balancing the polarity that we can learn to stand free of these patterns.

The Shadow within the Collective

Within wider society and cultures, we see this same dynamic being continually expressed. For example, the anger and enmity between the Israelis and the Palestinians is a classic, yet very sad, expression of this powerful patterning. Both sides project out onto the other their unresolved, unintegrated passions. The Israelis claim that Hamas is a 'terrorist' organization, yet then uses, in the name of self-defence, 'terror' tactics through bombs and bullets, regardless of life, to try to control the inhabitants of Gaza, seemingly forgetting their own Jewish history when they too, as a people, were the scapegoats of the Nazi regime. All governments and peoples of this world can be guilty of these tendencies, for these powerful energies sit within both the individual and the collective.

The way forward, in these cases, has to be through dialogue. It is imperative that we do not demonize those who we see as our adversaries. We need to recognize them as human beings, with their own sets of grievances and agendas. We have to try to understand them, to walk in their moccasins, so that we can reach some level of rapprochement. The troubles in Northern Ireland were finally brought to a close by the Hillsborough Accord, demonstrating that it is possible to find agreement and consensus as a step towards peace and reconciliation. Military force should only be used as a very last resort, when confronting the destructive or malign *shadow*, and then only to protect the rights of individuals and peoples so that they too are able to live in freedom.

Personal Interest in the Shadow

My own interest in the *shadow* was born from two sources. The first was my simple desire to try to understand myself, particularly when things went awry within my life. There is nothing like a good crisis to make one take stock, to look at what might be going on, at a deeper level. Throughout my life I have been aware of a spiritual guidance that I could access for help and advice. More often than not, my *ego* got in the way or blocked out these sage whisperings. I found I had to look deep within to try to understand why I acted or did not act in particular ways. In trying to understand why I felt hurt, sad or angry in certain situations I came to recognize that this reflected the hurt, sad or angry parts of me that then linked to past traumas. Initially I saw these aspects as simple psychological states. I now recognize them as real personalities, residing within my psyche, with their own feelings, perceptions and free will.

When I initially contacted these sub-personalities, which is the term I now use, they were locked in the trauma that had brought them into existence. The four-year-old child was still being beaten by his mother; the six-year-old was still grieving for his pet dog, somehow thinking he was responsible for its death, and so on. By learning how to drop into a semi-trance state, I was able to dip below the level of my normal waking conscious self, to connect with these traumatized parts of my being and then begin to heal them. In this context, learning meditative exercises can be valuable, because the process that leads to inner exploration is not dissimilar.

My inner guidance used to tell me that my inner world was every bit as vast and peopled as my outer world. I am slowly starting to grasp the significance of this statement. I am in constant amazement, when working with clients, at how their higher selves or their higher power brings forward to their conscious minds some character that holds their pain and suffering. These psychic beings can take many forms, initially reflecting back our perception of them. They can be ugly, hideous and loathsome or vast and terrifying. Our initial response can be to recoil in horror and to reject them. In one case, a client became aware of a huge slug-like repulsive monster confronting her. By learning to dialogue with it, to send it light, love and healing, the outer form dissolved and underneath she discovered a distraught seven-year-old child, traumatized by having been called 'fat and ugly' by her father. The pain of this split-off feeling needed to be reintegrated within the client's psyche so the child could begin to find a new sense of peace and contentment.

The process does not always entail seeing inner monsters or demons. On many occasions, simply re-establishing a connection with the traumatized child is enough. The child needs to be rescued and its emotional feelings reabsorbed within the adult psyche, assuring the child of one's love for it and affirming that it no longer needs to relive these harrowing situations. Most of us have traumatized children, or child sub-personalities, waiting to be rescued.

Therefore, the first reason for delving into my *shadow* has been for my own self-healing and desire for wholeness and in this exploration hopefully to be a better practitioner in assisting my clients in their therapy. The second and equally important element has been the recognition that we are all part of the collective psyche of humanity. While I might not be directly experiencing the traumas going on in different parts of the globe I am, nevertheless, linked to them. Their pain, in one sense, is my pain, and in recognition of this fact it is very easy either to divorce oneself from watching the news or to be sucked into the strong emotions which can be easily invoked. It is possible then to feel a sense of outrage and hatred towards those who are creating these circumstances. Our thoughts have energy, and sending thoughts of anger and hatred only empowers the collective negative *shadow*, which is why Christ implored us to learn to love those who do us harm.

We cannot suppress our emotions, but in acknowledging them we can then discipline ourselves to send out thoughts of healing and balance to whatever situation is going on. If the world could accept and integrate its own *shadow* projections, conflicts could be resolved peacefully. To change the world, as the sages say, we first need to change our selves.

Consciousness

The word 'consciousness' is used more than a hundred times in this work and is therefore worthy of a definition. It is defined here as that which is 'alive' and able to respond to its environment in a constructive and meaningful way. Woven into this definition is the implication of free-will choices, no matter how small or limited. In other words, the responses are not just mechanical but have opportunities for variation and optimal selection. The term 'alive' pertains not just to the physical manifestations of Earth's smallest organisms, such as viruses and bacterium, through to the most consciously aware, like us. It also includes the suggestion, based on evidence from a variety of reliable scientific sources, that consciousness can exist independent of the physical body and is an inherent construct of the universe.

The Sections of the Book

This book falls into three sections. The first, Illuminating the Shadow, covers the background to shadow work, starting with Jung's original definitions. It explores in detail the way this energy flows through us artistically, finding outlets in film, literature, mythology and fairy tales. For those wishing to get to the meat of the book, Chapters 2 to 5 could be lightly skipped through, although they do contain a number of activity exercises that provide insights into your own *shadow*.

The second section of the book, The Shadow's Manifestation, explores the way the *shadow* operates as a universal principle and then more specifically both within us and within the collective. This section starts by considering the concept of the cosmic *shadow*, and argues the case that this is a fundamental part of Creation. Through this process, new insights are given into the nature of the universe. As part of this chapter, the atheist view of life is challenged on the basis that this is not congruent with an ultimate expression of evolution, which sees consciousness as a fundamental part of the process as systems grow in complexity. At this level the cosmos only makes sense if consciousness is not limited to the body but goes on 'experiencing' after the cessation of physical life.

The section then explores the nature of the personal and collective *shadow*, seeing its reflection in many areas of our life. Within this context, the nature of 'evil' is considered first within humanity and then explored at a spiritual or cosmological level. For example, why does mythology contain *shadow* beings, such as Lucifer, whose aim would appear to encapsulate all that is anti God? It explores the role of darkness within the collective psyche of humanity and the ways we can learn to differentiate easily between right and wrong.

The last section of the book, Transmuting and Healing the Dark Side of the Psyche, looks at the many practical steps we can take to understand and integrate our *shadow* selves. This section contains a variety of self-help exercises, which can be played out individually or within a group. Once recognized it becomes easy to discern when our *shadow* is getting in the way and then to do whatever is necessary to help release the blocks that stop us reaching our full potential. The two major issues that we all have to address is how to confront our fears, which generally stem from traumatized, split-off, bits of our psyche and secondly how to redeem those parts that hold our guilt and shame. To heal these parts we need, above all, to learn how to be loving and forgiving of ourselves.

Within this process, there is the larger aspiration of realizing our dreams. To be able to work through those parts of the self that appear to limit us. However bad or inadequate we feel about any subject, the opposite element has to be part of us. If I perceive myself as a hopeless dancer, somewhere inside resides a budding ballet star or the 'lord of the dance'.

Achieving greatness comes through belief and persistence. We need to evaluate what is possible against what is not. For example, at my time in life, it is very unlikely that I will ever be able to run a four-minute mile, even if I had the desire, which I do not. However, I can aspire to fulfilling my maximum potential within this present life and then take steps to achieve this ambition. Examples abound within society of individuals who have achieved their goals through dedication, self-belief and hard work. These individuals affirm that they could not have achieved what they have without the assistance of others, which leads on to one of the most important elements of this book.

Running through this third section are the methods we can use to access the powerful inner support and guidance that stems from our Higher-Self (H-S). This aspect of our being has direct connection to an insightful level of wisdom which we might call our *Spirit*. From there it can access guides, helpers and other beings of higher consciousness that can support us on our journey. Effectively, we can learn how to become our own gurus; to connect to a most profound level of empowering spiritual knowledge and understanding. It is our connection to the Divine and therefore has access to the highest level of consciousness. This element cannot come into play unless we actively seek its help. In the great mythological tales, the heroes and heroines achieved their goals by being open to, or inviting in, the help and support of others. We likewise need to call upon our higher power for insight and guidance, and to learn how to listen to the 'still small voice within' and be aware of its promptings.

This book is aimed at everyone for, as already stated, we all have a *shadow*. I have tried to weave in different elements to suit diverse minds and preferences. The book is full of references for the academically minded but also contains a number of personal anecdotes and experiences that reflect my own journey of self-discovery. If this eclectic mix causes confusion or irritation then I apologize. I have attempted in this work to reach out in the widest possible way.

The book is also directed to all those who wish to address their inner issues, to discover new insights about themselves and learn how to break some of the destructive patterns that flow through their lives. Individual crisis will often prompt a desire to look inside; it certainly did for me. However, many people whose lives seem generally balanced and fruitful could benefit from greater insight into their *shadow* selves. The golden treasures of our being are waiting to be discovered by those who have the courage and resilience to explore within. As Christ so rightly stated: 'The Kingdom of God is within' (Luke 17:21), and 'Seek ye first the kingdom ... and all else will be added unto you' (Luke 12:31).

Finally, if any part of this book produces a strong negative response or reaction, you can be sure that your *shadow* is communicating with you. Read on and you will discover the tools to gain further insights into yourself.

Shall we begin?

SECTION ONE
Illuminating the Shadow

Chapter One

What is the Shadow?

Where love rules, there is no will to power; and where power predominates, there love is lacking. The one is the shadow of the other.

Carl Jung

We cannot change anything until we accept it. Condemnation does not liberate, it oppresses.

Carl Jung

The awareness of our potential for good and evil has been part of human consciousness from ancient times. The metaphorical eating, by Adam and Eve, of the fruit of the tree of knowledge of good and evil in the Garden of Eden is one of the primary Creation stories of the Bible (Genesis 3:5-6). In ancient Egyptian belief, before being allowed to enter the realms of eternal life, the deceased soul was brought into the Hall of Judgement, presided over by Osiris, King of the Dead. There they had to recite up to forty-two negative confessions about the life they had just given up. These declarations took the form of simple statements such as 'I have done no evil against any man; I am not a murderer', and so on. Failure to provide truthful answers would entail the heart of the deceased being eaten by the Great Devourer, and their spirit cast into darkness (Geddes & Grossett, 2001: 97-101). This powerful incentive was a way of trying to ensure that people lived virtuous lives; if not, punishment would assuredly be meted out in the afterlife.

Similar ideas have found their way into other cultures and religious belief systems, such as the Christian and Islamic. This battle was not just internal, for early Christian theology portrayed an individual being influenced by good and bad angels, each vying for the human soul. The classic play *The Tragical History of the Life and Death of Dr Faustus* by Christopher Marlowe (2009) is a prime example of this inner world tussle, with Faustus selling his soul to Lucifer through the enticements of the dark angel Mephistophilis. For hundreds of years, throughout Christendom, it was widely believed that angelic or demonic beings could wrestle for human souls, inciting individuals to act one way or another, through either the temptation of worldly success or the fear of going to damnation in the afterlife. If justice for evil acts could be apportioned in the earthly life, so much the better, but, if not, a greater Judgement would ensure that no man or woman would escape from their sins.

The tussle between good and evil or the light and dark aspects of human nature have been and still are a part of our journey, so how does the concept of the *shadow* fit in?

Jung and the Shadow

The recognition that the rational mind is not the only aspect of the self that impels us to act one way or another was Sigmund Freud's great contribution to psychology, through his exploration into the unconscious or subconscious elements of the psyche. Freud was only one of a long line of distinguished thinkers, including William James and Frederic Myers (Ellenberger, 1981), who acknowledged the reality of the unseen domain of the psyche. Jung, as one of Freud's early disciples, took his mentor's ideas and slowly developed them through the course of his life. The idea of a personal *shadow* emerged gradually from Jung's writings. Although dealing with *shadow* concepts, Jung's *Psychological Types*, published in 1921, had only three references to the *shadow* (Casement, 2006:97).

According to Jung, the personal *shadow* contained all the repressed or unacceptable elements of a person's psyche, which could include anger, greed, indolence, jealousy, and so on. He recognized that an individual could have a positive *shadow* when they projected a form of hero worship onto another. However, in these cases, putting individuals onto a pedestal created the danger that eventually they would topple off. Indeed, in Jung's own life this happened spectacularly between himself and Freud when the two psychologists fell out. This highlights one of the principles understood by those ancient Chinese philosophers when they stated that pushing yang or yin to an extreme would cause it to revert to its opposite: 'When extreme, reversal is inevitable' (Liu, 2010:16). This idea can be observed in the saying, 'The darkest hour comes just before the dawn.'

Jung perceived that *shadow* elements generally stem from childhood situations, when the infant ego first starts to grapple with their surroundings. In the simplest form, the child learns to project onto their parents or their siblings what they perceive as their good (acceptable) and bad (not acceptable) parts of themselves. In some cases, the parents also collude in this process by assuming the roles of the good and bad parent. That is to say, one parent might choose always to appease while the other chastises, whether this be physically, emotionally or mentally. In growing towards adulthood these patterns become ingrained within the psyche and then go on playing themselves out in the drama of life. In the adult environment, other people, whether friends, colleagues or acquaintances, unconsciously receive these *shadow* projections, perhaps of idolization or rejection, and then act them out accordingly. This process goes on repeating itself until the individual recognizes these patterns and they are healed and reintegrated.

In another example, the child who has grown up with a sibling that has been favoured, perhaps because of their demeanour, sex or intellectual ability, will generally hold feelings of anger, hatred and jealousy towards their rival. These can be repressed within a childhood environment but this energy will inevitably leak out, in the later stages of life, with the adult being driven by feelings of suspicion and jealousy towards those close to them, thereby poisoning their relationships.

One might summarize this idea by stating that when those who have felt betrayed as a child move into adulthood they will likely be drawn, by their *shadow*, to people who will betray them; those who have been abused to abusers; those who have been emotionally rejected to those that reject, and so on. As part of a pendulum swing, individuals will often, in whole or part, switch the role that has been inflicted upon them and become abusers, rejecters and betrayers, with their psyche alternating between victim and persecutor by consciously or unconsciously acting out their inner patterns. In cases that may be diagnosed as borderline personality disorder this is known as 'switching'.

The Positive Shadow

Jung's initial idea of a positive *shadow* was where an individual idolizes a person in hero worship, the *shadow* element in this case being the non-acceptance, or lack of integration, of the corresponding parts within the person's own psyche. This can often occur within therapy where the therapist takes on *healer* projection from their clients. In these cases, it is important for the therapist to keep reinforcing the client's own inner abilities and healing skills, so that they can begin to access and own these corresponding parts within themselves. If the therapist accepts the projection, in a process known as *transference*, they can begin to have an inflated image of their own self-importance and then project a feeling of superiority over their clients, which is known as *countertransference*. Being mindful of these elements is very important in good therapeutic practice (Casement, 2006:95).

While the projection of the heroic or idolized image onto another is one element of the positive *shadow*, it is not the only one. All that you perceive you are *not* holds the potential of all that you can become. Therefore, another dynamic held within the positive *shadow* is the fulfilment of your full potential. As Marianne Williamson states (Williamson, 1992:190):

Our deepest fear is not that we are inadequate. Our deepest fear is that we are powerful beyond measure. It is our light, not our darkness that most frightens us. We ask ourselves, Who am I to be brilliant, gorgeous, talented, and fabulous? Actually, who are you not to be? You are a child of God.

As soon as you set limitations on yourself, you invoke your positive *shadow*. Setting goals and then realizing them is a way to make this aspect of your *shadow* conscious. It may take an enormous amount of effort and energy but then the rewards will be correspondingly great.

The Repressed or Rejected Shadow

The repressed or rejected *shadow* holds the negative elements of the psyche that sit beneath the surface of the conscious mind. Very often, these aspects control or determine our life, or at least parts of it, despite the best attempts of the *ego* to control their impulses. One cannot, by persuasion, compel the OCD sufferer not to wash their hands, if that is their compulsion, for the inner urge completely overwhelms any conscious rational control. This raises the question of the nature of those aspects of the psyche that have so much power. Most *shadow* influences are not so overt, yet, nevertheless, sitting beneath the surface of the conscious mind they manipulate the psyche, when aroused, in all sorts of subtle ways. Their origins stem from trauma, whether in childhood, adulthood or a past life. To understand why these aspects exert so much influence over us, we need to delve into the realms of the subconscious mind, but before doing so something needs to be said about the nature of evil.

The Malign Shadow

When these traumatized, repressed and rejected aspects of the psyche reach an extreme position they can sometimes take over control of the *ego* mind, which then can become very susceptible to carrying out malign or evil acts against others or against society. Our prisons are full of such individuals. It should also be appreciated that these *shadow* influences have a power of their own and can flow down through families, as well as expressing themselves through the collective group psyche. This expression of the *shadow* can be termed the 'malign *shadow*', a concept that will be fully covered in Chapter 8, although we will also come across its expression when considering films, literature and mythology.

The Subconscious Mind

We are normally fully aware of the conscious elements of the psyche, the part that claims to be the 'I' aspect of our being, which we might identify with our *ego*. This part operates in normal waking daily life and exerts a primary level of control over the body. When we fall asleep, a different function takes over, the conscious control is relaxed and we can have direct access into our subconscious mind. Originally, this was called the 'unconscious', which is somewhat of a misnomer as the mind is always conscious, at some level. During dream sleep, we can be directly aware of the images and messages from the subconscious and, with a little practice, learn to remember their contents.

The dream world is rich in symbolism, predominating in images and feelings rather than words, although these can occur. It is not the intention here to explore the full significance of dreams and their meanings, as this is readily available from other sources. What is helpful to take on board is that the inner characters we encounter in dreams nearly always reflect parts, or aspects, of our selves even if these appear as friends, acquaintances or family members. In other words, a dream about your mother or father is the portrayal of a part of you that is reflected in your mother or father. These parts are known as sub-personalities, which leads on to considering the role of these characters within the psyche.

Sub-Personalities and Traumas

From the moment the foetus starts to develop within the womb it is affected by its environment. If this is a benign experience then there are no real issues until birth. However, let us take the case of the mother who does not want the child, or indeed goes even further and tries to abort the embryo. Even at such a tender age, the foetal psyche can be aware of this intent, and then go on to create an aspect of itself to hold the trauma. This simple defence mechanism allows us to deal with adversity when we are not in a position to cope with it, protecting the psyche from being overwhelmed. Initially, then, until healed and reintegrated, sub-personalities, 'ego states' or 'alters' are created by the core self or soul as a vessel to hold trauma and once created each has its own free will imbued with its own individual soul-fragment.

The terms 'ego state' or 'alters' are sometimes used for these inner world characters because they can assume executive control of the mind and body in specific situations, particularly when the core trauma is being activated again. However, through this book the term 'sub-personality' will be used.

Depending upon life circumstances, this splitting-off process continues through childhood and into adulthood, where we then need to deal with the parked energies of these sub-personality parts. As already mentioned, each sub-personality has its own free will and individual consciousness. They are not simple psychological states but real characters, existing in their own psychic space (Zinser, 2011:123). Depending upon the cause of the trauma, these sub-personalities can be associated with specific areas of the physical body. For example, the trauma of being asked a question in class, and then being unable to answer or made to look a fool, could cause, through blocked expression, a restriction in the throat. Additionally, because it was brought into existence at a specific moment, it is generally locked into a set period. These sub-personality characters, while sitting beneath the surface of the conscious mind, are always aware of what is happening to the *ego* self. When an outer world event mirrors the original trauma, the sub-personality is activated, releasing some of the emotional charge of the primary pain. For example, the sub-personality part of a child who has been attacked by a dog will become very agitated whenever dogs are around. Effectively, these parts hold our phobias.

These sub-personalities can exert considerable control over the mind when stimulated. For example, the strap thrashings I received from my mother, at the ages of four, five and six, brought into being several sub-personality children who cowered within, waiting to be beaten. Any intimation, in my outer world reality, that something similar might happen again caused enormous reactions within these child parts. If one of these characters sensed a threatening mother figure in my outer world, it would react strongly, with fear, anger or aggression. This was simply a *shadow* part of myself being activated by some life event.

In order to heal this situation, I had to go inside and communicate with these children, telling them that they no longer needed to feel the pain and fear, before leading them into a place of safety. The process by which this can be done is one of the themes of this book. The important point that needs to be stressed is that a considerable number of such characters abound within our inner psychic space. Debbie Ford, in her book *The Dark Side of the Light Chasers*, recounts meeting dozens of such sub-personalities (Ford, 2001:94). Psychologist Dr Tom Zinser suggests that nested, or groups of, sub-personalities can be numerous, particularly when connected to past lives (Zinser, 2011:172-179). From my therapeutic work experience and inner journey explorations, I would concur with these perceptions. The way that the psyche creates these characters will be discussed more fully in Chapter 10.

Paradox and Polarity

Another important theme of this book is the recognition of how both paradox and polarity appear to be fundamental components within the cosmos, working through us in many different ways. This can be demonstrated scientifically, using Young's famous double slit 'light experiment', where a projected beam of light, passing through both slits onto a neutral background, can be perceived either as waves or as discrete particles, although not both, simultaneously (Cameron, 2014). In classical physics theory, this is an impossibility, thereby creating a paradox which can only be understood using the strange theories of quantum mechanics (Penrose, 1989:299-305; Cameron, 2014). From this simple experiment, first conducted in the early 1800s, several other observations have been derived, such as *complementarity*. This states that all objects have complementary or dualistic properties, which cannot be accurately measured, at the same time. The more precisely one aspect is measured, the less accurately can the other be quantified. Put another way, the greater the clarity or focus on one property, the less defined is the other, which nevertheless is still present (Faye, 2014:note 4).

Four thousand years before Young's experiment, Chinese sages started to grapple with similar ideas. This eventually led to the development of the concept of a twin complementary force that flowed into all elements of life and the cosmos. The poles of this polarity were defined as yang and yin. Yang is essentially a male principle and relates to everything that might be termed positive or outgoing, while yin reflects the feminine and that which is negative (in electrical terms) and inward-looking. The day and light are yang, while the night and darkness are yin. As with Young's experimental inheritance, this polarity is perceived as complementary, like the head and tail of a coin – you cannot have one without the other. The stream of chi or life energy flows seamlessly from yang to yin, like walking from leg to leg across a stage, in the drama of life. The development of this simple principle lies at the heart of all Chinese medicine, particularly acupuncture. It is an intrinsic part of Feng Shui, which aims to create harmonious spaces, and is the essential component to the Chinese divinatory classic the *I Ching*.

As the *Tao* states (Tao, 2015:2):

> When people perceive something as 'beautiful',
>
> Other things become ugly.
>
> By affirming something as 'good',
>
> Its opposite becomes evil.
>
> For difficult and easy complement each other.
>
> Long and short define each other,
>
> High and low balance each other.
>
> Pitch and tone make harmony together.
>
> Beginning and ending follow each other.
>
> Having and not having are part of each other.

What has this to do with the psyche?

It implies that opposites are held in all psychological states, whether it be love or hate, peace or strife, joy or sadness, and so on. By focusing on one element its opposite or complement is always held, as an intrinsic part, within it. As long as I acknowledge this dynamic then my psyche will allow me to express different emotions in a balanced way. I can be happy, fulfilled and joyful, as long as I am willing to experience their opposites and not reject them. If I continually try to avoid that which causes me distress, then I can be sure that I will be drawn, inexorably, one way or another, into that polarity.

I sometimes consider that life can be a bit like a fairground roller coaster ride. One moment I can be up high, in a happy state, surveying all of the scenery and the next, plunging down a steep slope into the bottom of the trough of sadness or depression. Bipolar illness is an example of this principle, taken to an extreme. The mood swings of this illness, particularly when descending into the 'pit', can be overwhelming, often needing medical intervention. Fortunately, for most of us these extremes are not common. When these patterns move through us, the trick is not to apply any metaphorical brakes because, if one does, the momentum is lost and it then becomes much harder to ascend back to the top. If you allow yourself to flow with this rhythm, you will experience what your psyche needs and come through to the other side.

If I happen to wake up in the morning feeling sad, I acknowledge that sadness, breathe into it and then exhale, letting it go. I might need to comprehend why I am sad and, when the insights come, I can breathe out the sadness and inhale its opposite of joy. It is a distorted perception, fostered by fantasists, that we can be happy and joyful all the time. The reality of life is that we need to go through some level of hardship and suffering and to express what are sometimes perceived as negative emotions, such as anger and hatred, in order to find balance.

Loving What Is – Byron Katie

The concept of turning things on their head is not new. Under the heading 'The Work', it has been developed by therapist Byron Katie into a very effective process of treatment. Focusing specifically on relationships, or our projections onto others, Katie asks us to write down a series of comments about our partners, neighbours or work colleagues. Then taking each statement in turn we need to ask four simple questions (Katie, 2002:15):

1. Is it true (yes or no)?
2. Can you be sure that it is true (yes or no)?
3. How do you react, or what happens, when you believe that thought?
4. Who would you be without the thought?

The next part of the process is most telling and revealing, for Katie asks us to turn each statement on its head. For example, in the statement 'Paul does not understand me', the turnaround is 'I do not understand myself'. Katie then requests that we discover at least three examples of this statement in relationship to our life. The next turnaround is 'I do not understand Paul', where again exploration can be made into all of the situations where this occurs. Further turnarounds can be applied such as 'Paul does understand me', and so on (Katie, 2002). This process of continually turning concepts and statements on their head is most insightful, showing where projections are occurring within our lives and giving insights into what we need to do to heal our inner world. I would thoroughly endorse the work of Katie in this respect.

The Hanged Man

One of the tarot cards, known as the Hanged Man, beautifully captures this concept. In the Rider Waite pack, we see a man hanging by his right foot from a tree in the form of a Tau Cross (see Fig. 1). The man has a halo around his head, indicating illumination. The Tau Cross, a symbol adopted by St Francis, represents salvation as well as Truth, with a capital 'T'. A number of meanings have been ascribed to this card, such as the need for self-sacrifice. However, I have always felt that the most important is that truth can never be fully comprehended unless it is turned on its head. Effectively, we need to keep applying the process of turning things on their head or turning them around in order to unpick the truth of any situation.

Fig. 1 – The Hanged Man from the Rider-Waite tarot deck.

Darkness and Light

The origins of the term *shadow* lay in what Freud called the light and dark sides of the unconscious (Casement, 2006:94). At a human level, this can be perceived as to whether the conscious self is fully aware of some pattern or not. All that is held within the subconscious and not readily acknowledged might be considered an aspect of the dark self, while that which is conscious is our light. We might also reflect that without the *shadow* we would never fully understand or comprehend the light. On a bright sunny day, everything is brought into sharp relief by the shadows. The dynamic flow between light and darkness can also be considered at a cosmic level, embodying ideas of God and the Devil. To what extent might unseen forces be manipulating the course and pattern of our lives? Are we caught in some cosmic battle between light and darkness? When looking at different polarized situations on the planet, such as the conflicts in the Middle East, one might be forgiven for thinking so. These are deep issues that need to be addressed as part of our journey through life if we are to achieve some sense of balance. These questions will be considered at different stages through this book.

Detecting our Personal Shadow

There are two basic ways in which we can learn how to detect when our personal *shadow* is being activated. The first is by looking at our emotive responses or reactions to people, situations or, more often than not, to personal comments about our selves.

> *Activity 1:1*
>
> Think for a moment about the last time you reacted strongly to a situation and consider what triggered the emotive response and the nature of underlying emotion, i.e. anger, resentment, fear, sadness or even love, and so on. To develop this further you can write down any perceptions about this situation and whether this was a one-off occurrence or something that has happened regularly within your life. If the latter, it almost certainly relates to part of your *shadow*.

The second way that we can determine the expression of our *shadow* is to look at our friends, colleagues and acquaintances. Who do you get on with and who do you not? Our *shadow* will be carried by both those that inspire us (positive *shadow*) and those that cause us some form of grief (negative *shadow*).

> *Activity 1:2*
>
> Make a list of six friends, colleagues or acquaintances, choosing three that you get on with and three that you do not. You can then write against the names the qualities that these individuals carry that either inspire you or cause you some form of negative reaction. In all cases, try to identify what might be the specific trigger. For example, you might have a friend who is a great raconteur and inspires you with the things they say. On the other hand, a colleague at work might irritate you in some particular way. Try to identify what the trigger might be and then reflect on how this relates to you as an individual.

The personal shadow will be covered fully in Chapter 7, but the exercises given in Activities 1:1 and 1:2 can give some insight into our personal *shadow* responses. Once the triggers have been identified, we need to discover the source of the related past trauma and then adopt strategies to help balance and heal their problematic qualities. The terrified child, locked away in a blackened cellar as punishment, most likely is still cowering in the darkness, full of fear. We need to go back to those moments to rescue those childhood parts and bring them into the light. To do this we need courage, perseverance, acceptance, love and forgiveness.

The Shadow in Myths and Fairy Tales

Shadow elements are central to many myths and fairy tales. These will be tackled in more detail in Chapter 4, but it is worth emphasizing, at this stage, two important complementary themes. The first is the heroic journey, in which the hero or heroine has to confront and overcome their fear, sometimes with extreme courage, in order to defeat that which opposes them. Usually, in these tales, it is only by obtaining supernatural help that that challenge is met. Monster and dragon-slaying myths fall into this category. The second, found more often in fairy tales, is the way love transforms that which is perceived as hideous or ugly. These tales give insight into the two central tenets of *shadow* work. Facing that which holds us back through fear is the first, and learning to love and integrate that which we perceive as the unlovable aspects of the self, is its complement.

Fear has had its part to play in ensuring our survival on this planet. Yet, when this fear is misplaced, it can limit our full expression as an individual. For example, the fear of being rejected might then stop an individual entering into a relationship that might otherwise be beneficial for them.

Learning to love and forgive the ugly and shameful aspects of the self is, from my therapeutic experience, the harder and generally greater challenge. The example, in the Introduction, of the woman who discovered that her inner demon was a seven-year-old child, called 'fat and ugly' by her father, is a demonstration how we need to face and transform that which is abhorrent to us. Parents, whether through accident, ignorance or intent, can make comments that can be deeply wounding to the child, creating traumatized sub-personalities that feel abandoned, betrayed, abused, denied or rejected. We need to bring these parts back into consciousness and affirm, from our adult perspective, that they are loved, accepted and forgiven. This powerful therapeutic process is of paramount importance for our psychological health and well-being.

Summary

The *shadow* is a term, first coined by Jung, to describe the unconscious self. Since then it has grown to encapsulate a wider definition that holds the potential of all that we might be, as well as all that we consciously repress. Held within our *shadows* are those troubled sub-personalities that hold our pain, which are waiting to be released. In this healing process, we need to comprehend how opposites or polarities run through our lives. If we go through a period of elation, we will often then experience being in the dumps. One cannot have one without the other. This can sometimes occur in religious experience where a feeling of meeting the illuminating essence of the Divine, an epiphany moment, is then followed by a nosedive into confrontation with the *shadow* elements of the psyche. I have met many such individuals who, discovering the blazing light of illuminated consciousness, are then plunged into what is sometimes called the 'dark night of the soul' (St John of the Cross, 2003). This is a natural cycle and, although uncomfortable, needs to be accepted as one of the primary rhythms of the cosmos. Only by learning to balance these opposites can we move beyond these pendulum swings.

Finally, the great mythological tales offer two routes to redemption. Firstly facing that which we fear, either within or without, and secondly redeeming the ugly and unlovable elements of the psyche, wherein sit our guilt and shame. These are the challenges that we all need to consider as part of our life experience.

These elements can be summarized as follows:

- Our positive *shadow* holds all of our potential for who and what we might be. In this sense your shadow will always expand, for the greater you become the greater is your potential to become.
- Our negative *shadow* holds all of the repressed or traumatized parts of the psyche that have not yet been fully integrated within the self.
- Our malign *shadow* operates when the traumatized parts of the psyche take over and then perpetrate acts of violence against others. In other words, all of those actions which might be deemed as being evil.
- The *shadow* operates both at an individual level as well as through the collective, where the unresolved or unintegrated aspects of the psyche

are projected onto others. An example of a collective psyche projection took place prior to the Second World War when the Jews were blamed for all that was wrong in Nazi Germany.
- To work through *shadow* dynamics we need to understand the concept of polarity and how this flows through every aspect of experience. The challenge within the individual is how to balance and integrate these polarities within the psyche. This will be dealt with fully when we come to look at the personal *shadow* in Chapter 7.
- Mythologies and fairy tales offer two important routes for working through personal shadow issues. The first is learning how to confront and go through our fears and the second is learning how to love and integrate the unacceptable aspects of the psyche.

In the ensuing chapters, we will look at how these themes weave through films, TV and literature, before moving on to look at their cosmological role in myths and fairy tales. In each chapter, there will be some activity exercises to allow you to explore the *shadow* through different genres and to get some idea of your own personal *shadow* by exploring its reflection in your outer world. In the second section of the book, we will address how these elements operate both within us and within society. We will also consider the concept of the cosmic *shadow*, presenting a cogent case for the continuation of consciousness beyond physical death. The final section of the book presents a series of exercises for healing and balancing our *shadows*.

Chapter Two

The Shadow in Films, TV and Video Games

We are shaped by our thoughts; we become what we think. when the mind is pure, joy follows like a shadow that never leaves.

Buddha

The expression of the *shadow* in film, television, drama and literature is a vast subject on which a whole book, or several books, could be written. One cannot hope to cover this topic in any great depth but the intention within the next two chapters is to give some insight, using selected material, into how the themes outlined in Chapter 1 have been expressed through these media. This chapter will focus first on films and then conclude with a brief look at television and video games. In the next chapter, we will look at literature, drama and poetry.

In the earliest stages of human development, the only means to portray these elements was through tales and pictures. The former found their way into the great myths and folk tales, from all regions of the world, which we will cover in greater depth in Chapter 4. Graphic art has been with us from ancient times as can be evidenced in the drawings and paintings in the caves of Lascaux and Chauvet in southern France, which date back some thirty thousand years to the Palaeolithic era. There is some evidence that certain scenes represented shamanic trance states, such as the Lascaux painting known as the Sorcerer, showing a man's head, adorned with antlers, and a body that is part human, part animal.

In the modern world, we have expanded this range to include motion pictures, fly-on-the-wall documentaries and interactive video games. The scope is endless but, before proceeding further, it is worthwhile pausing for a moment and carrying out the following activity.

> *Activity 2:1*
>
> Try to answer as fully as you can the following questions:
>
> 1. Which genre of film do I most enjoy and why?
> 2. What is my favourite film and what is it that appeals to me so greatly about this movie?
> 3. Which are my favourite television programmes?
> 4. What is my favourite video game, if I play them?
>
> Once this list is completed, consider how any theme that runs through this genre might reflect an aspect of yourself.
>
> Now create a similar list by answering the following questions:
>
> 1. Which genre of film do I most detest and why?
> 2. What is my least favourite film and what is it that I dislike so much about this movie?
> 3. Which are my least favourite television programmes?
> 4. What is my least favourite video game if I play them?
>
> Finally, consider how these two lists complement each other. What do they tell you about yourself?

From these two lists you might start to get some insight into the way your *shadow*, your sub-conscious self, might be operating through you. We will return to this theme in the second section of the book, to look at how we can learn to balance, or give voice to, the *shadow* within us.

FILMS

There are many places where we first could have started this exploration. I cannot, however, avoid being drawn to those films that have most touched me as an individual and which, inevitably, reflect something of my own *shadow* self. Fortunately, I am not alone in some of my selections, particularly in this first movie choice, for in the 2001 UK census close to four hundred thousand people listed their religion as Jedi Knight (Rogers, 2012).

Star Wars

The first *Star Wars* film, later known as *Episode IV: A New Hope*, first hit the screens in 1977. It was followed by two more films in 1980 and 1983, creating a trilogy which had sufficient completeness for the series to remain dormant for another sixteen years before it was revived. This revisitation explored the background to the themes and characters of the original movie. Much has been written about the *Star Wars* story. One of the debates revolves around whether these films express the genre of science fiction or science fantasy, because one of their components is a mysterious energy called The Force. This touches one of those paradoxical elements on the nature of truth and reality, the factual world of physical science and the magical inner world of consciousness.

The central theme of the first three films is the expression of the negative *shadow*, personified by Darth Vader, whose aim is domination and control of the Galactic Empire using the 'dark side of the Force', which works through hatred, deception, greed and, above all, fear. Set against these powerful forces, which control a vast destructive potential, are a group of unlikely heroes and heroines, two of which, Luke Sky Walker and Princess Leia, turn out to be the twin children of Vader. Luke in particular has to go through many adventures and initiatory experiences before being able to face his father and the Dark Lord of the Sith, who sits behind him. In this process, Luke learns how to contact his own inner mental powers and to be open to telepathic guidance from Obi-Wan Kenobi, one of Luke's early mentors, who had deliberately sacrificed himself in a duel with Vader.

In the final scenes of *The Return of the Jedi* (1983), Luke confronts both his father and the Dark Lord, who urges him to give in to his anger and hatred and thence become under the domination of the dark side, like his father before him. Luke has to fight his father in a duel, using light-sabres, but despite winning he refuses to kill him, stating continually that he senses the good within him. The Dark Lord then turns against Luke and tries to use all of his powers to destroy him, and the hero appears doomed. However, Vader himself, when confronted with the imminent death of his son, turns against his dark master and casts him into an abyss. Father and son are reunited and, in this act, Vader regains his place as a Jedi Knight and his rightful name of Anakin Skywalker, before dying from his wounds in the arms of his son.

The appeal of these films, particularly through the number of individuals who wished to be identified with the Jedi religion in the census return, shows the power of these different elements within the human psyche. The *Star Wars* films exemplify the heroic element of human nature; the refusal to be cowed by fear and domination, even if this means giving up one's life. Yet they also include the compassionate element. We see that Luke, despite defeating Vader in the duel and being offered the opportunity by the Dark Lord to choose power and domination himself, refused to kill his father, preferring to die rather than follow that path.

Superhero or Superheroine Films

All superhero or superheroine films, such as *Superman*, *Spider-Man*, *Superwoman*, *The Avengers*, and so on, present a black and white confrontation between good and evil. Human equivalents, as in the *Indiana*

Jones films, James Bond or Lara Croft in *Tomb Raider*, do the same thing yet in a more humanized way. The weaknesses of these characters are generally minimized, although they all have to draw upon some extra inner strength or insight in order to overcome their adversaries. For example, in *The Avengers* (2012), in which a group of superheroes and heroines come together to save the Earth from the evil Loki (the god of mischief from Scandinavian mythology), Iron Man knowingly prepares to sacrifice his life to save the world. As part of good cinema, he is miraculously saved in the end to fight another day.

Some interesting and more subtle *shadow* elements are occasionally woven into these films, such as in *Spider-Man 3* (2007) where, in addition to confronting the usual antiheroes, Peter Parker (Spider-Man) is himself insidiously infected by a malign force that has come to Earth to exaggerate the destructive ego-driven side of the human psyche. For a period, Peter allows the evil side of his nature to dominate his actions before realizing what has happened to him. This series also shows the interrelationships between Peter, his sweetheart Mary Jane and his best friend Harry Osborn, so that different projected *shadow* aspects are reflected between the three characters.

More nuanced *shadow* elements are woven into the *Pirates of the Caribbean* (2003, 2006, 2007, 2011) series, in which the primary character, the pirate Jack Sparrow, expresses many characteristics which would normally be regarded as expressions of the negative or malign *shadow*. In some situations, he is more antihero than hero. The other two primary characters, which make up the trinity in this film, are Elizabeth Swann and Will Turner, who are more normal in their heroic portrayal.

E.T.

Another classic science fiction film, which hit the screens in 1982, was *E.T. the Extra-Terrestrial*. This film revolves around two primary characters:

a ten-year-old boy called Elliott and a stranded extra-terrestrial called E.T. Although slightly comical, E.T., standing slightly smaller that Elliott, would be considered very ugly and ungainly in normal circumstances. The plot tells how Elliott, his elder brother and a few friends try to keep E.T., who has some supernatural powers, from being discovered by the authorities and help him 'go home'. Elliott increasingly comes to identify himself with E.T., and when speaking to his brother he refers to himself as 'we'. Living on an alien planet causes E.T. to become seriously ill. After being captured by the government agents he appears to be dying and Elliott himself is seriously ill. Both are taken into an isolation tent and E.T. appears to die, with Elliott coming back to himself. He then, in an emotional moment, affirms his love for E.T., which is the magical ingredient that brings E.T. back to life. In the last part of the film, we see Elliott and E.T. escaping with the help of magical powers (telekinesis) into the woods where E.T. can be rescued and taken home. In the final scene, just before ascending into the spaceship, E.T. points his finger at Elliott's forehead, telling him that he will always be there inside.

This film expresses the other side of *shadow* work: learning to love what appears to be ugly. E.T. can be seen as an aspect of Elliott's *shadow* self, holding all of his magical potential, including resurrection. When we accept and love these elements of the psyche, they release their powers to us. The emotional potency they exert through the heart is enormous, although some people might find this too overwhelming. If so, they will then block off the emotion, which is a natural emotional self-defence mechanism that is triggered to protect a vulnerable inner child.

Avatar

Like the two previous films, *Avatar* was an instantaneous hit when it was released in December 2009, creating an enormous response around the world and ending up becoming the highest grossing film of its time. The plot of the film is probably well known to most readers. It involves a group of humans, in the year 2154, mining for a precious mineral called unobtanium on a distant planet called Pandora. The planet is inhabited, like Earth, with a diverse range of plant and animal life and a semi-hominid group of people called the Na'vi. Earth scientists have discovered a method of creating for themselves a Na'vi body, while in an altered state of consciousness held within a special chamber, and thence to discover aspects of the Na'vi's life and understanding of their home environment. We discover that these indigenous people have a deep understanding and respect for the connectedness of all life, which runs counter to the greed and violence of the mining officials who are driven only by their desire to obtain the mineral at all costs.

As with most action films, the Na'vi have to fight for their right to live in peace in their world, which they do with the help of one of the Earth scientists called Jake Scully who, although physically crippled in his Earth body, is a hero when entering into his avatar Na'vi form. He also needs to learn mastery of this realm and to gain control over some of its elemental creatures, such as the dragons. An invocation to the collective spirit of the planet, called Eywa, finally helps the Na'vi, along with the forces of their natural world, to defeat the human invaders and expel the mining company. To some people this may resonate with the struggle of indigenous cultures around the world being eradicated or enslaved by greedy and unscrupulous empire-builders. World history holds many accounts of the failure of indigenous people to defend themselves in the face of such overwhelming odds, such as the North and South American tribes and the Aborigine of Australia, among many others, who fell to the expansion of western imperialism during the seventeenth, eighteenth and nineteenth centuries.

The *shadow* elements of the story are clearly portrayed in the greed of the members of the mining company, who would go to any lengths, regardless of other life or consequences, to achieve their ambition. At the heart of all greed lies fear, which is why greed was perceived as one of the seven deadly sins. The realm of Pandora reflects a spiritual perspective about the interconnectedness of all life and presents a vision of how it is possible to live in harmony and cooperation with all that is around. Jake Scully's acceptance of his aspirational *shadow* self allows him to transcend the limitations of his human body and ultimately find union with a Na'vi female called Neytiri. This might be likened to the inner initiatory journey of finding atonement with our corresponding animus or anima. The film reflects a number of stereotypical polarized images, which some critics have called racist. One fall-out from the film has become known as the 'Avatar Effect', where individuals have felt depressed and suicidal about not being able to visit the utopian world of Pandora.

Maleficent

Premiered in 2014, this is the most recent of the films explored in this chapter. The summary of the film states 'A vengeful fairy is driven to curse an infant princess, only to discover that the child may be the one person who can restore peace to their troubled land.' This is a reworking of the story of Sleeping Beauty, although taken from the perspective of the wicked fairy who curses the infant Princess Aurora. Before this event, we learn that Maleficent had originally been a happy fairy living in a magical land called the Moors. One day she meets a young man called Stefan and eventually they fall in love. Stefan has a deep *shadow* in his desire to be king and this leads him to betraying Maleficent and cutting off her wings to disempower her. Presenting the wings to the king, he earns the right to ascend to the throne on the king's death, which he eventually achieves. He marries Princess Leila and they have a daughter, Aurora.

At the christening of Aurora, Maleficent appears, vowing revenge, and proceeds to issue the well known curse that the princess will fall into an eternal dreamless sleep after pricking her finger on a spinning wheel needle on her sixteenth birthday. Stefan pleads for his daughter's life, and because of their former love Maleficent responds by saying that only a true love kiss will restore the princess back to life again. The terrified king then has all spinning wheels destroyed and hands Aurora over to three incompetent pixies to be looked after and kept away from the palace.

The curiosity of Maleficent is aroused and she starts to keep an eye on the princess from afar, stepping in secretly to help her when the pixies fail in their duty. Aurora finally meets Maleficent when she is fifteen and begins to build a relationship with her, calling her 'my fairy godmother'. At this point Maleficent starts to regret her curse and seeks to undo the spell, although this proves impossible because of the way it was created. Although a handsome prince appears and is greatly attracted to Aurora, her sixteenth birthday comes before they can cement their love and the curse enacts its spell, causing Aurora to fall into a deep sleep. Thinking that the prince can break the spell, Maleficent smuggles him into the palace but his kiss proves futile. Feeling distraught and desolate at the loss of someone she has come to love, Maleficent herself kisses the princess as a last goodbye. Aurora then awakes because the 'true love kiss' had come from Maleficent, not the prince. Stefan, still full of rage, is determined to kill Maleficent, using every means at his disposal, and in the final scenes Aurora comes to the rescue of her godmother by releasing her imprisoned wings, allowing Maleficent to soar above her assailant and defeat him.

The essence of the tale shows how easy it is to take impulsive, rash action and seek revenge when feeling hurt and betrayed. How often might we have verbally lashed out at someone when they have touched part of our wounded self? The film also shows the overambitious *shadow* side of Stefan, who is determined to win the kingdom at all costs, even if this means wounding and betraying the one he loved. The crown proves a hollow reward, as everything he has loved is slowly stripped away from him and, ultimately, consumed by his anger and hatred, he falls to his death.

These fictional fantasy films pick up different aspects of how *shadow* elements, either covertly or overtly, can work through the characters. Even when an individual allows themselves to be subverted by their *shadow* self, it is never too late for redemption. Both Darth Vader and Maleficent achieve this transformation. The heroic element of facing that which terrifies, and learning to love and forgive, can be seen in all these films. They all, additionally, incorporate a supernatural element which taps into the deeper, magical aspects of our psyches, providing an antidote or polarity to the materialistic perspective of modern science. The strength of fantasy lies in its ability to create a diverse range of characters that highlight specific qualities, such as Gandalf, the archetypal wizard, in *The Lord of the Rings*, or the robot character R2D2 in *Star Wars*.

Reality films need to present more rounded characters, which come to the fore in the next two films I have chosen, *The Pianist* (2002) and *Schindler's List* (1993), which are both set in Nazi Germany in the later stages of the Second World War. The Nazi Party gave full expression to the malign *shadow* through its use of fear, control and ego inflation (the superiority of the Aryan race). It makes a chilling backdrop and shows the challenges individuals have to face in responding to this insidious destructive element. Both of these films are based on true stories, which were first published in books, although these did not have the same outreach as the film versions.

The Pianist

This film, directed by Roman Polanski and released in 2002, tells the story of Wladyslaw Szpilman, a Jewish virtuoso pianist and composer, who was trapped in Warsaw during the Second World War. The film graphically portrays the horrors of the Warsaw Ghetto and the inhumanity inflicted on the Jewish inhabitants during the Nazi occupation. Szpilman is shown not as a hero but a survivor and a victim, driven by the primary will to live. In this he is fortunate, for his exceptional gift as a musician comes to his aid in a number of different ways. He is recognized as a talent and this helps him initially gain work in the cafés of Warsaw. Later, when the deportations start in 1942 for Treblinka concentration camp, he is spotted and rescued by an authority guard and used instead as a slave labourer but eventually manages to escape.

In the final scenes of the film we see a starving and desperate Szpilman hiding in the attic of a large deserted house where there happens to be a piano. He thinks he is alone but is discovered by a German officer and fears he is about to be shot. However, the officer, Wilm Hosenfeld, is intrigued when he discovers that Szpilman is a pianist and asks him to play a piece, which he does, choosing Chopin's *Ballade in G Minor*. The quality of the playing so moves Hosenfeld that he resolves to do what he can to save Szpilman, bringing him food and showing him a safer place to hide. Despite the apparent odds against him, Szpilman survives the war. At different moments in the film, it seems as though an invisible guardian force steps in to rescue Szpilman, with him taking little specific action or decision himself. The thought 'Why me?' must have been present in many such survivors, when other members of their families had perished.

Malign *shadow* elements are expressed throughout the film but we also see how courage, belief and humanity counter the ever-pervasive fear. In the final scenes it is the beauty of the music that softens the heart of Hosenfeld, allowing his redeeming compassionate qualities to come to the fore so he can reject the orders that he would normally have obeyed.

Schindler's List

Like the previous film, *Schindler's List*, released in 1993, should be considered in the book section under the title *Schindler's Ark*, which was written by Thomas Keneally, an Australian novelist. Although the book won what was then the Booker Prize in 1982, the film had a higher profile and went on to win many awards, because it gave great insight into the brutality of the Nazi regime and the horrors of the Holocaust.

The story tells of Oskar Schindler, a Nazi supporter and ethnic German businessman, who through lavish bribery and deceit was able to gain the support of the Wehrmacht (German armed forces) and the SS to build a factory for making enamelware. To make the most of cheap labour, Schindler contacts Itzhak Stern, who has links to the Jewish business community, and together they enlist Jews into the factory as workers. Throughout the film, Schindler maintains good connections with the very brutal commandant Amon Goeth, who is in charge of the local concentration camp, and witnesses horrific and gratuitous violence which profoundly affects him. Thereafter Schindler does everything in his power to protect the Jewish workers, using lavish bribes and the deception that he is using the labour to make much-needed munitions for the war effort. These workers are eventually saved when he creates a 'Schindler's List' of the people who are to be transported back to his home town to work in a new factory.

The *shadow* elements within the film, shot interestingly in black and white rather than colour, are clear and obvious. The overt, malign *shadow*, when given voice and expression, has little regard for life, operating through fear and domination. The commandant Amon Goeth expresses this brutality in all its stark harshness. There are many memorable lines within the film, one of which is when Goeth, after shooting a young woman in the back from his office window, turns to Schindler, who is watching, and boasts that to kill someone like that is real power. Schindler contradicts this statement, saying that real power is having the power but then using it to spare a worthless life rather than taking it.

As the film develops we see the transformation taking place within Schindler, as his humanity and regard for life come to the fore to help those in greatest need, despite the peril in which this places him. He uses all of those *shadow* forces of deceit, treachery and greed against the Nazi regime and thereby is able to save eleven hundred people who would otherwise have perished. The primary difference between Schindler and Szpilman from *The Piano* is that Schindler is not an obvious victim. He had a clear choice about whether to co-operate with the Nazi regime or to try to pervert it, thereby saving so many lives. Towards the end of the film we see Schindler, in deep remorse, bemoaning the fact that he did not do enough to save more people. In reply, Stern responds that there are eleven hundred people still alive because of what he did.

He then gives Oskar a ring bearing a powerful Talmudic inscription 'Whoever saves one life, saves the world entire' (Wikiquote, 2015). This statement has caused some controversy because another version of the same text, from the Babylonian Talmud, inserts the words 'in Israel' after the word 'life', which somewhat changes the film version's broad humanitarian proclamation (Hoffman & Critchley, 1994).

The film is harrowing to watch because of the brutality it portrays, yet the elements of courage and the refusal to be bowed by this terror are plain to see. It also demonstrates that malign influences can be infectious, causing otherwise good men and women to carry out acts of brutality through fear of their own lives.

It's a Wonderful Life

This final film, directed by Frank Capra and released in 1946, tells the tale of insurance agent George Bailey. He is pitted against the miserly and rapacious Henry Potter, who is only interested in gaining financial control of Bedford Falls, the town in which they live. These two characters represent the *shadow* sides of each other. At a certain point in the film, George feels utterly defeated when a large amount of money goes missing from his Building and Loan company and he attempts suicide. However, he is rescued by his guardian angel, who shows George what life in the town would have been like had George never lived. He comes to realize that good deeds have beneficial consequences and that the intentions of the destructive Henry Potter need not have the upper hand. In the end George is saved from disaster by his friends, who rally in support, and the machinations of Potter are shown in their true light. After a very slow start, this film achieved international acclaim, being cited as one of the most inspirational American films of all time.

Many other films could have been chosen for this section, whether science fiction or otherwise, that display *shadow* elements, and this takes us back to the original questions at the start of this chapter: which films inspire or touch you?

TELEVISION

When I grew up in the 1950s and early 1960s, television was in its infancy and films and documentaries were presented in black and white terms, both literally and metaphorically. Cowboy Westerns had their clearly represented 'good' and 'bad' guys. The 'good' guys were clean-shaven and wore white hats, while the 'bad' wore black hats and were scruffy and unshaven. When they appeared, the Native American peoples, such as the Apache and Comanche, were invariably cast in a negative light. As television and the media have evolved, this stereotyping has given way to a more rounded view that can perceive the light and *shadow* operating within any one individual. Some of these nuances are reflected in the very popular soap operas.

One of the most interesting programmes, to my mind, which reflects these elements is a programme called *Wife Swap*. This is a British reality programme, created by Stephen Lambert for Channel 4 and first broadcast in 2003. Despite the title, the show does not focus on sexual relationships but rather on the lifestyles of two completely different sets of home establishments in which the two wives are swapped round for two weeks. In the first week, each wife has to abide by all of the rules of the home she is visiting and in the second week she can bring in any changes that she wishes, which the members of the household then have to abide by. This often leads to conflicts within the family because their routines and status quo are being challenged.

At the end of the fortnight both sets of families come together to share their experiences, which can often be very emotional and sometimes acrimonious. A month later, the cameras revisit the homes to see whether any changes have been instituted within the families, which invariably proves to be the case. The strength of the programme lies in pitting opposites against each other. For example, the family that is neat and orderly being pitched against one that is untidy but where other priorities are important. As can be seen from the programme, some of the situations that arise are cathartic, because it is often very difficult to step into the *shadow* sides of ourselves. While the experiences of the participants are generally challenging, it is very rare for them not to have been profoundly moved by their involvement and to make, sometimes, radical shifts in their family relationships, moving to a more balanced position.

This form of television gives excellent insights into the working of *shadow* elements within us. The bringing together of opposites highlights these dynamics and in these cases forces individuals to confront that which they do not want to consider within themselves. The two most fascinating parts of the programme are first where the 'new' wife has to deal with the opposite type of lifestyle to that to which she is accustomed, such as the stay-at-home wife stepping into the shoes of a career businesswoman who juggles many different jobs in her 'motherly' role. The second is the reaction to the challenges which the father and children have to face when the routines are reversed under a new set of rules. Some knuckle down and accept these changes but most rebel against them in some form, showing how difficult it can be to move into a new place of balance.

VIDEO GAMES

Before concluding this chapter, brief mention needs to be made of a new genre of gaming entertainment that first emerged with the development of personal computers in the late 1970s and early 1980s. The speed of development of the computer industry has allowed for more sophisticated gaming that allows individuals to challenge themselves against either the computer or other players, who could even live in different countries. Such games can be great fun but also, potentially, enormously addictive. The subconscious aspects of our psyche often communicate through visual images, which is why we dream in pictures rather than words. Interactive computer games allow for a connection to these deeper elements of the psyche through the images they present, and invariably they have light and *shadow* sides woven into them. Games that educate and inspire reflect the positive elements of this genre, while those that extol aggression, violence and gratuitous sex express the negative *shadow*. Acting out these elements within a game format can be one way for an individual to gain insights into their own *shadow* self and to balance these aspects within themselves. The danger is that, in some cases, these games can inspire individuals to play out these roles in their material daily lives, where the fantasy then moves into reality. How humanity deals with this form of *shadow* expression is going to be one of the challenges of the twenty-first century.

Summary

In this chapter, we have explored a few examples of the *shadow* within films, television and video games. In the next chapter, we will look at these same elements within literature and drama, where we move, in the case of literature, from an overt image into an internalized one. Both have their strengths and points of connection to our emotions. The key to all these forms of artistic expression is to keep asking yourself the question: 'What do I feel about this film, scene or drama?' That which touches you strongly at an emotional level will almost certainly connect to some aspect of your *shadow* self. It is then possible to start to look for patterns in your response to these outer world forms, which will bring to the surface those parts within you that need attention. It is important also to try to identify the type of emotion being invoked, such as anger, sadness, love, hatred, resentment, and so on.

For example, for many years I was always affected by stories involving young children which, in this case, reflected something of my own childhood traumas that still needed attention. However, it is important to remember that the *shadow* also holds all of our potential for the future, so the emotional response can be one that inspires or uplifts. Films that show stories of struggles against adversity, in overcoming obstacles and achieving some positive goal or outcome, highlight our potential to accomplish the same. Superhero films fall into this category.

Chapter Three

The Shadow in Literature and Drama

No, no, I am but shadow of myself:
You are deceived, my substance is not here;
For what you see is but the smallest part
And least proportion of humanity:
I tell you, madam, were the whole frame here,
It is of such a spacious lofty pitch,
Your roof were not sufficient to contain't.

William Shakespeare, *The Second Part of King Henry VI*,
Act II, Scene III

In the previous chapter we explored how *shadow* elements are represented within films, television and video games. In this chapter we will explore these same elements within literature and drama. Once again the potential range is vast and I could have drawn on many different books that show clear expression of the *shadow*. Those that I have chosen reflect my own preferences. They are books or plays that have touched me deeply in different ways. As in the last chapter, you might like to reflect for a moment on the novels and stories you have read or the plays you have seen. What moves you in these tales and can you spot any particular themes that run through them?

Activity 3:1

Ask yourself the following questions and write down the answers:

1. What genre of book do I most enjoy and why?
2. What is my favourite book, and how do the characters portrayed reflect aspects of myself?

Having completed this list, consider whether any themes that run through the books might reflect an aspect of yourself.

Now create a similar list by answering the following questions:

1. What genre of book do I most detest and why?
2. What type of literature do you like?

You might like to compare this listing with the one you considered in relation to films. Are there any similarities that flow through both lists?

LITERATURE AND DRAMA

All books and plays will inevitably contain some *shadow* elements in order to make their plots engaging and memorable. The books chosen for this section show stark contrast between 'light' and '*shadow*' so that these elements can best be appreciated.

Illuminating the Shadow

The Tragical History of the Life and Death of Doctor Faustus

This play by Christopher Marlowe is mentioned in Chapter 1 and therefore it is worth looking more deeply into the themes it presents to tease out some of the ideas that it contains. Plays provide the options of being viewed in the theatre or read as literature or, ideally, both. We can read a play and give full rein to our imagination or we can see it performed. The origins of theatre go back to the early Greek tragedies, which allowed ideas to be conveyed to a largely illiterate people. As such, they can expand our levels of awareness and understanding and give insights into the ways that *shadow* elements weave through human nature.

When we first meet the doctor, in Marlowe's play, he is a highly successful and revered individual, with seemingly all the success that anyone might require in life. Yet this is not enough, for something within Faustus craves more. In Scene 1 he states:

> *The end of physic is our body's health.*
> *Why, Faustus, hast thou not attain'd that end?*
> *Is not thy common talk found aphorisms?*
> *Are not thy bills hung up as monuments,*
> *Whereby whole cities have escap'd the plague,*
> *And thousand desperate maladies been eas'd?*
> *Yet art thou still but Faustus, and a man.*
> *Couldst thou make men to live eternally,*
> *Or, being dead, raise them to life again,*
> *Then this profession were to be esteem'd.*
> *Physic, farewell!*

To ease this desire, Faustus resorts to the magical arts:

These metaphysics of magicians,
And necromantic books are heavenly; …
Ay, these are those that Faustus most desires.
O, what a world of profit and delight,
Of power, of honour, of omnipotence,
Is promis'd to the studious artizan!

Both bad and good angels then appeal in their different ways to Faustus, either to pursue this magical path or to repent. After some hesitation, Faustus resolves to follow the path of magic and conjures Mephistophilis to serve him. The doctor is convinced that he has the power to command demons, but Mephistophilis puts him right by saying that he came of his own accord because he is always on the look-out for immortal souls that might be dammed. As he states in Scene 3:

Therefore the shortest cut for conjuring
Is stoutly to abjure the Trinity,
And pray devoutly to the prince of hell.

Convinced now that the very act of seeking the aid of Mephistophilis will lead to his damnation, Faustus determines to proceed with entering into a pact with Lucifer, to sell his soul in return for world power for twenty years of his life, which he duly does. Despite all this material power and its manipulation, which we see through the play, when it comes towards the end we see in Scene 14 Faustus beginning to repent the folly of this desire.

Curs'd be the parents that engender'd me!
No, Faustus, curse thyself, curse Lucifer
That hath depriv'd thee of the joys of heaven.

In western society, it would not be fashionable to see this story as anything but a psychological metaphor, for it is not seen as feasible to sell one's soul to the Devil. Indeed, the consensus of modern society is that demons and angels do not exist. The simple answer to this enigma is that if one accepts the concept of the soul's survival beyond physical death, that we are also part of a spiritual reality, then the potential for benign as well as malevolent spirits must exist. This important theme will be considered in greater depth in Chapter 6, when we consider the Cosmic Shadow.

The Lord of the Rings

The concept of a powerful force for evil, known as Sauron, in *The Lord of the Rings* (Tolkien, 1970) lies at the core of JRR Tolkien's famous epic story of light versus darkness, which has now been made into three successful films (*The Fellowship of the Ring*, 2001; *The Two Towers*, 2002; *The Return of the King*, 2003). Sauron himself makes no appearance in the book or the films. His emissaries, the Ringwraiths and the Orcs, are the main malign protagonists, seeking to control and subvert by killing all that confronts them. Although set in the magical world of Middle Earth, the story has all the hallmarks of a heroic adventure challenge, with individuals confronting, through courage and endurance, the deep fears and dreads which they need to overcome. As stated, one of the main challenges of inner *shadow* work is facing that which we fear. The power of stories like *The Lord of the Rings*, although fictional, gives strength to our own courageous selves, when we identify with the characters and the challenges they face and overcome.

The demonic power of the Ring subverts all who wear it to the dark side of life. Although it bestows the gift of invisibility which Frodo, the Ring-bearer, has to use from time to time, this comes at a terrible cost. We see the evidence of this in Gollum, or Sméagol, who for many years had the Ring before losing it, only for it to be found by Bilbo Baggins (*The Hobbit*, 1970) and then handed to Frodo. The quest of the story is the destruction of the Ring and its malign influence in the realms of Mordor, wherein resides the Dark Lord in his tower of Barad-dûr.

Viewed in terms of *shadow* work, we might see Gollum and Frodo as *shadow* sides of each other. Frodo reminds Gollum of that which is good within him, while Gollum shows Frodo what he might become if he allows the malignant power of the Ring to dominate his psyche. Their paths are woven together for much of the book and, significantly, it is Gollum, not Frodo, who brings about the destruction of the Ring by falling into the volcanic fires of Mount Doom. It was only by collaborating with each other, co-operating with their *shadow* selves, that the quest was achieved.

Other initiatory elements flow through the tale. It was the struggles of the wizard Gandalf, with the Balrog, his *shadow*, that allowed him to assume the mantle of 'the White' instead of 'the Grey'. Aragon's taking on the mantle of his kingship, after wandering for many years in the wilderness, encourages us to take on the mantle of becoming the 'king' or 'queen' of our own lives. The friendship between Gimli, a Dwarf warrior, and Legolas, an elf, reminds us of the need to learn to work with those who seem different to us. Not all characters in the book are able to confront their *shadows*. Some, like the Steward Denethor, perish by their own hands, filled with despair, while others, like the wizard Saruman, a Faustian character, allow themselves to be subverted by the Dark Lord.

Perhaps the greatest failing in the book is the dearth of feminine elements. This possibly reflects something within Tolkien's own psyche. Only Éowyn plays any real part in the saga, although there are brief appearances by the Lady Arwen and Galadriel. The love element is not overt, except perhaps in the comradeship shown by the Fellowship, although the love of Lady Arwen, the elf maiden, for Aragon helped him to fulfil his part of the quest.

> *Activity 3:2*
>
> If you have read *The Lord of the Rings* or seen the film, create a list, with two columns. Put, in order of preference, the top ten characters you most identify with from either the book or the film. For example, if you feel the greatest connection with Gandalf, put him first. Once the list has been created, put into the opposite column the character who appears to hold the polarity of each character. For example, you might put Saruman in opposition to Gandalf. You might struggle in some cases, such as considering the polarity to the Ents. Once the list is complete, think about the characters and their opposites. Which themes do they reflect in your life?

Harry Potter

The first of this series of books, *Harry Potter and the Philosopher's Stone* by JK Rowling, appeared in 1997 and very quickly became enormously popular. Despite all the pronouncements of the material sciences, the magical aspects of our psyches yearn for a connection with that which relates to something deeper and possibly more profound. Like *The Lord of the Rings,* this is a tale about the confrontation between the forces of good and evil. It raises the question of what it is that makes one side 'good' and the other 'bad'. In terms of the psyche, that which conforms to the malign *shadow* will always seek control through three distinct elements:

- The inciting of fear
- The inflation of the ego
- The suppression of freedom of thought and action through control, generally by fear

In these tales, Harry, assisted by his friends Hermione Granger and Ron Weasley, goes through a series of challenges, involving magical elements and beasts, until Harry meets his nemesis in the form of 'He-Who-Must-Not-Be-Named', called Voldemort, who is the very powerful Dark Lord. The books remind us that the *shadow* is never far away but, by learning to harness our own powers, we can overcome that which would enslave us. Those who embark on their own inner journeywork, in a shamanic way, will have encountered many similar elements to the Potter stories, which attest to the genius of Rowling in intuitively capturing these elements in her books.

Harry and his friends confront a series of metaphorical challenges that touch many of the levels we all need to face in our daily lives. Do we give in to our fears? Do we succumb to greed and avarice? Are we prepared to sacrifice ourselves for others? These are some of the important themes that touch all of us, which is why books like JK Rowling's have proved so popular.

The Strange Case of Dr Jekyll and Mr Hyde

This classic story by Robert Louis Stevenson (1886) tells of the successful Dr Jekyll, who discovers a potion that allows him to transform into his negative *shadow*, Mr Hyde. The restrictions of Victorian Britain, where morality is contained within tight mores, caused the *shadow* elements of the collective psyche to be driven into the dark disturbing elements of the Victorian underworld. What needs to be understood here is that all of us, at times, need to fully acknowledge and, perhaps, act out that which is held within our *shadows*. Those in the acting profession are afforded this opportunity when they take on different roles and characters. However, this needs to be approached with some caution.

In the Middle Ages, on a certain day or a few days each year, the Lord of the Manor and the peasantry would reverse roles, with one of the locals being elected 'king' and the rest of the villagers being made courtiers who would then be waited upon by the ruling elite. A process of role reversal can be very helpful in balancing out different elements within the psyche, as in the case of the TV series *Wife Swap*. However, such an experience needs to be held within strict limits, for when this limitation is missing there is a danger of the 'dark' *shadow* taking over, as in the case of the Nazi regime.

And so it proved in the Jekyll and Hyde story. The more the doctor drank the potion and indulged his Hyde side, the more alluring and seductive this became until eventually there was no going back and the two characters switched sides or polarities, with the 'good doctor' then being held within the *shadow* of Hyde. The story has fed into our language with the term 'a Jekyll and Hyde character', implying a split personality, where two disparate or contradictory aspects of the psyche can manifest through one personality. This brilliantly told archetypal story reminds us of the need for balance when dealing with the light and *shadow* sides of our being. In the greater scheme of our spiritual evolutionary journey, we may need, as in the Prodigal Son parable of Jesus (Luke 15:11-32), to explore the world of physicality and some of the extremes that it can present. In this process, as the biblical tale implies, redemption is always there for us when we awake and return to our true source. In the Stevenson story there is no physical reprieve for either Jekyll or Hyde and the tale ends with both their deaths.

Frankenstein

Mary Shelley's novel (1818) is another classic Victorian Gothic horror story, which gives voice to some of the potential dangers of scientific hubris. The story emerged from a challenge between a group of writers that included Percy Shelley and Lord Byron to see who could spin the best horror story. The tale of *Frankenstein* came from a dream Mary had of a scientist who creates a monster. Our dream states allow us access into our *shadow* selves and Mary's story certainly captured public imagination and became hugely popular. Indeed, the story has spawned a series of similar books and films that are still in vogue today.

Hoping to create a beautiful being, Victor Frankenstein discovers that instead he has given life to a hideous creature who so appals him that he flees his laboratory in disgust and terror. The monster is mortified at being rejected by Frankenstein and goes in pursuit of his creator. We discover that en route the creature learns to read and communicate and even senses or feels love, when he lives for several months in an outhouse attached to a cottage in which a family resides. When eventually the monster is discovered by the family they are terrified and flee in horror. In a fit of rage, the creature burns their home to the ground.

Desiring now companionship at all costs, the monster succeeds in tracking down Frankenstein and pleading with him that if he is to be rejected by both his creator and by humanity then Frankenstein has to create another being to be the monster's mate. Frankenstein reluctantly agrees but then panics before the new creature can be brought into existence and destroys her. This creates intense hatred within the monster, who embarks on a path of revenge, killing one of Frankenstein's close friends as well as his new bride. The enmity between them both grows in its intensity until they finally perish together.

The message of the story is clear: when we reject our *shadow* it has the potential to end up destroying us. While this might seem overdramatic, we can certainly see this being enacted out within the collective of humanity. The rejection of the *shadow* and then the projection of it onto others can lead to the deaths of thousands of people, perhaps even hundreds of thousands, as in the terrible genocide that took place in Ruanda in 1994 or in earlier times with the Jews in Nazi Germany. In this I am reminded of some sage advice given to me by my spiritual mentor many years ago, which I have often reflected on, when he stated 'Evil is only evil as long as it is rejected.'

Many other stories in literature and drama, such as the plays of Shakespeare and Dickens's novels, are based on the tussle between the light and *shadow* elements of the psyche. They highlight the heroes and antiheroes that find rapprochement with their *shadows* by confronting the fears that they contain or learning to love and forgive that which was initially rejected. They also show that those who succumb to their *shadows* are dominated by fear, control and the inflation of the ego.

A particular genre of science fiction books, such as George Orwell's *Nineteen Eighty-Four* (1983) and Aldous Huxley's *Brave New World* (1977), focuses on a dystopian view of a future life by perceiving an element of the collective *shadow* and projecting it into the future. Such books tend to concentrate on a pessimistic perception of a future reality.

Cyrano de Bergerac

This play, written by Edmond Rostand (1897), is based on a real character who lived in the seventeenth century. The play fictionalizes Cyrano's life to express the power of love and, when this is not also applied to the self, the tragedy that then ensues. The Cyrano of the play is a larger-than-life character. He is a brilliant swordsman and poet, who can express his deepest thoughts with eloquence and passion. His only apparent flaw is the physical deformity of his large nose, which he considers so ugly that no woman could truly love him. He is admired and accepted by his comrades for his bravery and courage which serve him well when facing enemies but fail him completely in matters of the heart.

Into his life comes Roxanne, his beautiful cousin, full of grace and wit, with whom Cyrano falls hopelessly in love. For her own part, while accepting the friendship of her cousin, Roxanne's gaze is only turned to that which appears outwardly beautiful and she becomes besotted by Christian, a handsome youth in Cyrano's regiment. She enlists Cyrano's help to win Christian's heart, to which he reluctantly agrees because he is not able to express his own love for Roxanne in a direct way. Christian might be handsome but he lacks Cyrano's ability to express his emotions through words. In a famous scene in the play, Cyrano is hidden in the shadows, beneath Roxanne's window, and pours out his love for her as though he were Christian. It is the words and the powerful sentiments they express that capture Roxanne's heart.

Cyrano engineers a brief marriage ceremony between Roxanne and Christian before the two men have to leave to go to war. Despite being under siege, Cyrano manages to smuggle out daily letters to Roxanne, pouring out his love for her, yet all the while pretending to be Christian who is oblivious of Cyrano's actions and intent. Christian eventually discovers what is happening and realizes that Cyrano deeply loves Roxanne and that she in turn loves the poet in Cyrano that he could never be. Yet so convinced is Cyrano of his ugliness that he persuades Christian to never reveal his secret. Christian is then fatally wounded in battle, yet not before Cyrano has written a moving farewell love letter to Roxanne on the presumption of his death.

The scene then changes to several years later when Roxanne, knowing that Christian is dead, has ensconced herself in a nunnery. She still believes it was Christian who had held all of the qualities of eloquence, poetry and nobility that she loved so deeply. Once a week Cyrano comes to visit Roxanne, bringing news of the outside world, yet never daring to mention the truth of what happened, nor his continued love for her. However, on one fateful day, Cyrano himself is fatally wounded when a beam of wood is dropped on his head. Although barely able to walk, Cyrano visits the garden where Roxanne sits and asks to read the last letter which Christian had supposedly written. In the fading twilight, he reads the letter aloud and something in the words touches Roxanne's soul. She realizes that he is not actually reading but speaking the words from memory and then realizes that it was Cyrano all along who had been writing to her and not Christian. Although recognizing the truth that it is the poetic Cyrano who she truly loves, Roxanne is too late to save him from death.

The tragedy of this tale, which is a twist on the story of *Beauty and the Beast* (de Beaumont, 2008), is the failure of Cyrano to accept and love his own *shadow*, in the form of his long, disfiguring nose. Although deceived, Roxanne's failure was to focus on the outer personality and not be aware of the depth of soul that lies within. The challenge that we all face, at some level, is to be able to accept and love the unlovable aspects of the self. It is only when we can do this that we can find the path to wholeness and balance.

The Rime of the Ancient Mariner

This long poem by Samuel Taylor Coleridge (1798) has a rhythm which, like music, can allow ideas to access into the deeper levels of the psyche. It is a story of sin and redemption, with the hero mariner telling a wedding guest how he gratuitously shot dead an albatross with his crossbow, and the disaster that followed.

> *'God save thee ancient mariner!*
> *From the fiends, that plague thee thus! –*
> *Why look'st thou so ?' – 'With my cross-bow*
> *I shot the Albatross.'*

At first, the crew thought the mariner had done a good deed because a fair wind sprang up behind the ship but then they found themselves becalmed in a slimy sea, possibly the Sargasso, and running out of water.

Day after day, day after day,
We stuck, nor breath nor motion;
As idle as a painted ship
Upon a painted ocean.

The albatross was now hung around the neck of the mariner.

Instead of the cross, the Albatross about my neck was hung.

One by one, the crew members died and the mariner was left alone, with the dead albatross still hung around his neck.

Alone, alone, all, all alone,
Alone on a wide wide sea!
And never a saint took pity on
My soul in agony.

It was only when he watched the water snakes swimming around the ship that the transformation came.

O happy living things! no tongue
Their beauty might declare:
A spring of love gushed from my heart,
And I blessed them unaware:
Sure my kind Saint took pity on me,
And I blessed them unaware.
The self-same moment I could pray;
And from my neck so free
The Albatross fell off, and sank
Like lead into the sea.

Here we see the transformative power of true heartfelt loving prayer to release those albatrosses that we all carry or have carried in some form or another. Eventually the mariner is brought back to the shores of his home country and is then left to tell his tale, as part of his penance, to all those willing, or not so willing, to hear. Close to the end of the tale are these powerful lines:

Farewell, farewell! but this I tell
To thee, thou Wedding-Guest!
He prayeth well, who loveth well
Both man and bird and beast.

He prayeth best, who loveth best
All things both great and small;
For the dear God who loveth us,
He made and loveth all.

Dante's Inferno

To round off this exploration into the *shadow* through drama and literature, one cannot ignore a poem that is arguably one of the most famous of all accounts of the *shadow*. This is the descent into the inferno of hell by Dante Alighieri, which was written between 1308 and 1321. Dante's epic poem is divided into three sections: *Inferno*, *Purgatorio* and *Paradiso* (Dante, 1883). This allegorical tale tells of a journey into three levels of experience which could be described as hell, purgatory and paradise. It is the first of these that is most relevant to an exploration into the *shadow*, which in turn has spawned many paintings and writings including the famous drawings by Botticelli and Dan Brown's recent book *Inferno* (2014).

The poem starts with Dante, midway through his life, finding himself in a gloomy wood, having strayed from the direct path. He journeys on, lost and desolate, until he comes to a mountain which he starts to climb. He then sees a panther, which blocks his path. Seeking a new way up the mountain, he is confronted next by a lion and finally a she-wolf, all of which fill him with such terror that all hope seems lost. At this moment, he becomes aware of the figure that has come to help him, who turns out to be the poet Virgil. Dante pleads in desperation to be saved from these terrible creatures and Virgil replies:

Thou must needs another way pursue, if thou wouldst escape from out that savage wilderness.

Virgil then takes Dante on a journey into hell to see and meet the various beings that exist there. Hell is perceived as existing on nine levels, or circles, with an additional plane where Lucifer resides. At each level, Dante and his guide Virgil perceive and communicate with individuals trapped at those places. It is instructive to see how Dante perceived and graded these circles and their corresponding *sins*.

At the first level exists those virtuous people who have not acknowledged Christ and other pagans, who have otherwise led good and just lives. The second circle is reserved for those consumed by sexual lust and the third circle for gluttony; then follow, in turn, greed, wrath and sloth, and heresy. The seventh level is divided into three sub-planes relating to violence against people and property, followed by suicides and profligates, with the final stage relating to violence against God and nature. The eighth level is again sub-divided and related to fraud in all its forms, such as thieves, hypocrites, perjurers, corrupt politicians and sowers of discord. The ninth and last circle of hell is reserved for treachery in its different manifestations: to kindred, to countries, to guests and to benefactors. Here we find in torment Brutus and Cassius for their murder of Julius Caesar and finally Judas Iscariot for his betrayal of Christ.

Dante is eventually led back from hell before first visiting purgatory and then paradise. The story can be perceived allegorically as some of the aspects of the psyche that the soul must confront in its spiritual journey.

It reflects a period in fourteenth-century Italy when different conflicts between the Guelfs and Ghibellines, supporters of the Pope and the Holy Roman Emperor respectively, were tearing at the soul of the country. It also portrays some of the absolutes of heaven and hell that were then part of Christian theology, whereby sinners are dammed for eternity. While we might not see damnation as so fixed, tribalism and factionalism are still very prevalent throughout our world and have been responsible for countless millions of deaths since Dante's time.

Summary

In this chapter we have explored a few examples of the *shadow* within literature and drama. As can be seen, the *shadow* can express itself in either a positive or a negative way. The positive *shadow* challenges our limitations and asks us to be much more than we conceive ourselves to be; to embrace the polarity aspects of our psyche and to balance the opposites within. The negative *shadow* extols all of those elements that might be considered destructive or debased, that give expression to anger, hatred, revenge and fear. The challenge that humanity has to confront, within both the collective as well as the individual, is how we balance these elements within our psyches. In the next chapter, we will explore these same elements within mythology.

Chapter Four

The Shadow in Mythology

When walking through the 'valley of shadows', remember, a shadow is cast by a light.

Austin O'Malley

In Chapter 3 we looked at the *shadow* in relation to literature and drama. Although mythological stories are a form of literature, they would have stemmed originally from ancient oral traditions, prior to being written down. Myths provided an important role within society for they relayed a culture's ancestral history as well as providing an explanation of the spiritual forces, or deities, that permeated this world, sometimes, although not exclusively, associated with natural phenomena. Mythological stories are common to all countries and cultures and can be found even in the most primitive tribal societies.

When looking at ancient, long-dead peoples, like those that existed in Neolithic Britain, we can only dimly glimpse their understanding of the universe through the megalithic monuments and the few artefacts they left behind. We know from archaeological evidence that they interred the bones of their dead within long rectilinear mounds, called 'long barrows'. We might therefore infer that they had some form of ancestor worship, perhaps even communicating with their forebears in trance states, much as a modern spiritualist might do today. This, however, is pure speculation because we do not know what they believed or thought, we can only ponder. It is only when the stories have been transcribed and then studied that we can begin to gain insight into the beliefs that underpin them. These oral accounts can be extraordinarily complex, such as the great Finnish tales of the Kalevala. The Kalevala was only collated by Elias Lönnrot in the early nineteenth century, and not published until 1835 (Tarmio, 1985).

In our exploration into myth, we will look first at a number of overt *shadow* deities which can be found in some of the great mythological traditions. We will then consider some specific heroic stories pertinent to the *shadow*, showing how both heroes and heroines worked through the challenges that were presented to them.

Demons, Devils and Shadow Entities

I have been interested in mythology since childhood and, over many years of study, have been conscious of a number of common themes that weave through them. It is clear that our ancestors were well aware of the propensity for human beings deliberately to carry out evil or malign acts and needed to create some supernatural force to explain them. Those who claim psychic power, such as shamans, attest to meeting different beings when entering trance states. Indeed, many people who make no claim to psychic ability will have experienced some form of contact or communication with something supernatural at some point in their lives, which can sometimes be akin to St Paul's epiphany moment on the road to Damascus (Acts 9:3-19) or the mystical insights of Julian of Norwich (Norwich, 1998).

It is clear from many different mythological sources that the deities and spirits represented in the stories were considered to reside in another level of reality that was interwoven with the natural world. It is fashionable in today's world to see myths as simply stories, with perhaps, at best, some psychological element but no more. For example, *Oxford Dictionaries* (2015) defines myth in two forms, which can be summarized as follows:

1. A traditional story, sometimes involving heroes or divine beings, which is accepted as history and serves to explain a world view of a people or society.
2. A fictitious story or belief that misrepresents the truth.

The second of these definitions is invariably applied to most aspects of the first. However, we should be clear that this was not how our forebears perceived myths. The supernatural beings or deities that inhabited their world were considered real entities that both interacted between themselves and, when appropriate, with human beings. They were viewed as spiritual forces that both controlled and imbued the world. Seen in this light, we might envision another level of reality, infused with consciousness that runs in parallel with the physical world of the senses. If we consider ourselves mortal beings and nothing more, then scientific explanations are all that suffice. If, however, we believe that we are also spiritual, that the eternal soul has tangible reality, then we have to expand our vistas to consider these other dimensions. Our focus in recent years has been on mainstream mechanistic science and its paradigms, with all the material benefits it brings. This has blinded some to what our ancestors experienced, saw, believed and conveyed so eloquently through their myths.

When looking through the lens of different mythologies and the common threads that run through them, we can begin to glimpse this other-dimensional world and the beings that inhabit it. Like our own world, it is clear that not all of these entities are kind, loving and gentle; some most definitely are malign, full of deceit and demonic. The polarity vision, of the benign and the malevolent, flows into the spiritual hierarchies, presenting us with two distinct sets of deities which are antipathetic and, sometimes, in direct conflict with each other. The focus of this book is on the *shadow* side of this polarity, and to begin to peer into this realm we will go back in time to the myths of ancient Egypt, which first emerged, in written form, some four and a half thousand years ago.

MALIGN DEITIES

We will now examine some of the *shadow* deities believed by religions and past cultures to inhabit and influence this world.

Seth in Ancient Egypt

The main malign protagonist in Egyptian mythology is the god Seth, variously depicted as a crocodile, hippopotamus or ass-like creature (Wilkinson, 2003:197-199). The Heliopolitan cosmology tells us that at the beginning of time a supreme god, Ra-Atum, emerged from the waters of chaos and then brought into being two other divinities, Shu and Tefnut, who are associated with air and water. They in turn created the sky goddess Nut and the earth god Geb, who between them created two sets of polarity gods and goddesses – Osiris and Isis, and Seth and Nepthys (Wilkinson, 2003:17-18). The evil Seth was therefore one of the supreme gods of ancient Egypt, but what did he do wrong to gain this accolade?

The stories tell that Osiris, the eldest god, assumed rulership of the kingdom of earth, along with his sister and consort Isis, and together they civilized the Egyptian people. The benign Osiris then journeyed to other parts of the world, teaching people about agriculture and the benefits of civilization. While he was away, his brother Seth was left in charge of the realm. The pleasure of being in control so appealed to Seth that he determined to get rid of his brother when he returned. This he did by building a magnificent sarcophagus, which had been cunningly designed to fit exactly the body of Osiris. When his brother returned, Seth threw a magnificent banquet in the king's honour and offered the sarcophagus to anyone that it fitted, knowing that this would only be Osiris. After the many courtiers tried and failed, Osiris lay down within the box. Seth then immediately sealed the lid and cast the coffin into the Nile, where it floated away (Geddes & Grosset, 1997:42-48).

Fig. 2 – Statue of Ramses III with the god Horus on his right and Seth on his left.

Isis was distraught about what had happened to her husband and went searching in the reeds of the Nile for her beloved. Meanwhile, the cunning Seth had already discovered the body. He dismembered it by cutting it into fourteen pieces, which he then scattered throughout the land of Egypt. Discovering what had happened, Isis once more set forth to gather together all of the pieces, which she finally succeeded in doing, save only his phallus which had been devoured by a Nile crab.

Through magic, Isis was able to breathe life back into her husband and to unite with him by creating a new magical penis, from which union the hawk-headed god Horus was born. After these trials, Osiris resolved to retire from the physical world and ascend to heaven, leaving behind his son Horus to battle the evil Seth. We can see depictions of this tussle in the great Egyptian temple of Horus at Edfu, where Horus, aided by different gods and goddesses, battles to subdue and contain Seth, who variously appears as either crocodile or hippo (Geddes & Grosset, 1997:42-48).

The origins of Seth in Egyptian mythology are obscure, although he appears to have been present from the earliest of times. He is associated with the desert and was often depicted with flaming red hair, full of anger, rage and violence. The desert was a chaotic place full of potentially evil things, so in this form Seth became associated with all that opposes order (Maat), and therefore stands in opposition to Horus, who symbolizes the grounding of divine order in the physical world. The kings of ancient Egypt were always perceived as an aspect, or son, of Horus. Seth was a god of enormous strength, and when this power could be harnessed it could be turned to the benefit of the king. A triad grouping from the reign of Ramses III, dated to circa 1150 BCE, shows the king striding forward, with Horus facing his right shoulder, balanced by Seth on the left. Both the gods have their hands upraised in benediction, touching the backing stela of Ramses (Fig. 2). In this form, the strengths of Seth could be utilized. Order and chaos were therefore seen as two balancing opposites that needed to be both accepted and propitiated (Wilkinson, 2003:17-18).

Seth was not the only deity in Egyptian mythology to be associated with evil. The great adversary of the sun god Ra was seen as the serpent Apophis, who embodied the qualities of dissolution, darkness and non-existence. He was depicted as a serpent which would attack the sun god each morning, just before dawn, in an endless round of aggression. In this guise, he was sometimes associated with the god Seth (Wilkinson, 2003:221). Apophis was a personification of all that is evil. His malign intent had to be protected against, leading to the creation of many spells which invoked the help of protective deities, particularly in relation to the soul's journey into the afterlife. Below Apophis came a range of minor demons, subject to his control, that we also need to defend against (Wilkinson, 2003:81).

Egyptian mythology abounds with many different gods and goddess that could be considered to represent different aspects of the psyche. However, they were also considered to exist in their own right, as described earlier in this chapter, and could interact with human beings in their daily existence. It was the duty of the king and high priests to propitiate these deities, invoking their support and protection. Despite some *shadow* elements, most were predominantly seen as forces for good. Their beneficent assistance could be invoked in times of crisis, whether at a personal or collective level, and, as such, they could be equated with the benign angelic beings of Christianity. The mythology surrounding these many deities, who ultimately came under the jurisdiction of the sun god Ra, is rich in symbolism. Moreover, the *shadow* was not always feared and rejected, but where appropriate could be harnessed for good.

Lucifer in Christianity

We now turn to a deity that has become equated with the Devil, or Satan. As Prince of Darkness, he became central to Christian mythology as the personification of all that stood against God and His son Jesus Christ. The name 'Lucifer' appears once in the Bible in Isaiah (14:12), meaning, paradoxically, 'bringer of light', and has been associated with the 'morning star' Venus or, in some cases, with the moon (Delahunty and Dignen, 2014). The origins of the association of Lucifer with Satan are obscure, as he was not initially seen in a negative light by the early Latin Church. However, this angel came to be seen as the embodiment of evil in later Christian development. He was originally understood to have been one of the hierarchy of archangels who aspired too high and rebelled against God, only to be cast into the world. He is often associated with the serpent that deceived Eve, which reminds us of the snake Apophis in Egyptian mythology. Satan is a translation of the Hebrew word for 'adversary'.

Lucifer, or Satan, as the inspirer of all that is bad and evil within the human psyche, carries a dynamic that can be found in many diverse traditions. As a spiritual force, he encourages and incites hatred, violence, revenge and fear. Unlike the ancient Egyptian myths of Seth, there is no sense of Lucifer being accommodated. His energies must always be challenged and rejected. This creates a very clear boundary between light and darkness. Within many branches of Christian belief, this polarization creates a tendency to brand anything that is perceived to stand against biblical teachings as satanic.

In the biblical story, Job, beloved by God, is tested by Satan in his tribulations and torments (Job 2:2-13), yet still remains true to Yahweh. We might therefore see Satan as a necessary part of human experience that challenges us to understand the light by seeing and or experiencing the *shadow*. In Job's case, despite all of his tribulations, he finally regains everything that he has lost.

A similar theme can be found in the temptations of Christ, where Jesus is tested in his resolve to remain true to God and not to use his powers in a selfish or inappropriate way. At the end of the temptation, we read in Matthew 4:10 that Jesus commands:

> *Get thee hence, Satan: for it is written, Thou shalt worship the Lord thy God, and him only shalt thou serve.*

A slightly different version is given in Luke 4:8, where Jesus states:

> *Get thee behind me, Satan: for it is written, Thou shalt worship the Lord thy God, and him only shalt thou serve.*

In this second account, there is the implication that the *shadow* is always present (behind us) waiting to test our resolve or understanding. As long as one remains true to one's higher principles, there is nothing to fear. For if we project fear onto the *shadow*, we only empower its self-destructive element.

The Devil in Islam

Islamic mythology contains three distinct groups, which are classed as angels, humans and jinn. In these beliefs, only humans and jinn have free will and hence are subject to being either good or evil. One of the jinn, called Iblis, refused to acknowledge and bow before Adam. He was consequently cast from heaven, into the world, and henceforth known as Shaytan. In other respects, the jinn are generally akin to the demons and devils of Christian theology and are responsible for inciting evil acts within people (Esposito, 2014).

Loki in Scandinavian and Teutonic Mythology

Loki, as one of the Aesir, or supreme gods, is initially just a mischief-maker and trickster before becoming more directly associated with evil. He often found himself in scrapes and, to save his own skin, was not averse to betraying his kindred gods or goddesses. For example, after being captured by the giant Geirröd he agreed, in return for his freedom, to bring back the mighty god Thor, unprotected by his hammer, iron gloves and girdle. Cunningly persuading Thor to visit Geirröd's abode while unarmed, Loki betrayed the god through deceit and trickery. Thor would have been destroyed had he not fortuitously met on the road the giantess Grid. She warned Thor of Geirröd's malice and Loki's treachery and Thor was able save himself (Tonnelat, 1994:266). Possibly, through association with

Christian ideas, Loki increasingly came to be associated with malice, hatred and revenge (Tonnelat, 1994:266). His contempt for Balder 'the beautiful' led Loki to discovering the one element that could destroy the otherwise immune god, which was the mistletoe plant. He then engineered a contest in which Balder agreed to have different objects thrown at him, thereby demonstrating his invincibility. Handing the stem of the mistletoe to the blind god Höd, Loki directed his aim and Balder was slain. Loki is finally killed along with the other gods and goddesses of Asgard in the Götterdämmerung, 'the twilight of the gods', the final conflagration between the Aesir and the giants. Loki himself had been heavily involved in engineering this conflict, which started with the death of Balder.

Many other deities, both major and minor, are represented within Germanic mythology which, like the ancient Egyptian, is peopled by different supernatural beings that inhabit the natural world. These include the spirits of elves, dwarves, nixies, valkyries, and so on. The souls of deceased people were also considered to roam, as shades of the night, if their funeral rites had not been properly instituted (Tonnelat, 1994:277-280). We see again in these myths a complex spiritual world that overlaps with the physical. There is continued enmity between the gods and goddesses of the Aesir and the giants, but it is the betrayal by Loki, one of their own kin, which leads to their eventual demise.

Ahriman of the Persians

The primary malevolent deity of ancient Persia is the god Ahriman, who lived in permanent opposition to the wise being Ahura Mazdah (Cotterell, 1989:56). Persian cosmogony, and its derivations through Zoroastrianism, is based on a dualistic principle of *good* and *evil*. These twin forces were perceived to operate throughout the world, attracting individuals into either one or other camp. For every good deed that Ahura Mazdah performed, Ahriman would do his utmost to counter it by sowing seeds of hatred and revenge wherever he could. These two forces were perceived as being at war with each other, without any hope of reconciliation or balance. The potency of this mythology expanded beyond the boundaries of Iran finding its way into Judaism, through the symbolism of Yahweh and Satan, and then subsequently into Christianity. Ahriman in his quest for domination created a number of minor demons who operated under his jurisdiction. These included a three-headed dragon called Azhi Dahka, plus a number of other lesser known Hindu gods and goddesses (Cotterell, 1989:56).

Other Malevolent or Demonic Beings

As has been mentioned, the spirit of evil can take many guises and has found its way into most mythologies, in one form or another.

The ancient Greeks did not have any one particular major deity that personified evil. This was best represented by the hundred-headed monster Typhon, the 'scourge of mankind', who had been born, some say, from the earth goddess Gaia and, by others, from the goddess Hera. Within the myths, Zeus and Typhon are endlessly locked in combat until eventually Zeus manages to imprison him within Mount Etna, on the island of Sicily (Cotterell, 1989:171). Malefic intent is expressed through the actions of Zeus's wife Hera, who is ever jealous of her husband's infidelities and his support of different human beings. Her vindictive spite and revenge are often directed towards those that Zeus loved or favoured. Some myths suggest that, in anger at Zeus giving birth unaided to the goddess Athene, she invoked Gaia and the imprisoned Titans to create for her a child and then gave birth to the monster Typhon. The mighty Hercules, or Heracles, was one of her victims, and she continued to do what she could to punish the hero throughout his life. Heracles married Megara, but their marriage was doomed when Hera sent Lyssa, the Fury of madness, to Heracles. Driven to insanity, he mistook his wife and children for his enemies and massacred them. In penance for this crime, Heracles had to perform the twelve famous 'Labours' (Guirand, 1994:170).

The main demonic entity from Assyro-Babylonian mythology is the she-dragon of chaos called Tiamat, who is perceived to have existed long before the world was created. She engages in a battle with Marduk, who eventually prevails in overcoming and destroying her. He then sets out to create the world from her body, so bringing human beings into existence (Cotterell, 1989:168). Even though Tiamat no longer existed, some of her energy pervaded other spirits who could incite mischief and evil acts within the minds of human beings. These malignant forces, known collectively as *utukku,* fell into two groups. The first, known as *edimmu*, were the souls of the dead, who had not been given proper burial, whose funeral rites had been neglected. In their disturbed state, they created problems for living individuals. The second group known as *arallu*, were evil genii who ascended from the infernal regions of the Earth and incited hatred and torment. They had no regard for prayers or supplications and did everything in their power to spread discord amongst people. According to Guirand (1994:65), the only way that they could be cleared was by an exorcist who, in the name of the god Ea, commanded:

> *Evil alu, turn thy breast and depart!*
> *O, inhabitants of the ruins, get thee to thy ruins;*
> *For the great Lord Ea has sent me:*
> *He made his incantation for my mouth,*
> *He has given into my hand the cauldron for the Seven,*
> *According to the holy ordinances.*

It is clear from this incantation that the concepts of exorcism and the cleansing of malign spirits has been around for a very long time as these myths stem from around 2000 BCE.

Hindu mythology and its offshoot Tibetan Buddhism contain many references to demonic beings. One group of supernatural beings is divided into the *devas* and the *asuras*. The former rejected lies, espousing only truth, while the latter rejected truth, operating only through lies and deception. We might liken these two groups to the 'angels' and 'fallen angels' of Christian theology (Masson-Oursel & Morin, 1994:334-5). While the *asuras* were in perpetual conflict with the gods, another group of beings, called the Rakshasas, focused on human beings, inciting some of the most despicable passions of lust, gluttony, violence and mendacity. Their role might also be seen as akin to the Fates of Greek mythology who would attach to an individual, who needed to experience these conditions, as part of their destined incarnation (Masson-Oursel & Morin, 1994:337). Chief amongst them was the demon king Ravana, generally depicted with ten heads and twenty arms, who was often in conflict with Vishnu, one of the supreme gods of the Brahma pantheon. Ravana was finally slain by the avatar Rama, through the assistance of the monkey god Hanuman (Cotterell, 1989:234).

Within Buddhism, it is the god Mara who holds the main adversarial role in countering the Buddha's teachings. He can take three forms, representing the qualities of inciter, deluder and destroyer. Like Satan with Christ, Mara does everything in his power to deflect the Buddha's mission on earth, because he knows that his teachings could potentially remove evil from the world. In this sense, he represents a polarity to the Buddha, carrying all of the negative *shadow* aspects of these teachings (Cotterell, 1989:125).

Slavonic myths have two deities – Bylebog, the 'white god', and Chernobog, the 'black god', which reflect light and darkness, good and evil. All good things came from Bylebog, who brought wealth, abundance and prosperity, while the converse was attributed to Chernobog, who with the introduction of Christianity became associated with Satan (Cotterell, 1989:190). These two deities would appear to be very similar in concept to Ahura Mazdah and Ahriman of Persian mythology. As we can see in these myths, polarities run through them which reflect the perception, held within many diverse cultures, of this innate pattern of experience. Essentially, we cannot have one without the other; both polarities must exist on all levels.

DIVINE BEINGS AND THE SHADOW

In their mythological stories, the great gods and goddesses of different pantheons will often experience and explore *shadow* elements of themselves. We have already seen how the great goddess Isis, in the Heliopolitan mythology, went in search of her husband Osiris in order to bring him back to life, so that she could be reunited with him again. This represents an initiatory journey of the psyche, which has to delve into the *shadow* self to discover what is hidden or lost. To achieve her quest Isis had to resort to many different stratagems, including tricking the supreme sun god Ra to give up his secret name, so that she could breathe life back into her dead husband. In order to overcome certain challenges we have to access the very highest levels of spiritual knowledge to achieve our goal.

In a similar vein, Demeter, one of the supreme goddesses of the Greek pantheon, embarked on an epic search to discover the whereabouts of her daughter, Kore, who had been abducted by Hades, the god of the Underworld. Kore was born from the union between the corn-goddess Demeter and Zeus, the king of the gods. Children, in myths, generally represent aspects of ourselves and so it was with Kore, whom Demeter loved dearly. When she grew into a beautiful maiden, her father Zeus, unbeknown to Demeter, offered her as a gift to his brother Hades. One day, when Demeter and her daughter were exploring the countryside, Kore was attracted to a narcissus flower. At that instant, Hades emerged from his realm in a golden chariot and seized Kore, taking her down into the Underworld. Here we see an aspect of the psyche which, beginning to fixate on itself, is immediately drawn into the *shadow*.

So quick was the abduction that Demeter did not see it and was distraught to find that her daughter had disappeared. She then embarked on a journey of discovery to find out what had happened to her. Often, spiritual journeys start with some adversity in our lives. A sudden illness, the loss of a job or a bereavement can impel the soul to take stock and re-evaluate the patterns that make up the life. Although she was a great goddess, Demeter was not immune to having to deal with these *shadow* elements. In her search, she travelled to many different lands and, after various adventures and challenging encounters, she eventually arrived in disguise at Eleusis, where King Celeus and his wife Metaneira entertained her hospitably. She agreed to take on the task of being a wet-nurse to the newborn prince Demophoon. As a gift to the royal pair, Demeter decided to make him immortal by bathing him every night in the celestial fire. Sadly for the prince, Metaneira saw what was happening and, without realizing its import, rushed into the room screaming, so breaking the spell. The fear elements of the psyche can often block or impede the transformational process.

Demeter now revealed herself to the couple in her divine form and offered to bestow great gifts on Triptolemus, one of Celeus's other sons, who had brought news to her of Kore's abduction, citing Hades as the probable culprit. Demeter eventually discovered the truth from Helios, the sun god, who saw everything. Armed with this knowledge, she toured the earth, forbidding the crops to grow and thereby bringing the race of men to the verge of extinction. Zeus was ashamed of his ruse in giving Kore to Hades and, desperate to save humanity, forced his brother to release her back to her mother. Before she emerged from the Underworld, Kore ate a few pomegranate seeds which Hades had given her, thereby cementing their union. Demeter was overcome with joy at seeing her daughter again but despaired when she discovered the binding union that Kore had unwittingly made. Eventually an agreement was made that Kore, now named Persephone, would spend three-quarters of the year with her mother and the remainder, during the winter, with Hades (Graves, 1960: 89-96).

These myths are generally interpreted as an explanation of the seasons but the inner mystery, perhaps explored in the famous Eleusinian Mystery School which Demeter and Persephone founded, was the need for the conscious elements of the psyche to periodically delve into the subconscious *shadow* self in order to gain insight and knowledge. Zinser, in his book *Soul-Centered Healing*, describes this as entering the 'dark spot', which is a cycle we all periodically enter as part of human experience. Zinser states (2011:261):

Everyone periodically passes through his or her dark spot. Depending on the person, that sojourn through the dark can be relatively easy or extremely painful. The conscious self can even become stuck in this dark spot.

The final myth we will explore in this section stems from Assyro-Babylonian mythology and relates to the tales of Inanna, the Queen of Heaven. This goddess was one the great deities worshipped more than five thousand years ago by the peoples who lived in the valleys of the Tigris and Euphrates in what are now Iraq and Syria. Known sometimes as Ishtar, Inanna was principally a goddess of love, joy and sexual expression. As part of her initiatory experience, Inanna decided that she needed to descend into the Underworld to face the hideous Ereshkigal, her sister and the queen of the Underworld.

Before her descent, she put on her crown, her regal clothes and all the regalia of her status as queen of Heaven. She told her faithful companion Ninshubur that, if she had not returned within three days, she should inform the people and the gods of what had happened to her. At the first gate of the Underworld Inanna knocked and called out 'Open the door, gatekeeper! Open the door, Neti! I alone would enter.' Neti enquired who she was and why she had come. Inanna replied that she had come to this realm to participate in the funeral of her sister's husband Gugalanna. Neti then asked her to wait while he took orders from his queen, Ereshkigal. She told Neti to strip Inanna of one item of her clothes or regalia at each gate of the Underworld. As she descended through the seven gates of hell, Inanna was stripped of everything she possessed and eventually stood naked and bowed before her sister Ereshkigal, who now fixed the eye of death upon her. As a rotting corpse, the body of Inanna was hung on a meat hook.

When Inanna did not return after the allotted three days, Ninshubur set out in despair to notify the people and the gods about what had happened and to plead for assistance in rescuing Inanna. Eventually Enki, the god of the waters, agreed to help and, by creating two magical creatures, he was able to trick Ereshkigal into releasing Inanna and restoring her to life (Wolkstein and Kramer, 1983).

Here we see again a depiction of the descent into the *shadow* self to discover what is hidden there. Ereshkigal carries Inanna's polarity, representing the depraved elements of the psyche. Stripped of all that she possessed, Inanna had to face her *shadow* to become whole. When we descend into physical incarnation and connect to our *shadow* self, there is always some part of our being that remains in the 'light' and can set up the means to rescue us. I have worked with a number of clients whose task in this incarnation has been to help rescue and release some aspect of themselves from a previous life that was trapped and still 'earthbound'. The means of help are always available.

HEROIC MYTHS

The accounts of malign deities reflect aspects of the negative *shadow*. Heroic myths express the challenges we need to overcome in order to grow, and so express the positive *shadow*. They can be broadly divided into two categories. The first are the hero myths, which demonstrate courage when facing fear and adversity. These myths are often, although not exclusively, presented through male protagonists, who embark upon quests to overcome some great challenge. The second broad grouping relates to transforming situations through love, compassion, wisdom and forgiveness. It needs to be stressed here that these mythological principles relate to all of us, both men and women. For example, Joan of Arc, in her quest to unite France and drive out the English, was working through the male heroic, warrior principle. Christ, in giving up his life to demonstrate forgiveness, worked through the feminine principle.

HEROES

One of the early great epic accounts, within Assyro-Babylonian mythology, is the story of Gilgamesh, which probably dates back to the second millennium BCE. After his close friend and companion Enkidu unexpectedly perished, Gilgamesh embarked on an epic voyage to discover the meaning of life and death, which sometimes brought him into conflict with great deities, such as the love goddess Ishtar or Inanna (Guirand, 1994:66-72).

We find hero characters in all cultures, inspiring us to be greater than whom we seem, and extending us far beyond the limitations of the normal world. In some cases, the heroes have to slay mythic beasts, displaying fearlessness and resolve in meeting the challenge. In others, they have to transform the situation through compassion and forgiveness, such as the tales of St Francis. Certainly, the more ancient stories tend to focus on the warrior element, rather than that of the healer. Super, or semi-divine, heroes can be found in many diverse stories and are still being created today. In the Anglo-Saxon epic, Beowulf has to slay the monster Grendel (Cotterell, 1989:189), while in Irish myth, Cuchulainn fulfilled this heroic element in his many exploits and defence of Ulster. These heroes often had divine parents. Cuchulainn's mother was Dechtire, the wife of an Ulster chieftain, whilst his father was considered the sun god Lugh (Cotterell, 1989:79). The father of Hercules or Heracles is Zeus, king of the gods, while his mother is Alcmene, the queen of the Tiryns (Cotterell, 1989:100). These divine conception stories find an echo in the divinity of Christ and the dream of Queen Maya before the birth of the Buddha.

Perseus

Another of Zeus's mortal children was the hero Perseus, whose mother was the princess Danaë. A prophecy had foretold that Danaë would give birth to a son who would kill his grandfather, King Acrisius. To prevent this happening, Danaë was locked away in a tower. Zeus appeared to the princess as a golden shower, impregnated her and then spirited her away with her child, to be brought up by local fishermen. Growing to manhood, Perseus came to the attention of the local king, Polydectes, who saw him standing in the way of his desire for Danaë and so plotted to be rid of the young upstart. To achieve this end, Perseus was sent on a seemingly impossible quest to bring back the head of the Gorgon Medusa (Guirand, 1994:183).

The Gorgons had originally been three priestesses who were the guardians of an Atlantic temple that was dedicated to the goddess Athene. Two were immortal, while the third, Medusa, was mortal. One day the sea god Poseidon turned himself into a magnificent black stallion and seduced the priestesses. In outrage, Athene turned them all into hideous creatures, with hair of snakes, and banished them to a distant land. Anyone who then looked at these creatures was immediately turned to stone. The quest that had been given to Perseus looked like certain death.

Perseus, nevertheless, was able to call on the assistance of the gods. Hermes, the winged messenger, loaned him a golden sickle and a pair of magic sandals, so that he could fly to the land of the Gorgons. Athene gave him a magic shield, and Hades a cap of invisibility. Armed with these gifts, Perseus was able to track down Medusa. By looking at her image in the shield Athene had given him, he was able to cut off Medusa's head and to put it into a sack. However, this was not end of Medusa because from her body and blood sprang the white winged horse Pegasus and the golden warrior Chrysaor. Perseus, easily eluding the other two Gorgons with his cap of invisibility, then returned to Polydectes and presented the king with Medusa's head, instantly turning him to stone. Perseus then offered the head to the goddess Athene, who placed it on her shield (Mavromataki, 1997:216-7).

The Medusa myth touches many levels in its relationship to the *shadow*. Firstly, there is the implication of some misdeed in the past, perpetrated by the feminine, that had led to the creation of a malign force. This has echoes in the biblical story when Eve persuaded Adam to eat of the tree of knowledge of good and evil, and in the curiosity of Pandora who releases all of the woes of humankind, saving only hope. This might be a simple projection of rational male inadequacy onto the intuitive feminine. However, the soul is sometimes perceived in feminine guise and the myth might allude to some perception of a fundamental imbalance, or flaw, residing deep within our psyches, perhaps as a form of original sin.

Being turned to stone equates with the Buddha's greatest sin – that of mindlessness. In looking at the different elements on this planet, many of its fears and attractions can chain or lure us into a mindless or unconscious state. *Shadow* work demands we bring that which is locked within into the light, for while it remains unconscious it will inevitably curtail our actions. The heroic challenge demands that we delve deep to confront our fears and overcome them. However, this is always best done by calling on divine assistance, as Perseus did. The inspiration that comes from the higher aspects of our psyche gives insight into the best way to tackle our issues. When we confront and slay our fear demons, they release new energies to us, which in the case of Perseus was a white winged horse and a golden warrior.

Pegasus, the white winged horse, went through a number of adventures before Zeus placed him in stars, as the constellation of the same name. There is a belief, amongst some, that we are now moving from the Age of Pisces into the Age of Aquarius. When viewed in the heavens, the constellation of Pegasus sits between these other two signs; therefore, to move from one Age to the next we need to go through the transformation process that the birth and myths of Pegasus invoke. The slaying of Medusa, or any such myth of conquest, is simply the challenge of facing and overcoming our fears. At this level, nothing is ever destroyed, only transformed.

Heracles

The greatest of the Greek heroes was Heracles, or Hercules as he is sometimes known. We have already mentioned his conflict with the goddess Hera. In these tales, she represents his spiritual *shadow*, by challenging him with the adversities he then has to overcome. She caused Heracles to undergo the trials of his twelve Labours, which he ultimately achieved, thereby gaining immortality. Each of his Labours can be seen as a confrontation with different aspects of his *shadow* and the steps he took to overcome the challenges they represented. The twelve trials might be considered the spiritual test for each of the signs of the zodiac (Esonet, 2015). To achieve these goals, he had to use many different skills, aided at times by different gods, goddesses and mortals. For example, in his eleventh Labour he was told to bring back the golden apples of the Hesperides, which had been Gaia's gift to Zeus and Hera on their wedding night. Enchanted by their beauty, Hera had planted them in a garden where the giant Atlas lived, whereupon a tree sprang up bearing the fruit of golden apples. Hera had protected this tree with the huge hundred-headed dragon called Ladon and four nymphs, known collectively as the Hesperides.

At first Heracles could not find the road to this land but eventually did so by capturing Nereus, one of the sea gods, and compelling him to give the right directions. Having now discovered the way, our hero, when crossing the Caucasus Mountains, came across the divine Prometheus,

Illuminating the Shadow

held in bondage and torment as a punishment for bringing the benefits of fire to humanity. Heracles slew the eagle that was devouring the liver of Prometheus and freed him. In gratitude, Prometheus encouraged Heracles to get the giant Atlas to gather the golden apples rather than perform the task himself. Heracles was able to persuade Atlas to take on this assignment by agreeing to hold the world on his own shoulders, while the giant carried out the mission. Atlas concurred and soon returned with the golden apples. However, the giant reneged on his bargain, saying that he would not take back the world. Instead of remonstrating with him, Heracles agreed that this was quite reasonable, but as the world was very heavy he would like to put a cushion under his shoulders. He asked Atlas to hold the world for a moment, while he made a cushion. As soon as Atlas took back the globe, Heracles gathered up the apples and returned to Mycenae. The apples were then offered to Athene, who in turn sent them sent back to the Hesperides (Mavromataki, 1997:163-4).

We see in this tale the different stratagems employed by Heracles to obtain his quest. The golden apples represent a divine aspect of our being that remains hidden. Apples are often associated with love, hence their gift from Gaia on Zeus and Hera's wedding night. Being gold, they also link to our spiritual side. To again access to these inner jewels, we first need to harness our intuition, symbolized by Nereus, before releasing our creativity, symbolized by the fire of Prometheus. The saying 'carrying the weight of the world on our shoulders' stems from this myth and the trials that life has to offer, which can sometimes seem like a terrible burden. Yet this myth tells us that these trials do not last forever. We can learn to let go that which we carry, and so gather the divine fruit from our spiritual self.

Another of Heracles' tasks was the slaying of the many-headed monster Hydra. Whenever one head was cut off two more grew in its place. Heracles achieved the task with the aid of his faithful companion Iolaus. Heracles first went to the spring where the monster resided and forced it from its lair with burning arrows. As he cut off each head, Iolaus cauterized the stump with a flaming brand, and slowly the monster was overcome. Heracles finally removed the last immortal head and buried it.

In this myth, we see the inner trial of confronting the different negative aspects of the psyche, the many-headed Hydra, which needs to be transformed by the fire of our spirituality; this is represented by the flaming brand of the soul, our true inner light. The final head is buried, indicating that it will always be with us, ready to challenge our resolve and determination.

In these stories, we see an aggressive approach to dealing with the *shadow*, which reflects something of the warrior male psyche as it was perceived in ancient times. This can still be evidenced today when we see how some elements, within different cultures, confront their *shadows*. If this were not so, armed conflict would be a rarity, which indicates how ingrained these elements are within us.

HEROINES

As already stated, myths relating to hero figures generally entail a challenge that has to be worked out by overcoming adversity and facing fear. Such individuals are often semi-divine, indicating the spiritual nature of the challenge that necessitates accessing this deeper level of our being. Heroine myths, on the other hand, are often more complex and when not aping the heroic masculine are generally woven around some element of love and self-sacrifice, such as the story of the ancient Greek queen Alcestis, which was made into a play by Euripedes.

Alcestis

Like all good myths, the story weaves together many different elements, both natural and supernatural. Alcestis is the daughter of King Pelias and Queen Anaxibia, and when the beautiful child comes of age she is offered as a bride to anyone who can achieve a seemingly impossible task. This entails hitching both a lion and a wild boar to a chariot, and getting this unlikely pair to pull the chariot for some considerable distance. One might have been forgiven for thinking that Alcestis was fated to die a maiden as a result of this bizarre edict. However, as in all good myths of this type, King Admetus, the hero of the story, has some tricks up his sleeve. He gains the support of the sun god Apollo, who is quite capable of taming these two wild beasts, and so the king wins his bride and brings her back to his kingdom.

For a few years, the couple live in wedded bliss and Alcestis gives birth to a little boy and girl. The fates, however, have decreed that Admetus will only live a short mortal life, like many heroes before him. As the time fast approaches for his demise, his divine mentor, Apollo, manages to get him a reprieve, on the one condition that someone close to him is willing to sacrifice their life in his stead. Admetus pleads his cause to his two elderly parents who are nearing the end of their lives. Yet they have none of it, saying they have done all of their duties by him, are enjoying their old age together and that this is his problem and he needs to sort it out for himself. At this point of the tale, seeing the dilemma, Alcestis steps forth.

Recognizing that kingship is important for the stability of the realm, and that if Admetus dies there will be no one to protect her children, she chooses to offer herself in sacrifice. At first, Admetus declines her offer but then, seeing the wisdom of this choice, he agrees even though he is utterly distraught. He swears to Alcestis that he will not bring any other bride into his home and will continue to nurture and care for his children. This pact having been made, Alcestis lies down in her funerary robes and the 'shades' come to collect her. Admetus then completes all of the funeral rites and has her interred within a special tomb.

Into the scene now comes the hero Heracles, on one of his many adventures. Hearing of the plight of the couple, he descends into the realm of Hades to bring back the queen. This poses few problems for Heracles, as his last Labour had entailed venturing into these domains to bring back the three-headed monster dog Cerberus who guarded the Underworld. A quick excursion into the netherworld is a simple task and he brings Alcestis back to Admetus, with a black veil covering her face so that the king cannot recognize her.

Admetus knows and greets Heracles, and then enquires about the veiled woman standing beside him. Heracles tells Admetus that he has brought the king a new bride. Remembering his vow, Admetus refuses to accept her, and again Heracles presses her suit. The king is adamant, and after much argument Heracles finally asks Admetus whether he would like to remove the veil to see who the bride is. Not wishing to offend his guest, Admetus finally agrees and is astonished to see Alcestis standing in front of him. Heracles warns him that she will not be able to speak for three days, as she is still purifying herself from the ordeal. The king and queen then live happily ever after, or so the tale goes.

Here we see another level of spiritual initiation, where love and self-sacrifice are able to lift a mortal curse. In this beautifully balanced tale, both male and female qualities come to the fore, with both the king and queen willing to make sacrifices for their children. Ultimately, the power of love carries the couple through their ordeal, with both remaining true to the principles they have espoused. One is reminded in this story of John's comment, in reference to Christ: 'Greater love hath no man than this, that a man lay down his life for his friends' (John 15:13). Additionally, being unable to speak for three days is reminiscent of the three days that Christ spends in his tomb before his resurrection. Going into the Underworld is a symbol of going into the depths of one's being to access the spiritual self, which Alcestis does because of her love for her husband and children. These steps cannot normally be taken without divine help which, in this case, comes in the form of Apollo and Heracles.

Antigone

Our next story of feminine love and piety does not have such a happy conclusion. It involves the children of Oedipus, the legendary king of Thebes, who was prophesied to both kill his father and marry his mother, thereby bringing disaster on his family and kingdom. Despite his best efforts, Oedipus fulfils the curse and in a fit of remorse gouges out his own eyes. This story, made famous by Freud and his analysis, suggests that this myth represents the child's desire to slay the father in order to possess the mother. We might surmise that any child of such a union is going to carry some heavy ancestral karma, and so it proved.

Princess Antigone has two brothers, Polyneices and Eteocles, and a sister Ismene. After their father's death, Creon, their uncle, takes control of the kingdom. However, strife is never far away and Polyneices leads a rebellion against his uncle, which results in his own death and the death of Eteocles, who had supported Creon. After putting down the rebellion, Creon seeks revenge by proclaiming that no funeral rites or proper burial will be performed for the traitors, and their bodies should be left as carrion (Heaney, 2004, Loc.63).

Antigone is distraught at the loss of her brothers, and the thought that Polyneices will not be given a proper burial. Despite knowing that Creon has imposed a death penalty on anyone who opposes this order – 'Those that are not for me are against me' – Antigone determines to carry out the funerary rites one way or another. She first asks her sister Ismene for help but she is very unsure, and so Antigone resolves to do the deed alone.

Although the burial is successful, Creon discovers what has happened and determines, through right of the law, to punish his niece. She in turn appeals to a higher divine law, that of the gods and the rites demanded by them for proper burial ceremonies. Creon's heart, however, is hardened and, inflamed by Antigone's resistance, he orders that she will be sealed up alive in a tomb, with some food, so that the Theban people will not be implicated in her death.

Antigone's intended husband is Hæmon, Creon's son. In a modern version of the play by Seamus Heaney, Hæmon pleads for Antigone's life, stating that the local people regard her as a hero for having stood up for what is right and, instead of being punished, she should be honoured. He implores his father to reconsider his verdict. Both Creon and Hæmon then dispute vehemently with each other, presenting argument and counterargument. Finally, Hæmon concludes that if Antigone dies, she will not die alone.

Antigone accepts her fate, stating that her conscience is clear because she did what was ordained by the gods, and is sealed alive in the tomb. Onto the scene comes the great seer Tiresias, who warns Creon that he stands at the edge of a cliff and is about to fall over. For, says Tiresias, a ritual sacrifice that he had made on Creon's behalf completely failed, which he put down to Creon's headstrong nature and his determination not to forgive Antigone. Creon is oblivious to these insights, and claims that Tiresias is just a fake.

Despite his initial resolve, the situation eats away at Creon and, after much soul-searching, he finally relents. He determines to fulfil the burial obligations for Polyneices and to free Antigone. Sadly, it is all too late. Antigone has already hanged herself. In despair, Hæmon, her intended husband, stabs himself with his sword, and dies clutching the body of Antigone while cursing his father. Distraught by the death of her son, Eurydice, Creon's wife, also takes her own life. Creon is desolate and bemoans:

Woe is me, for the wretched blindness of my counsels!
The Chorus then concludes (Jebb, 1902):
Wisdom is the supreme part of happiness; and reverence towards
the gods must be inviolate. Great words of prideful men are ever punished
with great blows, and, in old age, teach the chastened to be wise.

In this story we see the determination of Antigone to surrender her life for the love of doing what she considered the 'right action' by her dead brother. Although this action led to her death, we might surmise that her soul remained unstained, while that of Creon would have been weighed down by guilt. Creon's fault in this matter is highlighted by having taken a rigid polarity position and then stuck by it. Truth and balance lie in being able to acknowledge and integrate opposites, as the wise Tiresias foresaw.

Summary

In these mythological accounts we have considered the major shadow deities and the ways that both heroes and heroines have dealt with the challenges presented to them. The propensity for human beings to perpetrate evil acts needed some explanation by our early ancestors. Perhaps the best way that this could be achieved was by seeing this projected onto a deity. War gods, such as the Greek Ares, are also common, indicating that armed conflict formed part of most ancient societies. Psychology is beginning to understand the mechanisms that cause some people to be psychopaths, or sociopaths, in an attempt to explain some of these perceived aberrations within the psyche. The challenge is how we collectively, as a species, deal with these traits that appear to be part of our innate nature.

It is also clear from these stories that a domain of spirit entities was perceived to exist. The world was 'peopled' by spirit beings, which wove into and out of the physical world we inhabit. One group of such spirits was human souls who had not been given proper funerary rites, or still carried some vindictive quality that kept them close to the physical plane. The perception of seeing, or being aware of, ghosts is a common thread that cannot lightly be dismissed. Once the concept of an eternal soul that transcends death is accepted, then a realm of spirit beings is the logical outcome. It is highly unlikely that early human beings worked out such ideas rationally, rather that they simply expressed what they saw and experienced.

Atheism denies the existence of a spirit realm as a valid concept. This stance is predominant within the scientific collective. It is eloquently expressed by individuals such as Richard Dawkins because the intangible, by its very nature, is very difficult to study in the crucible or under the microscope. However, it should be remembered that this is not the common experience of human beings through time. We will return to Richard Dawkins once more, when we explore the cosmic *shadow* in Chapter 6.

Heroic challenges generally entail facing insuperable adversities and then overcoming them. The bottom line is confronting fear in all of its manifestations. Indeed, it could be argued that one of the *shadow* reasons that humans engage in warfare is to confront their fear of death. Myths and stories relating to the feminine are more focused on love and self-sacrifice in its many different forms. Thus we may proclaim that fear is the opposite of love.

In the next chapter, we will consider the shadow in relation to metaphor and fairy tales, looking first at this theme through the eyes of various divinatory systems such as the tarot and the I Ching.

Chapter Five

The Shadow in Metaphor and Fairy Tale

I don't need a friend who changes when I change and who nods when I nod; my shadow does that much better.

Plutarch

As with myth, divinatory systems give insight into the subconscious patterns that inform our decision-making process. Developed over a long period, they are an attempt to make conscious the *shadow* or hidden elements of our psyche. One of the oldest of these systems is the I Ching, which sprang from the profound insights of the sages of ancient China. It is still used extensively by individuals wishing to delve below the rational conscious mind to gain another level of perception into personal, therapeutic and business decisions. Nor is it restricted to those of Chinese extraction alone but to anyone looking for another level of awareness about a specific situation. The I Ching has a reputation for bringing forward viewpoints that can be profound. As a system of divination, it was hardly known in the western world until Richard Wilhelm's translation in 1951. Before then most fortune-tellers resorted to other methods, such as palmistry, astrology and the tarot.

It is the latter of these systems that provides most insight into the workings of the *shadow*. The tarot first emerged from a series of court cards in the Italian Renaissance of the fifteenth century (Giles, 1993: 7:9). They developed into the modern decks we see today, although probably the most influential is the Rider-Waite (1909) pack that was created by the writer and occultist, AE Waite. The deck was illustrated by his colleague Pamela Colman Smith. Waite himself wrote (Giles, 1993:44):

The tarot embodies symbolic presentations of universal ideas, behind which lie all the implicits of the human mind, and it is in this sense that they contain secret doctrine, which is the realization by the few, of truths embedded in the consciousness of all, though they have not passed into express recognition by ordinary men.

In this chapter, as well as considering the metaphors of the I Ching and the tarot, we will explore the role of fairy tales which, like mythology, show different methods for dealing with the *shadow* when their messages can be understood. The universal mind is symbolic, which is why we dream in pictures. Our dreams give insight into what is going on in the subconscious. When we hear or read stories they generate images in our mind from the descriptions given. These are then picked up by the deeper parts of our psyche, or by our sub-personalities. In resonating with these subconscious components, the stories give intuitive insight into the steps we need to take to deal with and heal the *shadow* elements of our being.

METAPHOR

We now will look in more depth into the I Ching and the tarot before moving on to consider fairy tales.

The I Ching

The origins of the sixty-four hexagrams of the I Ching are thought to date back to the time of King Wen, in the twelfth century BCE, although earlier origins are likely, possibly from the earliest stages of Chinese civilization (Marshall, 2002:3-7). It was based upon the expression of movement of the two fundamental principles, already mentioned here, known as 'yang' (–), represented by a single straight line and 'yin' (- -) represented by a single broken line. These principles were never seen in absolute terms in the way that they are expressed today in the development of electrical circuitry, when a system can be either on or off. To the Chinese mind, even within extreme yang there was yin, and vice versa. Indeed, in going one stage further, they perceived, either through insight or observation, that when a system went to an extreme it would then revert to its opposite. The bipolar mood swings involved in being on a high before descending into the depths of depression in a low is a human psychological expression of this idea.

The Chinese sages were not restricted to seeing just the two principles in operation but considered what might be the influences if they brought them together or combined them in some way. The first stage in this process was to consider the four possibilities presented by any two paired lines. When placed one above the other, we can have two yang lines, two yin lines, a yang line over a yin line, or a yin line over a yang line. This simple mathematical progression also reflected the development stages within a family structure. We all have two parents and four grandparents. Your father's father could be represented by two yang lines, your father's mother by a yin line under a yang line, your mother's father by a yang line under a yin line and your mother's mother by two yin lines (see Fig. 3).

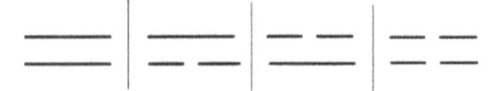

Fig 3 – I Ching, Development Stage 1

Intuitively, there was an understanding that polarities within themselves are often unstable. There is always a tendency to swing from one polarity to another. To stabilize a system a third component is required, creating a triangle, which was perceived to be the most stable pattern within the universe. Trinities, or triangular relationships, are part of universal awareness and therefore must be considered as a fundamental part of the human psyche (McGoldrick and Gerson, 1985). We find many expressions of trinities within family dynamics, mythology, fairy tales and religious literature.

Within the family, the fundamental triangular unit is the mother, father and child. Without the child component, there can be a tendency for the adults to split apart. In such cases, family psychologists have discovered that an unconscious patterning will generally draw in another person or pet to anchor this polarity. Not all triangles are harmonious. Within some families, they can cause great conflict, yet there is always an unconscious power that binds them together. When more siblings come along, a series of triangular relationships is created, which can be complex (McGoldrick and Gerson, 1985).

Within both mythology and religious belief we find many instances of trinities of gods, goddesses and child, such as Isis, Osiris and Horus from ancient Egypt, or the Holy Trinity in Christian theology of Father, Son and Holy Ghost. Questions and challenges are generally made three times and knowing the answer to three guesses is often a component in fairy tales. So while polarity is one fundamental in the universe, trinities appear to be another. With this thought in mind, let us now return to the development stages of the I Ching (Fig. 4).

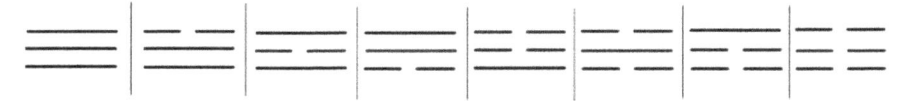

Fig. 4 – The Trigrams of the I Ching

It can be found that a combination of three yin or yang lines can be put together, one above the other, to create a trigram. This arrangement gives eight different combinations, which again expresses the dynamic of the family for we all have eight great-grandparents. In a similar way

Illuminating the Shadow

the ancient Chinese saw this eightfold combination as a family with a mother (three yin lines) a father (three yang lines) and six children with three sons and three daughters. These combinations were perceived as eight distinct principles, which in turn were perceived to flow through different aspects of life. For example, Kun, the receptive mother, related to all maternal things, including the earth, motherhood and relationships. Seven of these trigrams represent benign qualities: K'an, the second son, relates to that which has the potential to be malign, evil or dangerous (Wilhelm, 1968). The I Ching itself is based on the combination of any two of these trigrams, creating what is known as a hexagram. When we multiply eight by eight we have a total of sixty-four hexagrams, which make up the I Ching. Each hexagram has a commentary, giving insights into the perceived qualities involved with that particular combination. For example, in Hexagram 11, which has the title 'Peace', where the Receptive (mother) principle stands above the Creative (father), we read (Legge, 1899):

In Thâi (we see) the little gone and the great come. (It indicates that) there will be good fortune, with progress and success.

However, when the trigram K'an appears in the reading we can be sure that some form of problem or difficulty is indicated, with the *shadow* elements being overt and present. For example, in Hexagram 39, known as 'Obstruction', we have the image of a 'dangerous abyss' in front of us with a 'steep inaccessible mountain rising behind' (Wilhelm, 1968).

Effectively then, a potentially destructive problematic element is built into the I Ching relating to different expressions of the suppressed, negative or malign *shadow*. To reiterate this point, of the eight primary archetypal principles contained within the trigrams, one relates to the negative aspect of our psyche and the way that potentially malign *shadow* patterns flow through us. In *An Anthology of the I Ching* by W. Sherill and W.K. Chu (1977), the attributes or associations of K'an are listed as: danger, hardships, trouble-makers, evil doers, sick persons, troubled individuals, strongly sexed persons and the dead.

What is fascinating about these particular elements of the I Ching is that they are mirrored within the tarot deck. Two widely spaced systems of inner inquiry, in both region and time, reflect similar patterns and, like Newton's apple, suggest universal principles, at least within the human psyche.

The Tarot

Tarot cards are divided into two groups: the Major Arcana has twenty-two cards and the Minor Arcana has fifty-six cards, making seventy-eight cards in all. The Minor Arcana cards were further developed to become the traditional playing cards we use today for many different games, such as whist and poker. While the playing cards have become common it is the twenty-two Major Arcana cards that are the most interesting in giving insight into the *shadow* and linking to the I Ching. In my book *Develop Your Intuition and Psychic Power* (Furlong, 2008), I explore the significance of the tarot card associations in some depth, as the following pattern is not generally recognized. I suggest that these twenty-two cards can be further divided into three groups of cards, which can listed as:

- *Eight archetypal character cards, which reflect the eight trigrams of the I Ching*
- *Twelve astrological cards*
- *Two cards that relate to us as human beings*

The eight character cards comprise the Fool, the Magician, the High Priestess, the Empress, the Emperor, the Hierophant, the Hermit and the Devil (Fig. 5). The twelve zodiac cards are as follows: Aries – The Chariot; Taurus – The World; Gemini – The Lovers; Cancer – The Moon; Leo

– Strength; Virgo – The Hanged Man; Libra – Justice; Scorpio – Death; Sagittarius – Wheel of Fortune; Capricorn – Judgement; Aquarius – The Star; Pisces – Temperance.

The two remaining cards – the Sun and the Tower – represent the incarnate spiritual soul and the physical body or material life. In the Tower card, we see the descent of the spirit into the physical world, symbolized by the lightning flash, with two characters falling headlong and the crown at the top of the tower being displaced. This card informs us that when we incarnate into the physical body we lose our connection to the spiritual realm, represented by the displaced crown. This card was originally known as La Maison de Dieu (The House of God), which reminds us that the body is the temple of the soul (Willis, 1991:84-5). The tarot deck can be seen as a system of initiation that takes us back to reconnecting with the Divine when we are ready (Furlong, 2008:151-8).

In a similar way to the I Ching, we find the seven character cards of the Fool, the Magician, the High Priestess, the Empress, the Emperor, the Hierophant and the Hermit that portray balanced principles and one, the Devil, that clearly relates to the *shadow*. Within tarot readings, its appearance in a spread indicates some malign or problematic influence involving, anger, oppression and restriction (Almond and Seddon, 1991:86-88). To further emphasize this point we also find, within the Heliopolitan cosmogony of ancient Egypt, eight main gods and goddesses (Osiris, Isis, Horus, Hathor, Thoth, Nepthys, Anubis, and Seth) whom we have already met in the chapter on mythology.

There is not space within these pages to explore this concept further, except to flag this up as another potential pattern that we can see expressed within very distinct cultures at different historical periods. These ideas are more fully explored in my book *Develop Your Intuition and Psychic Powers*

Fig.5 – The Devil Tarot card.

(Furlong, 2008). The suggestion implied is that a component exists within the human psyche that exaggerates and emphasizes the *shadow* elements within us. This theme will become more apparent when we explore the cosmic *shadow* in Chapter 6.

Let us now look at how the *shadow* is represented within fairy stories.

FAIRY TALES

Fairy tales, as a complement to mythology, can be found in many different cultures of the world. They differ from mythology because these tales primarily relate to individuals, often children, acting in a magical landscape full of fairies, dwarves, goblins, wizards and witches. They invariably reflect some element of *shadow* work, which is why their stories are so enduring and are told and re-told through many different formats. The reworked Sleeping Beauty story in the film *Maleficent*, already mentioned, is one such example.

Fairy tales fall into certain groups, often involving a heroic journey or quest which can lead to the winning of the handsome prince or the beautiful princess. To understand these two elements we can consider that the prince or princess relates to our inner soul essence, which needs to be first recognized and then won, in order for us to become whole and balanced. In these stories the prince, or hero, needs to overcome different obstacles to win his princess, while the princess, or fair maiden, generally needs, through love, to discover her handsome prince. The story of *Beauty and the Beast* (de Beaumont, 2008) is such a tale and it is this aspect of *shadow* work that interests us here.

Beauty and the Beast

In this story a wealthy merchant, who has fallen on hard times, goes to a local port to see if one of his ships has returned safely. He has three sons and three beautiful daughters (note the trinity), two of whom are grasping and cruel, while Belle, the youngest, is loving and gentle (in polarity balance to her sisters). The merchant promises to bring back to his children some gifts if anything remains from the sale of the ship's goods. The two greedy girls want jewels and fine clothes, while Belle asks only for a rose (as symbol of the spiritual self).

When the merchant gets to the harbour he discovers the sale of the ship's goods is only enough to pay off his debts and he leaves to return home with nothing for his daughters. On his homeward journey, he passes through a dark wood (going into the subconscious) and there becomes lost. He eventually finds a castle and enters it to find it full of food, but nobody seems to be present. Being famished, the merchant helps himself to the food and then falls into a deep asleep, only waking up the following morning. There is still nobody around. On passing through the garden to find the road back home, he spies a beautiful rose and immediately remembers his promise to Belle. Picking the rose, he is then confronted by a terrible Beast that challenges him for his greed at not only eating the food but also stealing a rose. For this crime he must surely die. (Here, the ego self is not yet ready to access the spiritual because the inner work has not yet been done.) Trembling with fear, the merchant explains that he took the rose as a gift for his daughter Belle. The Beast states that he will spare his life on the one condition that he returns to the castle after delivering the rose. He must also tell no one of the bargain, particularly Belle. Having little choice, the merchant reluctantly agrees. The Beast then gives the merchant fine clothes and jewels for his other daughters and sends him on his way.

Back at home, he gives the presents to the daughters but knows that he soon must return to the castle. Belle senses that something is wrong and keeps pleading with her father to tell the truth of the situation, which eventually he does. Belle then insists on going to the castle in her father's place, to which he reluctantly agrees. Belle is then greeted by the Beast, who treats her kindly and states that she is now the mistress of the castle and everything she wants will be given to her.

So far in the story we can see the Beast as a rejected aspect of the merchant's *shadow* self and his children as other elements of his psyche. Roses in fairy tales relate to spiritual quests and the intuitive part of the merchant is symbolized by Belle, who knows that this is the only route to him becoming whole. It is this sensitive and intuitive part that is now needed to complete the task.

At first Belle is happy within the castle for there is much to see and explore. She enjoys the fine food and beautiful gardens, and every evening at dinner engages in pleasant conversation with the Beast, who always ends the evening by asking Belle to marry him. She refuses but at night, in her sleep, she keeps dreaming of a handsome prince and is convinced that the Beast has him hidden somewhere in the palace. During the day, she starts to explore the castle with its endless, enchanted rooms, but nowhere does she discover the prince. Here we see the intuitive part of the psyche being aware that there is something that needs releasing but not understanding what is being presented.

For several months Belle is happy within the castle but then starts to become homesick for her father and family and pleads with the Beast to let her go. Eventually he concedes but only on the express condition that she returns seven days later. Seven is another of our sacred numbers. She willingly agrees and goes back to see her father and her brothers and sisters. Her intuition, in realizing that the important part has not been discovered, now needs to return to the outer world of the senses. Before leaving, the Beast gives Belle several presents including a magic mirror, which allows her to see what is happening in the castle, and a magic ring that will allow her to return instantly when it is turned three times on her finger (note the trinity again). The rejected ugly self knows that Belle is the key to its redemption, giving her the magic gifts allows direct access into its energy.

Belle's father is delighted to see her but her sisters are jealous and try to do everything in their power to keep her at home in the material world. Here we can see the physical material parts of our being keeping us trapped from dealing with inner world issues. Each day after the seven allotted by the Beast, the cruel sisters plead with Belle not to go back and she reluctantly concedes. Eventually her intuitive part realizes that something is very wrong and uses the mirror to look inside, only to see the Beast lying heartbroken and nearly dead by the rose bush. Turning her ring three times on her finger Belle is immediately transported back to the Beast and, shedding tears, tells him that she loves him. The Beast then is transformed into the handsome prince. He tells Belle that a fairy had turned him into a Beast long ago, when he had committed an unkind act. The fairy told the prince that he would stay this way until someone loved him, when the curse would be broken.

This story relays a very important part of *shadow* work, which is learning to love and accept that which seems hideous and ugly within us. The suppressed and rejected *shadow* elements of our psyche hold both that which we fear as well as that which we loathe. Self-hatred is a very destructive element and leads to different tortured psychological conditions. It is only when we can learn to love and accept these aspects of our being that we can find wholeness and balance. To achieve this task we are asked to work with the spiritual intuitive part of our being that knows what steps need to be taken. In these cases, love often needs to go hand in hand with forgiveness. Two other fairy tales, which present similar themes, are *The Frog Prince* (Grimm, 1983) and *The Snow Queen* (Andersen, 2012).

The Frog Prince

In the first of these tales, a beautiful princess goes walking in the woods with her favourite golden ball (a symbol of her spiritual self), which she throws in the air to catch. However, on one occasion the ball slips from her hands and tumbles into a deep spring (our soul self knows the steps we need to take in order to be healed). Distraught at losing her ball, the princess declares out loud that she would give anything to get it back, including giving away her fine dresses and jewels. A frog sitting close by tells the princess that he is willing to retrieve the ball if the princess will love him and allow him to sit at her table and to sleep in her bed. Thinking this a silly idea, the princess agrees and the frog dives deep into the pool and returns the ball to her by holding it in his mouth. The princess, without even thanking the frog, seizes the ball and runs back home, thinking no more of her adventure.

Next evening, while sitting down to eat with her father the king and her mother the queen, they hear a knocking at the door. When the princess opens the door, she is astonished to see there on the doorstep the frog demanding that she keep her promise. In alarm, the princess slams the door and returns to the table but then confesses to her father what has happened. He tells her that as she has made a promise she must now stick to it (her father, the king, represents her higher wisdom). Rather reluctantly, the princess opens the door and allows the frog into the dining hall, where it jumps up onto the table and eats some food from the princess's plate. The frog then demands that it be taken up to her bedroom to sleep on her pillow next to the princess.

With some disgust, she accedes to this demand and allows the frog to sleep on the pillow with her. Next morning it jumps down from the bed and leaves the castle. The princess is relieved, thinking it has now gone, but the next evening it returns and the same process happens again. On the fourth morning of this tale, the princess is astonished to discover that, instead of the frog, a handsome prince is now gazing at her lovingly when she awakes. He proceeds to inform her that a curse had been placed upon him for some misdeed and only the love of a princess would rescue him and break the spell. In order to be whole, the princess has had to learn to love and accept that which appeared to be hideous and ugly to her. When she achieves this task, the prince is restored to his normal human form. This story has led to the famous humorous adage, 'Before you meet the handsome prince, you have to kiss a lot of toads.'

The Snow Queen

The Snow Queen is a similar tale of love transforming the *shadow*, although in this case Gerda, the heroine of the story, needs to go through a series of trials and tests before she discovers the whereabouts of Kay, her childhood sweetheart, because he has been beguiled by the Snow Queen. The story starts with a wicked hobgoblin or demon who makes a magic mirror that causes all who look into it to magnify even the tiniest flaw in that which is good and beautiful, causing it to appear ugly, and all that is hideous and ugly to seem normal and acceptable. Here we see an example of the workings of the law of polarity. The demon has a school and the pupils of this establishment are enthralled by the mirror to such an extent that they wish to show it to the angels in heaven. As they rise up towards the heavenly realm, the mirror becomes slippery and, falling from their grasp, tumbles to earth, smashing into millions of tiny fragments. These minute splinters get into people's eyes, causing them to see the world in a distorted way, and some also get into people's hearts, making them cold-hearted and callous.

The story then turns to the two young childhood friends, Gerda and Kay, who have grown to love each other as children. The symbol of their love is a beautiful rose. As they both grow up, a tiny shard of the hobgoblin's mirror gets into Kay's eye and another into his heart. He changes from being warm and loving into being cold and calculating, using his reason to always spot the flaws in his friends and that which is around him. Kay is then captured by the Snow Queen who takes him into her snowy frozen realm in the far north of Finland. Snow and ice, within fairy tales, indicate the aspects of our self that are stuck or frozen, rather like being turned to stone in the Medusa myth. Kay is quite happy in this place, thinking everything is normal.

After Kay disappears, little Gerda, who lives with her grandmother, initially believes that he is dead but the flowers and birds keep whispering to her that he is not dead, so she finally sets out to look for him. She puts on her new red shoes, which she loves very much, and ventures down to a river, throwing in the shoes as a sacrifice to the river to bring Kay back to her. The river, part of her spiritual self, knows that the task is not that simple and floats the shoes back to Gerda. She then picks them up and gets into a small boat that is berthed on the shore, to try to throw the shoes further into the stream, which she then does. However, the sudden movement causes the boat to become dislodged, and it drifts into the river with the current. Gerda is then taken downstream before being eventually rescued by a kindly old woman who takes her into her home to feed her. The woman is not really bad but wants to keep little Gerda there with her as a companion and, knowing that the rose is a symbol of Gerda's mission, makes all the roses in her garden disappear into the earth.

Gerda is then kept with all the material delights that she could ever want. For a while she is happy and forgets her quest to look for Kay. Yet something keeps nagging away at her and eventually she spots the symbol of a rose in the old lady's hat and remembers her quest. Hats in stories connect us to the spiritual part of our being, while shoes and feet link us to the earth. Little Gerda goes looking in the garden for roses and, not finding any, starts to weep. The tears falling to earth break the spell of the old woman and new roses magically grow up. She asks them about Kay and they tell her that he is not dead, so she knows she needs to continue her quest. She escapes the comforts of the old woman, which reflect the material lures of the world, knowing that she needs to continue her spiritual quest to find Kay.

Gerda goes through a number of adventures on her journey, meeting magical power animals (often a symbol for the intuitive or instinctual parts of our nature) as well as a robber girl, who reflects an aspect of her shadow self. The robber girl finally helps little Gerda by loaning her a pet reindeer that takes Gerda to the palace of the Snow Queen. To enter this palace Gerda needs to remember and repeat the Lord's Prayer to protect herself from the ice warriors that guard the palace, and she eventually finds Kay.

Her tears of love, joy and happiness fall on Kay's breast, so dissolving the tiny shards of the mirror in his heart. Gerda then repeats the verse she had made up, when they were both young children, which goes:

Roses bloom and cease to be,
But we shall the Christ-child see.

This causes Kay to weep and the tiny splinter of glass is washed from his eye so that he now sees clearly again, allowing both he and Gerda to be reunited in their love and appreciation of each other and eventually be married.

The tale of little Gerda and Kay exemplifies the feminine quest of learning to love and forgive. This is a very important component when working with clients in their inner worlds. They need to learn to first accept and then forgive those parts of their psyche that carry their rejected *shadows*. Love is the most powerful and protective of all transforming elements; as the Greek myths state, even the thunderbolts of Zeus fall harmlessly at the feet of those to whom Aphrodite (goddess of love) has bequeathed her girdle. Here we are talking about inner spiritual or psychological work, not necessarily the way it is expressed in the material physical world.

The Celestial Sisters

There is a wealth of interesting *shadow* material contained within fairy tale literature, too vast to be covered in this chapter. The last story that will be touched on here comes from the First Nation American tradition (Matthews, 1869). This story relates to the integration and balancing of the psyche by uniting the opposites within. It begins with a hunter called White Hawk, or Waupee, who is one of the most successful hunters of his tribe. One day in his travels he comes across a magic ring in the grass which appears as though it was made by someone dancing lightly on the ground.

Intrigued by the mystery he chooses to hide and discover the origins of the enigma. Circles and rings in myths and fairy tales generally relate to a spiritual quest, unless otherwise indicated. Presently, while lying in wait, White Hawk hears some gentle music and, looking up, sees a small object floating down from the skies. As it comes closer to the earth, he makes out a basket holding twelve beautiful maidens. When the basket lands the maidens leap out and start to dance in a ring, striking a golden ball to keep time.

White Hawk is entranced by their grace and beauty, and particularly by the youngest who dazzles him above all the others. Containing himself no longer, he rushes forward to grab the beautiful girl but in the twinkling of an eye the twelve damsels leap back into the basket and disappear into the sky. Distraught, White Hawk bemoans that he will never see them again and returns to his solitary lodge. However, he cannot rest or sleep and resolves to try again to win the maiden that he has now come to love. Here we first glimpse the inner spiritual self, luring us into taking steps to connect to its beautiful energy. White Hawk resolves to return to the same spot on the prairie and this time lies in wait as an opossum, which, as we know, can play dead.

After a little time the disguised White Hawk again hears the enchanting singing and sees the basket slowly descending to the ground. He watches enraptured as the maidens jump out and start to dance. Slowly he creeps forward but the ever-alert sisters spot him and leap back into the basket. This time they are curious but the youngest insists that they go, so they re-ascend into the heavens and once more White Hawk is left alone.

This time he knows that he has but one more chance to woo or capture the youngest sister, because two chances have already been wasted. He reflects long and hard on what to do. On his journey home, he passes by the stump of an old tree covered in moss and inhabited by mice. He considers that these tiny creatures could not cause any alarm and so resolves to transform himself into a mouse. He takes the tree stump, sets it down near the ring and, assuming his mouse form, waits for the appointed hour when the maidens will descend.

When the basket arrives the maidens spot the tree stump and, intrigued, go over to examine it. Being disturbed, the mice run out and the maidens chase them, killing them one by one except White Hawk, who is being pursued by the youngest sister. As she lifts her silver stick to hit him, White Hawk transforms himself back into his human form and seizes the maiden by the waist. The eleven other sisters, now terrified, ascend in their basket, leaving behind their youngest sister.

White Hawk has to exert all his skills as a human being to please his intended bride and win her affections. Leading her slowly back to his lodge, he relates all of his adventures and the wonders of being on earth. For a while their lives are filled with bliss and a beautiful baby boy is born to the couple. However, White Hawk's wife is the daughter of one of the stars and, as time passes, she begins to yearn to see her father and sisters again. Remembering the basket, she secretly weaves another, and when White Hawk is out hunting she places the basket in the magic circle and steps into it with her son. Singing now a mournful song, she rises in the air. Hearing the song on the wind, White Hawk races to where the basket is ascending but he is too late to catch it, for it is already beyond his reach and, as he watches, it becomes a tiny speck before disappearing into the sky.

Throughout the long winter that follows White Hawk is in despair for the love he has lost and also for his son. Meanwhile, carried away by the delight of being back in her father's household, White Hawk's wife begins to forget the life she had with him. However, as her son grows to manhood he reminds her again of the husband she has left behind. Then the star father tells his daughter that she should return with her son and that she should bring back White Hawk with her to his realm. As part of this quest, White Hawk has first to gather a sample of all the rarest and most beautiful of creatures and bring these back to the stars. Singing her song, the star daughter descends once more to the earth where White Hawk races to greet her, his heart filled with joy as the family is reunited again. Hearing now of his new quest he sets forth both night and day to gather the various animals, bringing a sample of them back to his lodge. Then comes the day when he has to bid farewell to the earth and his home and to ascend to the stars with his beloved and his son.

Great celebrations take place when they reach the starry realms. The star chief then invites all the star people to a great feast and bids them select one of the objects that White Hawk has brought with him, whether it be a claw, beak or feather. The star children are then transformed into the creatures from which these objects came and, descending to earth, then experience physical life as an animal, bird or fish. White Hawk, his wife and son each choose a white hawk feather and become beautiful hawk birds soaring above the earth, where it is said they can still be seen to this day.

In the latter half of this story, we see how White Hawk has to experience the opposites of the joy and happiness he once knew in order to become whole. Finally, in gathering all of his experiences, symbolized by the different animals, he ascends into the spiritual realm where he is reunited with his beloved wife and son forever. We cannot escape the gamut of human emotions if we are to be whole. All needs to be experienced and understood in the journey towards balance and integration.

Summary

Evidence from the divinatory systems of the tarot and I Ching suggests a recognition of a *shadow* component within the psyche, which is commensurate with other mythological systems. Curiously, both systems indicate one specific archetype within an eightfold pattern that particularly carries this *shadow* dynamic. This is similar to the one malign god Seth, from the ancient Egyptian Heliopolitan cosmology, who sits within an eightfold grouping of gods and goddesses. The significance of this patterning will become more apparent when we explore the cosmic *shadow* in Chapter 6.

Along with mythology, fairy tales give insights into the working of the *shadow* elements of the psyche and the steps needed to heal, balance and integrate the different components. A number of fairy tales highlight the importance of love and forgiveness in the redemption process, which might be interpreted as a more feminine approach to transmuting the *shadow* parts of our being.

SECTION TWO
The Shadow's Manifestation

Chapter Six

The Cosmic Shadow

Imagination is the real and eternal world of which this vegetable universe is but a faint shadow.

William Blake

The nature of God and what may constitute ultimate *reality*, along with our place in the universe, has been at the heart of human enquiry through millennia and has only been superseded in the last three hundred years with the development of the mechanistic sciences that are based upon Newtonian physics. All that can be achieved within this one short chapter is to give some insights or pointers and to open up this theme to further enquiry.

On one side of the debate sit the intelligentsia of the material sciences who, as a collective body, reject any concept of a deity, either through strong personal belief or simply because God cannot be measured or discovered within the mechanistic paradigm. As far as physical science is concerned, it is easier to ignore the challenge that is posed by incorporating a spiritual dimension into their material realities. On the other side stand the majority of humanity, who have some belief or acceptance of a spiritual dimension to which they are wedded. How can these polarized views be reconciled?

In the light of history, and given present-day experience, one can have some sympathy for those who reject religion and all that it embraces, particularly when considering some of the distortions and travesties that have been perpetrated in the name of a particular set of beliefs. Some of the most barbaric wars have been fought under the banner of different religious ideologies and, at the time of writing, religious extremism is still threatening the peace of the world. These issues need to be both understood as well as confronted. While war has been waged in the name of religion, the twentieth century showed that this was not the only reason why humans are prepared to kill each other, because different elements of the *shadow* have manifested themselves. The challenge of this chapter is to see whether it is possible to present a case that can begin to put all of these experiences into a context that can be understood as part of a greater whole.

Instead of first considering any idea of a God, which is the normal top-down religious approach, I will start this enquiry at a human level, to see whether a case can be built from the bottom up. This chapter will therefore first explore what happens to us when we die. The question we need to consider is whether the magnificent database of our individual experiences or stored consciousness is simply switched off at death, and all its information lost forever, or does some aspect of personal consciousness continue to survive? If so, what sort of journey might it be on? Only when these questions have been tackled, and some reasoned and supported arguments presented, can the wider question on the nature of any deity and notions of a cosmic *shadow* be explored.

One of the great benefits of technology is that it is now easy to gain access to widely divergent sources of information and experience to illuminate our enquiry. I have often stated that this is an amazing time to be alive for, at the touch of a button, we have the ability to both access and gain insight into many different belief systems. The gamut of religious faith over millennia is available to individuals across our planet in a way that was never possible in the past. For example, one of my interests is ancient Egypt and although the religion of that time is no longer practised as it was two thousand years ago, the writings, descriptions and temples provide ample evidence of the main tenets of Egyptian belief. We know that they believed in an afterlife and the existence of a spiritual realm presided over by different gods and goddesses. The advantage of this vast pool of collective knowledge is that it can provide insights into the way that the nature of truth and reality has been understood though history. We can draw not only from the pool of scientific wisdom but also from the powerful experiences of mystics, through the ages, in their visions of a spiritual dimension.

This chapter will therefore draw upon an eclectic mix of experience that considers both orthodox gnosis as well as that purporting to be from spiritual sources. Through the restrictions of word space, this mix must be limited to what is pertinent to the argument, which ultimately seeks to gain insight into the cosmic *shadow*. A case will be presented that supports the view that individual consciousness survives the death of the physical body, for the very good reason of the economy of accumulated experience, which at a physical level is expressed through Darwinian evolution.

These experiences add to the consciousness of the universe, and only make sense when a free will component forms an intrinsic part of the process. Machines that simply replicate what they are programmed to perform cannot and do not evolve. When learning and experience, derived from free will, are injected into the mix we have unique conscious evolution. This chapter will then argue that this occurs both physically, which Darwin described, as well as consciously, in realms normally known as the spiritual planes.

I will further contend that a Creative Intelligence exists which offers love, compassion and understanding. This benign force, through the free will element, allows spirits or individual consciousnesses the opportunity to accept or reject that impulse for however long or short a period of their experience they so choose. From this perspective ultimately all experience comes back into balance, yet at a human level we have to learn to deal with those individuals who choose deliberately to go against this caring process. We have to learn how to cope with those who wish to inflict pain and suffering on those around them. Nevertheless, at a greater level, our unique experiences add to this collective pool of knowledge and, in this sense, I believe we are all working out the cosmic *shadow*.

The Dawkins Challenge

Whilst many authorities could be drawn upon, one of the most articulate opponents of a belief in the existence of God is the biologist Richard Dawkins, who has taken on an almost messianic mission to challenge orthodox religion through the light of scientific enquiry. As we have seen so far in our exploration into the *shadow*, the need to work with opposites is an intrinsic part of the process. As soon as any statement is made, its polarity needs to be considered and understood. Scientists like Dawkins provide a valuable function in challenging established religious belief which, by definition, is rooted in the past. One might argue that if God or Allah truly exists, then the expression of such a deity should have been consistent across the planet and throughout time. When we find divergent beliefs throughout the peoples of this planet, particularly when these conflict with scientific knowledge, then this surely indicates the transient nature of the deity and the likelihood that this is just a mirage or creative projection of human experience.

The difficulty with this line of argument is that it ignores the fallibility and diversity of human expression. The evolution of the scientific worldview, for all of its amazing discoveries, has also been full of inaccuracies and shortcomings. For example, up until Einstein, the Newtonian model of the universe was considered complete. The birth of quantum mechanics turned this affirmed stance on its head. We know now that the universe is infinitely more complex than our nineteenth-century scientists could have ever imagined. It is full of paradox and wonder at a level that is truly awesome. Even more baffling to the cosmologists is the realization that around 95 per cent of the universe is composed of dark energy and dark matter, of which we know practically nothing (Efstathiou, 2013).

Furthermore, the theories and studies of quantum mechanics support the view of the mental nature of the universe – that the universe is a 'mental' construct, not a physical one. In an elegantly argued essay in the prestigious scientific magazine *Nature*, Professor Richard Conn Henry concludes by stating 'The Universe is immaterial – mental and spiritual. Live and enjoy.' (Henry, 2005:29). As part of his essay he cites another eminent physicist, Sir James Jeans, who stated in his book *The Mysterious Universe*:

> *The stream of knowledge is heading towards a non-mechanical reality; the Universe begins to look more like a great thought than like a great machine. Mind no longer appears to be an accidental intruder into the realm of matter … we ought rather hail it as the creator and governor of the realm of matter (Jeans, 1930:137).*

The problem that Henry (2005) highlights is that physicists in particular, despite overwhelming evidence to the contrary, still wish to see the universe as made up of individual particles of matter rather than aspects of mental energy. As he states, 'there have been serious attempts to preserve a material world – but they produce no new physics, and serve only to preserve an illusion'.

When considering the writings from past times of those who might be regarded as the spiritual sages of humanity, what is striking is not their differences but their similarities of viewpoint. They affirmed a spiritual dimension to life which touches a chord within many people across the planet because it also resonates with something deep within them. Further, it may also reflect their own spiritual experiences. Despite its desire for order and consistency, inconsistency has also been the hallmark of scientific enquiry. Axioms that were once the accepted truth are continually modified and adapted as new discoveries come along. All this is to the good because evolution has to be part of the plan of the universe.

In his book *The God Delusion* (2007), Dawkins sets out to prove that God does not exist and can never have existed. The primary aim of these attacks is against orthodox religions and, in particular, those descended from Abraham, which includes Christianity, Islam and Judaism. These religions, espousing old dogmas, need and deserve to be challenged. Indeed, it could be argued that one of the paradoxes of a religion that seeks truth is the desire of some of its adherents to want to kill or annihilate those who see things differently. This paradox is particularly true of Christianity, which is founded on the creed of someone who preached love, forgiveness and 'turning the other cheek' yet has so often in the past manifested the opposite, through religious intolerance and bigotry. Dawkins's book is full of such examples. It is clear that the limited notion of the Deity, found in orthodox religions, needs to be updated in the light of modern understanding, just as science does when new discoveries come along. In other words, a sufficiently broad definition of the Divine needs to be formulated that espouses all of the material sciences, and more. And it is the 'more' that specifically interests us here.

Dawkins presents a powerful case for the drivers of evolution (2007:190) and the way that:

> *Religion is so wasteful, so extravagant; and Darwinian selection habitually targets and eliminates waste. Nature is a miserly accountant, grudging the pennies, watching the clock, punishing the smallest extravagance. Unrelenting and unceasingly, as Darwin explained 'natural selection is daily and hourly scrutinizing throughout the world, every variation, even the slightest; rejecting that which is bad, adding up all that is good; silently and insensibly working, whenever and wherever opportunity offers, at the improvement of each organic being.'*

This simple yet compelling process is, according to Dawkins, the main oxygen of life, a universal principle that propels the world forward in its evolution. Yet, when it comes to individual consciousness, he would have us believe that it is simply snuffed out and extinguished fully when we die. What a complete and utter waste of accumulated experience, which is totally at odds with all that he has claimed for the planet's evolutionary consciousness. I fully agree with him that we need to raise consciousness and awareness in all areas of our lives. In this we should remember that it is strict religious dogma, not spirituality, that traps us in the past. Just as concepts and beliefs that no longer fit into the scientific paradigm need to be revised, so too the same principle needs to be applied to spiritual beliefs.

Throughout its life, however long or transient, every human being, every animal, every bird, insect or microbe acquires unique and valuable 'experience'. What a travesty it would be if, at the end of that life, all of that acquired information (consciousness) was simply lost. We know that genetic evolution ever seeks to go on replicating and refining itself, so why should this same process not happen to our consciousness when we die? It would be like turning one's computer off at night and losing all of the stored data of the day's activities. I am sure most of us who use computers would become pretty fed up if every day we had to start again from scratch.

The inanity of this idea reminds me of one of Douglas Adams's brilliant books, entitled *The Hitchhiker's Guide to the Galaxy* (1995), in which the Earth was destroyed by the Vogons to make way for a 'super space highway', and thereby extinguishes the computer set up to discover the meaning of life. Consciousness, no matter how basic, gives meaning to life and for that consciousness to be terminated at death, with the slate being wiped clean, is pointless and counter to all that we know about evolution.

Whilst Dawkins aims his main attacks against religious beliefs he neatly skirts dealing in any real depth with personal spiritual experience. Indeed, the word 'spiritual' only appears seven times in *The God Delusion*, most of which are quotes from other writers, which is an interesting insight into Dawkins's own *shadow*. In following our theme of building from the bottom up, probably the first and most important question we will all have to face at some stage is what happens when our physical body dies? Science acknowledges that there is a clear distinction between when a person, or other organism, is alive or dead. The cessation of heartbeat, the lack of breath and the flatlining of brain activity are the physical indicators of this process. Despite this clear distinction, there is very little difference in the number of atoms and molecules making up the organism prior to and just after death has been determined. Before death some force field keeps everything functioning together and it breaks down as soon as this energy departs. The open question that needs to be explored by science is whether this force-field consciousness continues to exist, in some other state, after the death of the physical body.

In the philosophy of the mind this view of reality is known as Cartesian dualism, after René Descartes, which suggests that brain and consciousness are two separate and distinct ontological entities. This was the accepted view of the intelligentsia in the eighteenth and nineteenth centuries but in modern times has been replaced by monism, which broadly sees mind and brain being the same, where one cannot exist without the other (Kim, 1995). Well-thought-out arguments can be presented for both standpoints, so which is correct? Here I will invoke Young's light paradox, which presents the conundrum about whether light is a wave or a particle in the quantum realm, because in scientific terms it cannot be both. Yet the experiment shows that it is indeed both. It all depends on how the experiment has been carried out.

A simple analogy to understanding this paradox is to stand and watch a sunset or a sunrise, which is something I am sure we have all done on occasion. From the observer's perspective it quite clear that it is the Sun that is moving, which our language supports in terms of the words 'sunrise' and 'sunset'. Yet, we also know through scientific observation that the Earth is turning, not the Sun. Depending upon our viewpoint, these paradoxes occur and we can learn to accept both positions at the same time. I would suggest that this could also be applied to the debate between dualism and monism, for the answer is surely that both are correct depending upon how we view life or carry out our experiments.

To return to the concept of dualism, Dawkins freely admits that religion is a universal phenomenon which is a challenge to the rational scientists. He attempts to address this issue without a very satisfactory outcome. Based on the research of psychologist Paul Bloom, he goes on to state (2007:209):

> *Religion is a by-product of instinctive dualism. We humans, he [Bloom] suggests, and especially children, are natural born dualists. A dualist acknowledges a fundamental distinction between matter and mind. A monist, by contrast, believes that mind is a manifestation of matter ... and cannot exist apart from matter. A dualist believes the mind is some kind of disembodied spirit that inhabits the body and therefore conceivably could leave the body and exist somewhere else.*

Why is this so important to know? In the atheist scenario, brain, consciousness and identity are all extinguished when death occurs. All personal experiences are then lost forever, and although some remnant of a life might continue in the form of an individual's creativity, their intrinsic self is no more. And yet no matter how great an artist, whether they be Leonardo, Mozart or Shakespeare, their manifested works are vastly less magnificent than the nuances and intricacies of their own particular life experience, for it is these experiences that make us uniquely gifted individuals. Why would the universe establish itself in a way that deletes something of inestimable value? We might go one step further and postulate a cataclysmic destruction of the entire earth and all its denizens in some global catastrophe in which all life is extinguished. What would be the point of the 'selfish gene' then, or indeed of Darwinian evolution? This theory only really makes sense if conscious or the stored experiences of life are held in a separate database, similar to the way we use the cloud as a form of storage for computers.

If, instead of being lost, our consciousness continued to live on then we might consider there to be some greater purpose to the life we are leading. The logic of Dawkins's and Darwin's profound ideas needs also to be applied to consciousness itself; to your consciousness, my consciousness, indeed to all consciousness across this planet. The desire to rightly tackle, and reject, outmoded religious beliefs has blinded Dawkins and his fellow atheists to one of the fundamentals of all religious tenets, which is the continuation of consciousness in some other state. Let us forget, at this stage, all concepts of heaven, hell and suchlike, which have been created by past cultures to meet specific ends, and instead let us focus simply on the concept that consciousness continues beyond the death of the physical body. This fully fits with the concept of nature maximizing against waste that Darwin postulated and Dawkins champions.

The atheist stance is a step on the path in the rejection of all that is distorted within religion, but it is surely not the full answer because it flies in the face of the evolution of consciousness at an individual level. And it is at an individual level that this consciousness is most potent. Reasoned arguments have been put forward for the atheist cause because mainstream physical science believes that we do not have sufficiently sophisticated scientific equipment to prove unequivocally that consciousness continues after death. This is a belief that needs to be, and is being, challenged. If you fundamentally choose to believe that consciousness ends at death, then evidence can always be found to justify such a stance because that is the way our brains are wired. However, if this subject is approached with an open mind and the evidence carefully examined, the case for continued conscious existence is compelling. Above all, it is 'evolutionary', which is a word that Dawkins loves to use; and more than that, it is purposeful.

Life After Death?

The scientific search for evidence of life after death has a long history that goes back to the nineteenth century. It is a question that prompted the founding of the Society for Psychical Research (SPR) in 1882 by a group of scientists, philosophers and intellectuals who saw a compelling need for science to investigate all so-called paranormal and supernatural phenomena. One of these men, Frederic W.H. Myers, spent twenty years researching these phenomena and, as a result of his accumulated evidence, came to the inescapable conclusion that is encapsulated in a summary of his life's work entitled *Human Personality and its Survival of Bodily Death* (1903). The SPR still exists and it continues its programme of scientific research into the paranormal to this day. In addition, Myers is now being recognized as a significant contributor to our understanding of human consciousness and the discovery of a realm of consciousness that exists beyond the conscious awareness (Ellenberger, 1970; Palmer, 2014). It is unfortunate that Myers's work has largely been ignored by mainstream psychology, much to the detriment of our modern knowledge and understanding. However, more recent research and anecdotal evidence is contributing to a revision of Myers's investigations as more discoveries come to light through the work of an increasing number of open-minded researchers. One of these contributors is Dr Raymond Moody.

Since Raymond Moody first published *Life After Life* (1975) on his studies into what has now been called the Near Death Experience, or NDE, this phenomenon has been studied by many other scientifically-minded individuals. NDEs occur when an individual reaches a point where he or she is perceived to be clinically dead and is then either revived by doctors or physicians or sometimes spontaneously comes back to life. Whilst the person is in this supposed death state, they can sometimes become aware of their consciousness being separated from their bodies. In some cases, this is simply seeing and recording what is happening to them from a different perspective, as though looking down from above.

Many years ago, in my later school years and long before Moody's book, I well remember a visiting medical doctor talking about a case he had attended – in those days doctors used to make personal visits to their patients. One evening a patient's wife called the surgery and said she thought her husband, who had been seriously ill, had died. Although it was late, the doctor drove to the house and found, on examination, that his patient was indeed clinically dead as far as he was concerned, as there was no sign of breath or pulse. As nothing more could be done that night the doctor said he would return next morning to deal with the situation more fully. His surprise was immense when the wife greeted him next day saying that her husband was now alive and sitting up in bed. On talking to his patient the man openly confirmed that he had witnessed everything that had happened the preceding evening, for he claimed 'he' had stood by the wardrobe in the room, watching the doctor's examination of his body, and then related all that the doctor had said to the wife. The man confirmed that he knew he could go on but had decided to stay. He then found himself back in his body and woke feeling very much alive.

Such anecdotal stories, in isolation, have little meaning, but when they are added together they begin to present a strong case for the continuation of consciousness beyond physical death. Various psychological arguments are put forward by scientists to counter the evidence of NDEs being a continuation of consciousness, such as oxygen deprivation causing the brain to hallucinate or temporal lobe epilepsy. These arguments are fully tackled by Dr Penny Sartori in the studies that formed the basis of her book *The Wisdom of Near-Death Experiences*, in which she shows that none of these concepts explains the lucidity that is present in NDE cases (Sartori, 2014: Chapter 6). Indeed, with the ability now to monitor brain function with sophisticated equipment, it has been found that NDEs have occurred when there is no higher-level cerebral activity. In a recent article in the *Daily Mail* (2014), neurosurgeon Dr Eben Alexander recounted his own NDE when he nearly died from meningitis. He stated, 'my survival chances were near zero' for he was in a deep coma and all of his higher brain functions were flatlining, showing no conscious activity, and yet, extraordinarily, part of his inner self still remained aware. For the next seven days he lay in an unresponsive coma, with no obvious brain function, yet the part of him that was conscious went on a series of profound out-of-body experiences beyond the confines of the physical world that completely changed his view of reality and the nature of the universe in which we reside.

Alexander then goes on to highlight that many other individuals in history, including mystics, shamans and ordinary people, have described glimpses into an ethereal realm. One such individual was Robert Ogilvie Crombie, who since childhood had felt a close rapport with nature and in particular with the ancient Greek god Pan. In the book *The Findhorn Garden* (1976:118-9) he describes a particular powerful spiritual experience he had whilst on a walk in the parkland of Attingham Park, a beautiful county estate in England:

> *I followed the path until I came to the Rhododendron Walk, which is considered by some to be a place of great power. At its entrance is a huge cedar tree with a bench beneath it. I sat there for some time, enjoying the beauty of the place, then rose and entered the Walk. As I did so, I felt a great build-up of power and a vast increase in awareness. Colours and forms became more significant. I was aware of every single leaf on the bushes and trees, of every single blade of grass on the path standing out with startling clarity. It was as if physical reality had become much more real than it normally is, and the three-dimensional effect we are used to had become even more solid. This type of experience is nearly impossible to describe in words. I had the impression of complete reality, and all that lies within and beyond it felt immediately imminent. There was an acute feeling of being at one with nature in a complete way as well as being at one with the Divine, which produced great exultation, and a deep sense of awe and wonder.*
>
> *I became aware of Pan walking by my side and a strong bond between us. He stepped behind me and then walked into me so that we became one, and I saw the surroundings through his eyes. At the same time, part of me –*

the recording observing part – stood aside. The experience was not of a form of possession but of identification, a kind of integration.

The moment he stepped into me the woods became alive with myriad beings – elementals, nymphs, dryads, fauns, elves, gnomes, fairies, and so on, far too numerous to catalogue. They varied in size from tiny little beings a fraction of an inch in height, like the ones I saw swarming about on a clump of toadstools, to beautiful elfin creatures, three or four feet tall. Some of them danced around me in a ring; all were welcoming and full of rejoicing. The nature spirits love and delight in the work they do and express this in movement.

I felt as if I were outside of space and time. Everything was happening in the now. It is impossible to give more than a faint impression of the actuality of this experience but I would stress the exultation and the feeling of joy and delight. Yet there was an underlying peace and contentment and a sense of spiritual presence.

This account is cited in depth because of the power of what it conveys. If Crombie is to be believed, what surrounds us, at levels we cannot perceive with our normal eyes, is an abundance of spiritual activity and consciousness. He was at one time part of a spiritual community called Findhorn, founded by Eileen and Peter Caddy and their friend Dorothy Maclean in the early 1960s. Findhorn became famous for growing amazing vegetables in otherwise impoverished soil and developing a deep connection with nature and the nature kingdoms. The community grew to several hundred people and is still flourishing today.

The Crombie account may be too much for some readers to take on board. Nevertheless, as we have encountered already, mythology is full of such beings, however diverse the culture that recounts them. To those who have them, these experiences are every bit as real as any other in their lives, and often more so. As the priest and mystic, Pierre Teillard de Chardin, is reputed to have stated, 'We are not human beings having a spiritual experience, we are spiritual beings having a human experience' (Furey, 1993:138). We need to wake up to our fundamental spirituality. What is also interesting from the diverse NDE accounts is that far from the afterlife being filled with a vindictive God, the exact opposite is the case. As Eben Alexander (2014) states, it is a place 'filled to overflowing with indescribable, unconditional love.'

It is quite understandable that the material sciences would not want to venture into such realms, although some anthropologists are beginning to explore these experiences as part of their studies. These fields should be the domain of scientific theologians, not stuck in the dusty past, but walking hand in hand with material scientists looking to uncover the true nature of our being that incorporates both a material as well as a spiritual component. Once the concept of the continuation of consciousness is accepted, the next step in the construction of our pyramid is to consider how that consciousness evolves and how it came to be created.

The Evolution of Individual Consciousness

With the development of hypnotherapy as a therapeutic tool to delve below the level of the conscious mind for the relief of suffering, some interesting and unexpected discoveries have been made. When tranced clients are asked to go back in their minds to the moment when the cause of a particular manifesting trauma first occurred, some have slipped back into past times and presented a situation from the perspective of a previous life. This event might have been a painful death in battle or suchlike. The clinician could accept this presentation as simply a metaphor and work with it to affect change. However, some therapists, intrigued by these memories, have sought to go deeper to try to unravel the source of these apparent experiences.

The concept of reincarnation or rebirth is not new. It can be found in the philosophies of Pythagoras and Plato and is an intrinsic part of Hindu and Buddhist theologies. Although some New Testament texts could be interpreted as suggesting that Jesus accepted reincarnation, the concept of the transmigration of souls has never formed any overt part of Judaic or Christian belief and was fully rejected in the Fifth Ecumenical Council of churches in 553 CE. Despite this religious rejection, the concept of rebirth found its way back into the west, in the nineteenth century, through the work of the French mystic Allan Kardec (1857), who was the founder of the Spiritist movement; the writings of Helena Blavatsky (1877), which led to the development of the Theosophical Society; and the work of Frederic Myers (1903), who was one of the founders the Society for Psychical Research. The hypnotherapeutic approach has been the latest, systemized examination of what lies beneath the surface of the conscious mind.

From these studies has emerged knowledge that each individual consciousness, whether we call it a soul or spirit, is on a journey of discovery which entails undergoing a series of experiences both within a physical body as well as in other dimensions. A fundamental component of this process is that each individual consciousness has free will to choose the life they have led or are leading because this gives meaning to their experience. Information and experience are cumulative and, most importantly (Dawkins, please note), nothing appears to ever be lost (Newton, 2002:211-2). All experience builds upon itself. Naturally, because perfection does not exist at this level, except as an ideal, mistakes are made. Yet, out of these mistakes we learn and grow; effectively we evolve spiritually, in complement to the somatic evolution of Darwin. This is reasonable, logical and in line with Dawkins's thesis for material evolution.

One of the hypnotherapists who have added to our knowledge of the spiritual realms is Dr Michael Newton, whose two books *Journey of Souls* (1994) and *Destiny of Souls* (2002) explored the space between lives. Newton achieved this insight through deep hypnotherapeutic techniques that allowed his clients to access their original database. What emerged, from hundreds of case studies, was an evolutionary realm, established to help support souls in their journey through experience. This realm, with its own hierarchy, would appear to be every bit as complex as the world in which we inhabit physically. The reports that came back from Newton's researches suggest that this level of experience is always warm, loving and very supportive. Some of his clients under hypnosis even mention the birthing of new souls, whose creation is to help further experience. In *Destiny of Souls* (Newton, 2002:127) a regressed client, in a trance state, describes the birth of new souls being held in their own incubators and are then 'are conveyed as small masses of white energy encased in a golden sac'.

The process that is captured from these many varied accounts is similar, in essence, to what we experience here on earth. After birthing, souls, or sparks of consciousness, start a journey of discovery which involves moving in and out of physical incarnation in its early stages. Newton's researches, based on the accounts of his regressed clients, suggest that some souls progress faster than others. Some easily learn a particular lesson from their incarnations whilst others do not. What is also apparent is that the gift of free will is sacrosanct. No soul is forced to do anything they do not wish to do.

This theme of the importance of free will is picked up by another hypnotherapist, Dr Tom Zinser, whose book *Soul-Centered Healing* (2011) deals with his experiences in working with many different clients to resolve psychological issues through hypnotic regression. Zinser developed his methods over a number of years. They involve accessing different sub-personality parts of his clients where trauma is held. Some of his clients resolved their issues very easily, whilst others did not and it turned out that the unsuccessful cases were to prove the most insightful. At a point when Zinser was considering abandoning his work, he met an individual who stated that she had a spiritual guide who wished to co-operate with Zinser in helping with problematic client issues. With nothing to lose, Zinser agreed to a sitting and was sufficiently impressed to resolve to continue.

Over the next fourteen years, on a weekly basis, Zinser brought his difficult cases to a guide named Gerod, who then gave Zinser insight into the causes of each client's condition and suggestions for dealing with the blockages that were occurring. Like Newton before him, Zinser built up a considerable body of knowledge on many of the psychological issues that occur within humanity. The efficacy of these methods was to be found in the restoration of health for numbers of his clients, who previously had been stuck. Gerod was able to pinpoint where the blockages occurred and the steps needed to clear them. Gerod also affirmed the free will element of soul choice and the way that this manifests on the planet and within clients. All spiritual beings working for the light adhere strictly to this provision, totally honouring the soul's free will choices; only those who reject the light do not.

In the cosmology that Gerod presented in giving insight into different conditions on earth, the Creator (for that was the name used) first emerged from darkness as a seed of light (Zinser, 2011:230). In this concept, we find echoes of ancient Egyptian mythology, where the supreme god Ra-Atum emerges from nothingness and brings into being the first divine twins, who are named Shu and Tefnut, which might be translated as air and water (Wilkinson, 2003:18). As the Creator grows, new spirits are brought into being which are endowed with the gift of free will, so they can grow in consciousness without pre-influence or control from the Creator. The only programme woven into them is that at some point in their journey they will return to the Creator, taking with them the sum total of all their experiences, so that the consciousness of the Creator will continue to expand.

Gerod goes on to state that in honour of the darkness from which the Creator emerged, all souls or spirits periodically have to spend a part of their experience within darkness, so that they can appreciate the light. A similar theme is recounted by another channelled guide called H-A, who has spoken regularly through Tony Neate over the past sixty or so years. During this time H-A has cross-referenced the experiences within the spiritual realm with what is happening on the planet, giving insights into the nature of the positive and negative energies that beset the earth. Like Gerod, H-A maintains that the Divine, or Ultimate Thought, which is the term he uses, offers only love, compassion and understanding and that far from being a single individual consciousness is actually a collective level of individual consciousnesses in a state of complete harmony and balance with each other (H-A, 1976:20). As part of the process of growth and evolution, this 'level of being' continually creates new spirits, all of which have the gift of free will, allowing them to experience as they choose. Because the light is ordered, the universe we know and understand is also predominantly orderly, although chaotic elements are also part of the equation (H-A, 1972:6).

The Nature of the Divine or God

The picture that emerges is that this Divine level of consciousness or supreme level of Creative Intelligence offers only compassion, love and understanding, as those who have had an NDE often attest, but does not, and never will, interfere with the free will choices that we might make either individually or collectively. This is our world and our life, we need to get on with it ourselves and not blame God or the Divine for any mess that we might and do make. We are led to believe from both Gerod and H-A, and indeed from many other similar levels of spiritual guidance, that help is always available to us if we ask for assistance. This help is offered unconditionally, on the proviso that it does not go against the free will wishes of the soul before it came into incarnation. In other words, if the soul wishes to go through some particularly difficult experience, the spiritual help will not take away that experience, only assist the soul in going through it. This concept accords fully with what we know in practice. It should also be stressed that God is not a person or single individual but the highest level of Creative Consciousness that underpins the universe.

In respect of evolution, the final point, which is made both by Gerod and H-A, is that there is a hierarchy of spiritual beings leading right up to the level of the Godhead. Imperfection or imbalances can transpire at any level or plane below the Divine and mistakes can and do occur (H-A, 1976:16-19). The Earth plane experience is fairly close to the bottom of this ladder and once souls have come to terms with being here, they no longer need to incarnate but go through finer levels of spiritual experience.

Insights from Studies on Twins

How do these insights translate into the known scientific facts of our world? Over recent years, extensive studies have been carried out on twins and, more specifically, identical, or *monozygotic*, twins. Exciting new discoveries have been made in the field of *epigenetics*, which considers how other patterns of experience that have not been predetermined by our genetic background, manifest themselves. Monozygotic twins have exactly the same genetic material and yet, as the studies tell us, they always present themselves as unique individuals. This can in part be explained by slightly different environmental backgrounds, which is the route that most epigeneticists are now pursuing. Yet, even in these studies, there are some extraordinary paradoxes.

Take, for example, two monozygotic twins named Lelah and Ladan. They had dissimilar personalities which were fully analysed using different psychological studies. Ladan liked animals whilst Laleh preferred computer games, which Ladan could not stand. One was left-handed, the other right-handed. Both were studious, with Ladan hoping to be a lawyer and Laleh a journalist. It was clear from the outset that Laden was the more extrovert and talkative of the two twins (Spector, 2012:2). The striking element of this example is not that the twins displayed very different psychological personas, which has been found in a vast number of twins studies, but that these two individuals were congenitally joined at the head as 'Siamese' twins.

They were wedded to each other in a way that most people would find very challenging and yet, despite almost identical environments, they were each very different. Indeed, as already stated, despite the similarities within identical twins, the sense of individual identity is paramount. In other words, the life force motivating each twin is totally unique and perceives itself as a separate entity and not as a clone of its sibling (Spector, 2012:283).

In Laleh and Ladan's case, this determination for each of them to lead separate lives was so overwhelming that they were bent on finding someone who would carry out the surgery to have them separated. This was considered by most authorities to be likely to be fatal to both of them. Sadly and ultimately, this proved to be the case. An operation was performed when the twins were in their late twenties and both died (Spector, 2012:3). The material or egocentric sciences can offer no logical insight into why these two distinct individuals were so determined to be different that they were prepared to sacrifice their lives in their desire to assert and express their individuality.

Spiritual science, on the other hand, sees two separate unique souls, working through their karma as part of their journey in the physical realm. I would suggest that spiritual evolution provides the most compelling explanation for the differences displayed in monozygotic twins. This cannot be genetic and can only marginally be ascribed to differences in environment. In other words, the differences in environment cannot readily explain the distinct personalities of Lelah and Ladan, whilst spiritual science offers a plausible and rational explanation. Two distinct souls will always perceive themselves to be unique individuals.

Why Do We Forget Where We Have Come From?

If the spiritual explanation is correct, an important point still to be addressed is why we should forget who we are and where we come from. This is crucial to understanding the role of our earthly experiences. Religion and religious belief play a part in this 'forgotten' memory which, at an optimum level, should help us link to the spiritual nature of our being. This is why, as Dawkins observes, religion is a universal phenomenon (Dawkins, 2007:194). In my many years working as a therapist, two primary reasons stand out for this amnesiac block that develops on our spiritual origins in early childhood.

The first is that the spiritual realm is always perceived as a very warm, loving and supportive environment. The soul who needs to face difficult trials in early childhood and beyond could be so overwhelmed by this challenge that they might make or take every opportunity to opt out of their soul's programme by committing suicide. I have come across many individuals who, when linked back to their soul essence, have expressed the view that they approached their present incarnation with the same level of relish as going to the dentist. Not wanting to be fully present in life can seriously impair a person's ability to achieve the objectives of the soul.

The second apparent reason is that the memory of past lives can cause imbalances to the present incarnation in all sorts of subtle ways. There is a period within adult life when a sufficient amount of grounding has been achieved so that it becomes possible to reconnect and heal past-life traumas. We need to do this from a safe space because the reliving of such horrors can be overwhelming if not handled wisely. These two reasons seem to me to be sufficient cause for the general populace to forget who they are and where they have come from spiritually. Perhaps in future times this block may not be so necessary.

Darkness, Free Will and the Shadow

We now need to explore the way that free will and darkness influence the shadow side of our being. In this we should remember that the shadow has been defined in three ways, or as carrying three different elements.

- The **positive** *shadow* holds all of the potential of what we might become, whether individually, collectively or cosmically.
- The **negative** *shadow*, at a personal or collective level, holds all that we reject or repress about ourselves or within society.
- The **malign** *shadow* holds the potential for evil and evil deeds, arising from a rejection of the light.

Like the myth of the birth of Ra-Atum from ancient Egyptian mythology, the spirit guide Gerod suggested that light or consciousness first emerged from darkness or chaos. In this situation, darkness is not perceived as anything destructive but simply as the absence of the light of consciousness. When we enter into what Gerod calls the 'dark spots' of our lives, which are part of all human experience, we are more in touch with the chaotic disordered part of our nature. It is during these times that we express what are often termed negative emotions, such as grief, anger, hatred, and so on (Zinser, 2011:207-14). In order to understand the light we have to experience the absence of light. However, because of the gift of free will, we might start to enjoy these negative emotional states. Indeed, to go one stage further, a soul, whether incarnate or not, might choose to reject the light and, for a period of experience, explore those elements that we have defined as the negative *shadow*. Through free will, all of these options are available to us. The Divine does not and will not interfere in this decision, for it is all part of our choice and experience.

From personal knowledge, I have come across and tried to help many spirits who have become stuck in the malign *shadow* aspect of themselves. Such spirits can cause a lot of mischief, trying to influence the minds of susceptible individuals by encouraging them to perpetrate what might be defined as evil acts, such as murder, rape, unprovoked violence, and so on.

These distinctions can be easily polarized for clarification. On the one side sits light, offering love, compassion, kindness, beauty and understanding, whilst on the other sits the evil or malign *shadow* encouraging, fear, hatred, violence, intolerance and control. I have often stated that the hallmarks of this aspect of *shadow* influence can easily be spotted from three simple questions (religions, please take note):

- Does the religion, belief system or ideology deliberately introduce fear at any level, e.g. fear of going to hell, eternal damnation, the firing squad, and so on?
- Does the religion, belief system or ideology deliberately try to control the thinking of its followers or people to generally inhibit free thought?
- Does the religion, belief system or ideology inflate the ego status of its adherents? For example, by buying into such concepts as 'We are a select or special people and therefore much better than those outside our group'?

Clearly, we need rules in order to run our societies in a benign and supportive way. The ultimate deterrent of the threat of being sent to prison, to ensure that these rules are adhered to, is legitimate, providing rules are applied equably. In all other instances, we can apply these three key tests across the board to the statements of individuals, the dictates of religious leaders, to professed ideologies and the pronouncements of politicians to determine the extent of the malign *shadow* that they may be expressing. In reading Dawkins's work and statements, I would suggest that the influence of these specific *shadow* elements is the main reason for his attack on religion.

The malign *shadow* is a large subject and will be covered fully in Chapter 9.

Summary

From what we have covered so far in this chapter a number of statements can be made. These can be summarized as follows:

- If notions of the Divine milieu have any meaning then they have to embrace all that science and scientific enquiry understand, recognizing that we are all part of an evolutionary system.
- This notion fully accepts the Darwinian model of natural selection espoused by material scientists but suggests also a complementary spiritual evolutionary process.
- It is argued here that it is illogical to believe that the magnificent computer of human experience should be switched off, and practically all of its contents lost forever, at the end of every life. If Darwin teaches us anything, it is the profound economy of the universe; experience is accumulated and only when it has fully served its purpose is it put into storage.
- Provided there is a willingness to be open to the concept, there is ample evidence supporting the claim for the continuation of consciousness through the examples of the Near Death studies. Closing one's mind, whether individually or collectively, to this idea is no better than the rigid adherence of religious leaders to their dogmas. In an interesting discussion I had with a psychologist on the one thing that psychologists do not study – the soul (psyche) – the psychologist in question was forced to admit that it was because collectively they do not believe the soul exists. What a wonderful, delightful and myopic paradox.
- Once the possibility of the continuation of consciousness is accepted, at least as a working hypothesis, then it becomes possible to build a construct that embraces both the material as well as the spiritual worlds.
- To attack spiritual notions because of religious beliefs based on tenets that date back more than a thousand years is no better than religious leaders deriding scientists for the beliefs they held in the eighteenth century. All needs to be updated and contemporary. Scientific enquiry should include both the material as well as the spiritual components of life.
- Hypnotherapeutic studies have helped therapists gain insight into the soul's journey in the spiritual realms, which suggests a level of complexity every bit as great as that which is contained in our physical

world. A fundamental component of this realm is spiritual free will that allows and empowers souls to explore experience in an unfettered way.
- Channelled accounts, from higher dimensional spirits, have fleshed out some of intricacies of the spiritual realm, which suggests a hierarchy of consciousness with an ultimate collective level of perfect balance and harmony. This *Source* offers love, light and understanding, and supports the directional flow of the evolutionary growth of the universe.
- The cosmic *shadow* can be seen as the unrealized potential for all consciousnesses within the cosmos, including that of the Divine. In this sense it is ever growing, for the greater the universe becomes, the greater is its potential to *become* in an expanding evolutionary process.
- Studies of monozygotic twins further support the view that psychologically unique individual consciousnesses inhabit each physical body, despite identical genetic make-up and similarity of environment. Twins display a sense of their own individuality which belies their similarities.
- Through the gift of free will, spirits can choose to work with all of the opposites of what might be termed 'good'. When they embark upon this path, they come under the influence of their malign *shadow* and other spirits working in a similar way.

Chapter Seven

The Personal Shadow

Above the cloud with its shadow is the star with its light. Above all things reverence thyself.

Pythagoras

Starting first with the negative *shadow*, this chapter will look at how different *shadow* components operate within our psyche. To do this we will also need to consider the steps required to bring its different elements into consciousness, for once we are aware of the subconscious patterns that are shaping our lives we can begin to do something about them. Those individuals who suffer a phobia or a condition such as OCD (Obsessive Compulsive Disorder) are fully aware of the outer manifestation of the issue and its impact upon them. What is not generally appreciated is that these conditions stem from buried trauma, and until the problem is tackled at its source the symptoms will not easily go away. It is possible, through different techniques such as aversion therapy or through medication, to block or override the original issue, but I will argue here that this is not the ideal approach. We need to learn to access and heal what lies within, not simply block its outer manifestation. This chapter will explore how trauma is tackled within the psyche and the steps we can take to alleviate inner issues and problems.

For those not suffering any obvious mental or psychological issue our *shadow* self will still be operating, manipulating our life in all sorts of subtle ways. To illuminate these impulses we need to discover methods for observing their actions within us. Fortunately, life provides some easy clues or mirrors to these elements so, for those who are willing, the task is not difficult. To conceive of this process you might like to imagine yourself as the teacher in a class of children of different ages. There may be some adults present as well. Each of these pupils carries, or has carried, some traumatized part of your psyche, and those needing help will often put up their hands to request attention. Some can be demanding and persistent, and these generally need to be dealt with as a matter of priority.

To further develop this metaphor, you could see your classroom divided into two distinct sides; on the right sit all the happy, integrated and healthy children, whilst on the left, on the darkened side, sit those who are unhappy or are still carrying some trauma. Your task is to move the dividing line to the left, so that ultimately all pupils are sitting in the light.

You might like to reflect for a moment on how you deal with those who sit in your shadow on the left, for you will certainly have some. Do you try to send them out of the room, lock them in a cupboard or, worse still, ignore them and pretend they do not exist? The teachers in our schools are working with their pupils in a very similar way to what needs to be applied within our own psyche. We need to learn how to deal with our class, particularly the half where the trauma sits. All pupils need to feel happy and fulfilled, allowing each to grow and flower to their full potential, thereby further integrating their positive *shadow* selves.

The first task then is to be very mindful when one of the unhappy children raises their hand asking for attention. They will do this by creating an emotional trigger response within you. Emotive reactions to people, events or situations, particularly when strong, are a symptom of your *shadow* expression. They are the unhappy, traumatized aspects of your psyche asking for help. In some cases, they may be obvious at an outer level. For example, you might find yourself becoming very upset or uncomfortable when a particular subject is discussed or experienced, such as sexual abuse or dealing with authority figures.

> *Activity 7:1*
>
> Think back to what you experienced yesterday and remind yourself of all the emotional responses that you had to different situations, particularly those that created some distress or irritation within you. If you are honest with yourself there will always be some. It might be feeling disturbed about what you have seen on television or heard on the radio, or annoyance about the actions of a colleague, partner or one of your children. Someone might have said something to you that caused you to feel hurt and angry. Whatever these responses are, make a note of them and consider which part of you – which of your class pupils – is being triggered.

Once the scene or situation has been evaluated then the underlying cause can be discovered. We all have an amazing higher power within us which can direct our awareness to a specific event or series of events in childhood, wherein lies the root cause of the problem. For example, if a child is made to look stupid in the classroom or by their parents, as an adult they will inevitably find themselves reacting strongly to any situation where stupidity is an issue, whether it is their own or within others. These emotional triggers are an important key to understanding where the original trauma might lie. There is a part of our psyche that has complete oversight and awareness of all of the traumas that have ever occurred to us and can direct the conscious mind to their origin. Throughout this chapter I will refer to this part as the Higher-Self (H-S). This is a phenomenal inner resource which, until acknowledged and accessed, also resides within our *shadow* self.

The next way to observe our *shadow* is through our friends, colleagues and acquaintances, for they will inevitably hold some of our negative *shadow* qualities and reflect these back to us. Those who irritate us, those that we despise, those that we hate, reflect corresponding parts within ourselves. In the second section of this book, we will explore different exercises and techniques for assessing the projected shadow but, for the moment, carrying out the following activity may give some valuable insights.

> *Activity 7:2*
>
> Note down three or four individuals who have caused you some distress over the past month or perhaps longer. Then connect to your emotions and be aware of what the quality might be that has most upset you. Perhaps it is how they have spoken to you, or how they react with others. Think of a few words that describe them, such as 'He is an arrogant bully', or 'She never listens to me'. Once this assessment has been done, reflect on how those particular elements have woven through your life. For example, using the above cases, were you the subject of bullying at school? Have you ever been a bully yourself? And, in the case of listening, when were you first conscious of not being listened to? Maybe your parents tended to ignore you as a child. Developing this further, you could reflect on the ways in which you do not listen to others, perhaps always interrupting people when they are speaking. The more that you can think about and, more importantly, feel into these situations, seeing them from both sides and owning your part in the process, the more rounded and balanced you will become. You can approach this process in the same manner as the work of Byron Katie described in Chapter 1 by continually turning the situation and comments on their head.

Towards the end of this chapter we will also explore what happens to a person when so much trauma has occurred within their life that they are tipped into wishing to carry out destructive or antisocial activities. Cases of rape and murder can be very disturbing. In the UK, the fallout from the Jimmy Savile case, in which celebrity individuals were found to have sexually abused young girls and boys, is still making headlines (Boffey, 2014). It is an easy response to portray these individuals as evil perverts. The question we need to face and address is, 'What are the underlying causes that impelled this to happen, and what steps need to be taken to prevent such situations occurring again in the future?' Such cases tip over into being part of the 'collective *shadow*', yet we need to be mindful that their inherent issues lie potentially within all of us. Who can hold up their hand and say that they have never done anything malign or abusive to another individual?

When resolving issues stemming from our negative *shadow* it needs to be borne in mind that these can, on occasions, hold a great deal of pain. They therefore need to be approached with a correspondingly high degree of care and compassion. This is why some people work through these processes with the help of therapists who can be there in a supportive, loving way. We need to learn to be gentle and tolerant of our selves and not to beat ourselves up for the failings that we manifest. No one is perfect and, within our lives, we will inevitably make mistakes from time to time. This is part of being human; indeed, it is a fundamental part of evolution, for making mistakes, however often, eventually leads to insight and change. I fully appreciate that, when considered within the context of a particular life, this may not always be apparent. Yet, as was argued in Chapter 6 on the cosmic *shadow*, I have tried to make a strong case that consciousness – your consciousness, my consciousness, all consciousness – is not limited to the physical body but goes on evolving and learning in realms beyond the material plane.

Finally, we will look at the connection with our soul consciousness and the Higher-Self (H-S), which for many people may be new terms. Until we can connect with these aspects of our being, they remain part of our *shadow*. From a therapeutic perspective, the H-S is an invaluable asset in helping us access and heal inner trauma.

The Start of the Journey

The material sciences are well aware of the development stages of the foetus from the moment of conception. From a spiritual perspective, the soul or life force consciousness makes a connection at an early stage of foetal development and then begins to programme it with its own identity. We have seen in Chapter 6 that this uniqueness is very apparent in monozygotic or identical twins, who hold the same DNA structure. Nor can epigenetic factors fully explain these psychological differences and the feeling within twins that they are separate individuals and not clones of each other. Once the foetus starts to develop it is exposed to the environmental influences of the mother, as well as the emotional and physical experiences that she is going through. If the mother has any traumatic experiences during pregnancy they can cause long-lasting emotional problems for the developing child that last well into adulthood. For the scientific evidence to support this view, see *The Secret Life of the Unborn Child* (Verny and Kelly, 1982). This process continues through to birth and beyond, with the soul essence consciousness taking greater and greater control of the body as the baby moves from infancy through to adulthood.

According to the material sciences, the brain is not fully developed until the age of twenty-five (Wallis, 2013). Rudolf Steiner, the founder of the Waldorf education system, suggested that the soul gradually takes possession of the body in a series of seven-year cycles culminating around the age of twenty-eight (Steiner, 1920). From my own working experience as a therapist, I am aware that some souls, even in middle age, are not fully grounded within their physical bodies. These cases are generally the result of childhood, or past-life, traumas to which they have been exposed. We are therefore dealing with a complex process which can be dependent upon many factors derived from environmental experience as well as the evolution of the soul that has taken possession of the body. More mature souls, as described in Michael Newton's regressions discoveries, are likely to make a better job of integrating into their body than a younger soul (Newton, 1994:103-5). We now need to look at what happens when the psyche is exposed to trauma.

Trauma and its Consequences

When the foetus, infant or child is exposed to trauma which it is unable to deal with at the time, the psyche splits off a part of itself to hold the emotional charge of the pain. It effectively creates a sub-personality or ego-state to hold that ordeal. This was first proposed by the nineteenth-century French psychiatrist Pierre Janet who proposed the 'dissociation theory' of trauma (Janet, 1976) and has more recently been developed by Tom Zinser (Zinser, 2011:262). Each of these sub-personalities has within them a tiny portion of the original soul essence. It is therefore imbued with its own individuality, although this is very much curtailed by the experience from which it has been created. Even a healthy childhood will still contain a number of these sub-personalities, for this is part of growing up. A childhood full of distress will give birth to many traumatized sub-personality parts, in turn generating considerable psychological disturbance and chaos.

As we grow into adulthood, through experience we can release some of the energy held within these sub-personalities, although many people remain stuck right through to old age. In working therapeutically with many middle-aged clients, numbers of these traumatized parts can be brought to the surface of the conscious mind and their energies released. This, in turn, creates a feeling of lightening and expansion within the individual.

When I first started my practice in the mid-1970s I used to see one predominant individual sitting in front of me. I am now aware that in addition to the primary personality there may be several dozen sub-personalities, each with their own story to tell, sitting within the psychic energy field of the client, in a similar way to the metaphor of the teacher with their classroom full of children. When exposed to similar experiences, such as abusive parenting, these sub-personalities often fall into groups, creating clusters. Effectively then we could have several sub-groups within the psyche relating to similar traumatic incidents. It is these sub-personalities, and their groupings, which generate the expression of the negative *shadow* within us.

Whilst this situation might seem very complex, I know from practical work with my clients that we all have another part of our being, our H-S, which can uncover these buried characters and bring them into full consciousness, enabling their energies to be released. Once the sub-personality has been accessed, it can then be sent light and healing to be brought into a state of balance within the psyche. The childhood sub-personality, locked in a cellar or cowering under a table waiting to be beaten, can be rescued and released from this state of fear. Nor are all sub-personalities limited to childhood suffering, because trauma can also occur to adults when we are exposed to terrifying events, such as accidents or war. The mind and soul conscious part, in dealing with such situations, can 'dissociate' part of itself from the body, sometimes causing a lapse into unconsciousness. The therapeutic process requires us to go into these incidents, to connect to the part that is suffering, and then send healing, balance, love and forgiveness to release the energy of the trauma.

Activity 7:3

Although this might be painful, it could be a valuable exercise at this stage to reflect on some of the incidents of your childhood that caused you pain. Some individuals find that writing down some of the events and the emotional responses to them can be very therapeutic. You might additionally reflect on how these incidents have shaped your life.

Psychological Groupings

From observation, the traumatized parts of the psyche often fall into one of five distinct categories. This idea was first brought to my attention by author and therapist Annie Davison, when she suggested the idea that we each hold one of five soul wounds, which can be listed as: *betrayal*; *rejection*; *abuse*; *denial*; and *abandonment*.

These specific groupings will be fully dealt with in Chapter 11, when we come to look at the different self-healing approaches to *shadow* work. What is important to flag up at this stage is that individuals will often find that one or other of these wounds tracks through their life. For example, the individual who is abandoned as an infant could find abandonment issues being a theme, whereby they either abandon people, situations or projects or, conversely, cause people to abandon them. They are caught in a cycle from which they cannot easily escape until they consciously become aware of what they are doing. These elements are deep-seated within us. I know my particular soul wound is rejection, and although I have done a lot of work to help heal the rejected parts of my psyche, my initial instinctive response is to say 'no' when new ideas are put to me, which is to reject what is being offered. It is only after consideration and reflection that I am able to change my stance.

Illuminating the Shadow

> *Activity 7:4*
>
> Try to identify which of the five soul wounds, listed above, might be affecting you. Normally one stands out above all of the others. When you have identified the soul wound, reflect on how it has influenced your life. To do this properly you will need to consider both being the victim as well as the perpetrator of the particular trauma. For example, if betrayal is your soul wound, you will need to try recall all of those moments or times when you have felt betrayed, as well as those times when you have betrayed other people, projects or, indeed, yourself. You might like to draw up a list, putting in one column the times you have felt betrayed and in the other where you might have been the betrayer. This requires a lot of personal honesty. I know, from long experience, that both columns should be of approximate equal length. If they are not you can be sure that you have not thought deeply enough into the issue, because ultimately all things are held in a polarity balance.

Observing Our Own Shadow

So far in this chapter we have been looking at the causes that give birth to our negative *shadow*. As previously stated, we can begin to discover our *shadow* through two simple and effective methods. The first is to look at all of those events where we have felt emotionally triggered, particularly when dealing with negative emotions such as fear, anger, hatred, jealousy, revulsion, and so on. In practically every case, these incidents will connect to some aspect of the negative *shadow*. The next step of the process is to uncover the particular sub-personality that is responsible for this reaction.

Because we do not easily see our own faults, the tendency is either to blame others for the response – the persecution complex – or we simply pass it off. When patterns go on repeating themselves we can be sure that one of our sub-personalities is involved. It is understandable that we do not want to look at any past painful, often deeply buried, situations, for it requires a great deal of courage to begin to delve within to heal the traumatized parts of our psyche. Yet this process is the only road that we can take if we wish to be healed.

> *Activity 7:5*
>
> Think about the last time you emotionally reacted to an incident, such as losing your temper or someone being angry with you. What went on within you and how did you respond? Are you aware of any pattern to the experience, such as something that regularly occurs in your life? What other underlying factors might be connected to this incident? Through reflection on past situations, we can begin to get a handle on what aspects of our psychological make-up are being triggered.

The People in Our Lives

As with incidents, so too do the individuals in our life, such as family, friends and colleagues, carry aspects of our *shadow*. This can also be applied to those in hierarchical positions such as doctors, teachers, work managers, and so on. The key test is to explore the emotional relationship you have with any particular person. Are you able to get on well with them generally, or do they have a knack of always pressing your emotional buttons? When your buttons are pressed, you can be sure that an aspect of your *shadow* is being agitated. As with incidents, the challenge then is to discover the particular sub-personality that is being triggered. When it is discovered, we can then take the steps needed for its healing.

Many years ago, in my late twenties, I had a job working for a builder as his architectural consultant. This particular individual was renowned for having an explosive temper, which he let rip at anyone who caused him upset. Built like a prizefighter, he had an intimidating presence which would cause most people in his company to feel very uncomfortable when exposed to his verbal rage. Although at the time he had never lost his temper with me, I always reacted inwardly when I saw him being aggressively angry towards others. This reached such a pitch that I began not to want to go into work. At this point, I decided I had to do something about my problem and I used a technique of confronting the person in my imagination, in a type of meditative exercise. I closed my eyes, connected to my higher wisdom and guides, and invited him into my inner world. I realized through this process that I needed to be able to stand up to him and not feel frightened. Effectively I had to learn to come to terms with my own anger and not run away from it.

Two days after this meditation he came into the office where I was working and headed straight for me, like an express train, mouthing all sorts of obscenities and in a violent rage about something I had designed. I was momentarily shocked at this unexpected verbal onslaught but then, instead of being cowed, much to my surprise I got angry back at him, and standing up I verbally confronted him with my anger against his totally unreasonable attitude. I can still see the look of surprise on his face as he stepped backwards. He ultimately went on to apologize for his action and I learnt a valuable lesson in integrating my anger and not being afraid of it.

This is an extreme case but highlights how individuals in our outer world subconsciously pick up and reflect back to us the hidden messages from our psyche. We are all broadcasting and receiving stations, intuitively picking up and projecting veiled information onto each other. The person who claims never to get outwardly angry will inevitably be surrounded, like moths to a flame, by angry people. In this process, we need to be ever mindful of the law of polarity. As soon as we affirm some quality about ourselves, we need to be aware of its opposite, which generally sits in the *shadow*.

Illuminating the Shadow

The following exercise highlights this process

Activity 7:6

Take an A4 sheet of paper and draw a large square on it. By taking the midpoints on the square, further divide this into four quadrants. Your paper should look like this.

Into the top left-hand quadrant write down six positive attributes that you might apply to yourself and then below that write six of your failings. You should end up with a list that looks something like this:

POSITIVE QUALITIES

- Kind-hearted
- Good at languages
- Good communicator
- Sensitive to others' feelings
- Intelligent
- Gets on well with people

NEGATIVE QUALITIES

- Easily stressed
- Workaholic
- Oversensitive to comments
- Hopeless at maths
- Low self-esteem
- Over-fussy about details

145

Once your list has been completed, reflect on how these qualities work through your life and the impact that they have. You might like to write down a few observations about specific incidents when these elements came to the fore.

In the next stage of the exercise, write down in the squares in the right-hand column the opposite of what you wrote in the left. For example, in the above list the opposite of number 1 in the positive list could be 'hard-hearted' and in the negative list 'calm and relaxed'.

As you will discover when doing this exercise, these dynamics can work through you in many nuanced ways. You may come to realize that, despite being loving and kind to others, you are very hard on yourself. The trick is to keep looking at the polarities of what is being presented or stated and, as Byron Katie suggests, keep turning them around or turning them on their head. This neatly leads onto the next theme.

Language and the Shadow

We also expose our *shadow* through our statements or comments about our self or the people around us. This becomes more emphasized when individuals have a pet hate or continually express particular ideas. To fully balance and incorporate the *shadow* elements of such statements we need to accept their opposites. For example, the person who believes or states that they are hopeless at maths has somewhere within them the potential to be an excellent mathematician. In another scenario, the person who habitually complains about an individual's character, such as saying 'John always looks out for himself and never thinks of others', is actually highlighting some imbalance within him- or herself. In this sense, all criticism of others is self-criticism, particularly when it is habitual or projected onto a specific person.

I sometimes play this game when listening to the pronouncements of our politicians. The Minister who states, after some issue, that they are not going to resign will generally be gone in a couple of days. Politicians who make firm promises will almost inevitably end up breaking them. Remember Prime Minister John Major's famous Back to Basics campaign, extolling the virtues of family life, while all the time he was having an affair with Edwina Currie? Those who proclaim they are speaking 'on behalf of the middle classes', or who say 'the National Health Service is safe in our hands', could well end up doing the opposite. This touches on one of Shakespeare famous quotes: 'The lady doth protest too much, methinks' (*Hamlet*, Act 3, Scene 2). Wise leaders know that opposites lie within all things and that ultimately we need to find a point of balance between extremes. The British Parliamentary system is built upon polarities, and it is the job of the Opposition to oppose and challenge the plans of the Government. As an ideal, the aim is to try to arrive at a form of consensus where extreme policies are filtered out; as history has shown, the process does work reasonably well, for much of the time.

> *Activity 7:7*
>
> Over the space of the next week try to make a habit of both listening to your own comments and statements as well as those of friends, acquaintances and people in the media. What might be the opposite of those statements? How is this reflected in their life or your life?

Fear and Revulsion

Before moving on to look at our positive *shadow*, something further needs to be explored in two themes already touched upon – fear and revulsion.

Illuminating the Shadow

The emotion of fear is a necessary element in ensuring our survival throughout our life. As children, we learn very quickly that when we fall over we can get hurt. We soon acquire the means to avoid pain, by learning how to walk properly. The fear of pain can be a great teacher. We can also learn from the experiences of others about what needs to be avoided. It is not sensible to walk out into a road in front of a passing car because we know the consequences could be fatal. Certain species on this planet protect themselves by learning how to become super-sensitive to potential danger, so that they can escape any threats to their life.

Within human life, fear can also be used manipulatively to control activity. The fear of a scolding can help a child to learn much-needed social disciplines and the fear of punishment can deter some potential criminals from their activities. However, this psychological element is a double-edged sword because fear can also be used in a most destructive and manipulative way, as Hitler so aptly demonstrated. It can additionally become a great inhibitor and controller of our lives. Dealing with our fears and phobias is an important part of *shadow* work. When we strip away the outer layers of most problems that confront both our society and us, we generally find an expression of fear lying at their heart. We need to be able to move into a position where our lives are not dominated by fear but by love and trust. We can only do this by confronting the fear within us which, as has already been alluded to, is part of the 'hero's journey'. This becomes particularly important if the fear is strongly inhibiting our life. Methods for tackling fear will be explored in the final section of this book.

The other deep-seated element within the psyche that needs to be addressed relates to that which we abhor or revile within ourselves, as these elements touch our shame and guilt. They become what author John Bradshaw calls 'toxic' secrets (Bradshaw, 1995:30). These events may well be remembered but, because the impact upon us is so deep, we do not want to relay them in any form to others. Sexual predators of children will often use this shame to prevent their victims from speaking out against them. Such secrets can become so introverted and distorted that we start to lie to others or cover up what has happened. People trapped by addictions will sometimes go to great lengths to hide what they are doing from their loved ones. Other cases could be the individual who loses their job but is then too ashamed to tell their partner or children. For a period, they might live out a lie by pretending to go to work, before generally being found out.

This type of shame is, in different degrees, very common. We all have secrets which we would rather others did not know. In past times, the religious confessional provided an outlet for people to give voice to that which they deeply regretted. In a more secular world, a therapist can provide a similar function. The first step is to fully own and accept what we have done, for these toxic elements can never be healed whilst they are being denied. We need to learn to love and accept all these facets of our character, to bring them into the light of the conscious self so they can be healed. The following activity will highlight how difficult it can sometimes be to fully own these remembered shames.

Activity 7:8

Sit quietly and reflect on your past. Then ask your higher wisdom to help you remember any deep-seated shameful event that you would not wish others to know about.

You might like to write this down on a sheet of paper. In some cases, it could relate to events that did become public, such as going bankrupt. Try to acknowledge all the feelings that you had about the incident. When completed, say out loud 'I forgive myself for ... [whatever the shame might relate to].' Sharing these emotional feelings with one other person is one step on the path to clearing our toxic shame, for the more we own our vulnerabilities and weaknesses the stronger we become.

Working with Our Positive Shadow

So far in this chapter we have considered how our negative *shadow* manifests, highlighting the imbalances or wounded aspects that it generates. Our positive *shadow*, on the other hand, can be projected out onto those that we admire or hold in high esteem. Individuals within society who have overcome great odds to achieve some goal provide positive role models as to what can be achieved. This is highlighted in the list of your failings in Activity 7.6, for the opposite bottom right-hand column holds your positive *shadow*. The trick here is to fully acknowledge and own where you are, and then to keep seeing or holding a vision of what you wish to become. To facilitate this process you might like to imagine that an historical or mythological character who epitomizes this quality is standing next to you, encouraging you to achieve your ambition.

The steps required to achieve your goals are expressed with great insight in Napoleon Hill's famous book *Think and Grow Rich*, which was first published shortly before the Second World War, in 1937. As the title suggests, the theme is presented as a way of achieving material financial prosperity, yet the principles are relevant to all other areas of life. The foreword contains one of Hill's aphorisms: 'Whatever your mind can conceive and believe, it can achieve' (Hill, 2014:2). As part of this process, Hill invokes a 'Master Mind' that we can all access in order to bring forth its benefits into our life. The book is still in print but is also available free in PDF format and is well worth reading.

Activity 7:9

Make a list of three things that you would like to achieve in your life and set them down in their order of priority. When you have done this, consider three people who best, historically, epitomized the particular quality needed for each of your listings. For example, if you have set your sights on being a teacher, you might like to think of one of your own teachers from school, as well as such historical figures as Pythagoras and Socrates.

You should have nine names in all. Select the first item on your list and imagine that those three characters are now standing next to you, supporting you in your endeavours and giving you insights into the steps you need to take to achieve your goals.

Try to be as open and creative as you can, perhaps even imagining that you are writing down their sage advice for any specific issue or challenge. The more that you allow them to empower you, the more you will be empowered.

The Malign Shadow

The malign *shadow* is not an easy area to contemplate because it can put us in touch with some of the baser elements of human nature. Yet we need to address the methods for dealing with its influence when it manifests, either within our life, or within that of our friends or acquaintances. This is a complicated area and there is no one simple answer. When reading of some disturbing murder or sexual abuse it is very easy to label the perpetrator as evil, yet the reasons that cause or lead to these situations can be very complex. An example is the recent case of the fifteen-year-old schoolboy Will Cornick, who murdered his Spanish teacher Ann Maguire by stabbing her in the back and neck. The judge, Mr Justice Coulson, called the murder a 'monumental act of cowardice and evil' and found the teenager's pride and lack of remorse over his actions 'truly grotesque' (Crone, 2014). It is clear from the evidence that has so far emerged that Cornick was interested in violent video games and had started to show psychopathic tendencies from the age of twelve, when he had been diagnosed with diabetes (Ronson, 2014). Cornick also claimed that he was 'hearing voices' (Brooke, Tozer and Bentley, 2014). Although we do not know all of the details of this boy's upbringing, it would seem that he came from a loving middle-class family. What then could have been the factors that led to this extreme form of violence against another individual?

From a psychological perspective, such cases can be baffling. Certain tendencies, such as a lack of empathy, can be isolated and these can be traced to the developmental stages of the brain. Yet why some people give in to such impulses to commit callous murder and others do not cannot easily be explained in purely physical terms. If we add a spiritual component then there are some further possibilities. The claims about 'hearing voices' is one factor, which raises the issue of the belief that some souls and spirits can become stuck close to the physical plane and can then influence the minds of living people. From my own working experience with clients who have felt beset by such interference, there is certainly a case to be made here. Cornick was addicted to extremely violent video games through which he could have been susceptible to subtle influences that exaggerated his hatred of others.

Clearly not all cases of mental imbalance can be ascribed to the intrusion or the influence of trapped or 'earthbound' spirits. Nevertheless, this is an important area for research. In his book *The Science of Spirit Possession*, Dr Terence Palmer (2014) presents a compelling case for the inclusion within psychiatric medicine of an understanding of spirit possession. Listing many different case studies and drawing on the work Frederic W.H. Myers, Palmer demonstrates that spirit attachment and influence can provide an explanation for many diverse psychological conditions.

The spiritual perspective also embraces the concept of past lives and spiritual evolution. Young souls entering into incarnation, like young children, could be more open to malign influences than a soul that had greater experience and maturity. Traditional religions around the world have rituals to protect the newborn child from malign influences. The Christian ritual of baptism has its origins in similar pagan traditions. Another factor could stem from past lives in which an individual could have felt extreme anger and hatred against society for something that had been perpetrated against them. In such cases, an individual, unjustly condemned to death, could have harboured extreme hatred for their peers and then nurtured a desire, either in the spirit realm or when returning to a new life, to inflict revenge against the authority figures who had unjustly punished them.

In other cases, dysfunctional family situations and childhood traumas can explain aberrant behaviour in adolescence and adulthood. Individuals caught up in crime can find themselves simply going along with the gang, perhaps in part for the adrenalin rush that it brings or the desperate need to be accepted by the tribe, family or group. Within society there are classifications of crimes committed, which is broadly in keeping with what might be understood from a spiritual perspective, where free will is acknowledged. The right to explore that free will gift is conditional on it not being used to deliberately inflict pain or suffering on others. In light of this consideration, offences against another person rank highest on the list of crimes, whilst those against property, such as theft, come secondary. Further down the pecking order come crimes against society in general, such as tax evasion and benefit fraud, and last of all come self-inflicted pain and suffering, such as attempted suicide or self-mutilation. Drug-taking falls into this latter category, provided that it does not lead to one of the other deviant behaviours.

The accounts from those who have regressed into the space between lives suggest that the spiritual hierarchy, in dealing with those who have perpetrated any of the above crimes, adopts a process not too dissimilar from the Truth and Reconciliation Commission introduced by Nelson

Mandela's government in South Africa. Souls are made to confront what they have done by becoming very conscious and aware of the suffering they have inflicted. This process is carried out in a loving, forgiving way and not intended to be any form of punishment but simply a method of helping souls recognize some of the consequences of their free will gift (Newton, 2002: 201-12).

As part of this process of reconciliation and rebalancing, a soul that has been responsible for causing hurt and harm to others might, in some future life, choose to become the victim in a specific situation where they too have to endure some similar hardship, pain or suffering. It is as though, in order to move on and progress, we need to balance those situations we have created from our past misdeeds. However, it should also be strongly stressed here that this does not imply that all who bear impediments from childhood must have carried out some misdeed in a past life. There can be many reasons, which have nothing to do with past crimes, why a soul might choose an imperfect body. Often life events will throw up such issues.

In my own case, I was aware as a teenager that I had been guillotined, in a previous life, during the French Revolution, which caused me some inner psychological distress. Some years later, while working to heal and balance this trauma and its impact on my life, I had a chance to visit Paris to clear any influence from that past-life period. When visiting the Place de la Concorde, where the executions took place, I reflected on the question 'Why did I choose to be guillotined?' The immediate inner response from my H-S was that I had been responsible in an earlier life for having other people's heads chopped off. This was one of those profound moments that turned all my thinking on its head. I knew immediately it stemmed from a life in China, where I had been in a position of authority and had been responsible for having people executed. I now realized that as well as sending out forgiveness, I needed to be asking for forgiveness for what I had inflicted on others and furthermore I needed to forgive myself, which I then did on both counts. As chance would have it, several months later I actually met one of those victims and I was able to resolve and clear up this particular piece of karma.

In working with many clients over the years, some of whom have experienced considerable trauma in their current lives, I have been struck by how often they have discovered and realized that they had been culpable, in a past life, for causing similar pain and suffering to others. This is not an easy experience to work through but I have never felt, nor have they, that they were being made to suffer: simply that they had chosen this particular 'cross' as a way of balancing a past situation.

In a wider context, every individual has the right to defend their life and that of their loved ones if they are threatened. If this means killing an assailant in the process then there is no stain or stigma attached to this situation, although souls can still feel a sense of shame and guilt over what they have done. At the time of writing (2014), we are remembering the suffering and sacrifice that was endured by millions of people during the Great War. In my therapeutic practice, I have had to help a number of clients heal and balance the 'remembered' past-life traumas from this conflict. These situations also form part of the collective *shadow*, although they are still felt and experienced at an individual level. They remind us of the extent to which human beings are prepared to go to inflict pain and suffering on each other. Whilst at a surface level there can be many different reasons that lead individuals to fighting and war, I have often reflected that one of the deep-seated *shadow* elements is the need to confront the fear of death. What better way to do this than to join the military? I am sure that those who enlist in today's fighting services must have this aspect at some level within themselves. For all their misguided reasons, the jihadists willing to kill others by committing suicide have something of the same mindset. Death for them is not seen as the end but the beginning.

The Higher-Self and Soul Consciousness

In the final part of this chapter I wish to devote time to considering the deepest layer of our psyche, wherein sits our soul consciousness and through which our Higher-Self (H-S) can be accessed. The spiritual sciences affirm that this aspect lies at the core of all human beings. We considered in Chapter 6 why we forget who we are and where we have come from as spiritual beings, yet a point can come within the adult life where we can begin to wake up this connection. When this is achieved, a source of support and inspiration is available for us which is of inestimable worth.

Whilst the soul consciousness is the main energy driver of the body, our H-S provides a direct link into the spiritual realm and a connection to those guides and beings that are trying to help us. These parts have access to the original plan and blueprint of our life. Additionally, your H-S, my H-S, continually monitors and records all that we do. It knows when the psyche splits off some aspect of itself and where those sub-personalities are parked and located. It can therefore put us in touch with the parts of our being that need healing. What the H-S will not do is interfere with our free will and generally only acts when help is requested. In this process, it will not necessarily take away issues and problems that confront us if those challenges are considered part of our life plan and based upon the lessons that our soul wishes to experience or understand. What the H-S will do is help us go through those experiences and, generally, it can be a very valuable ally in helping us to work through the different components of our lives. I firmly believe that when the lessons have been learned we no longer need to suffer.

It is not difficult to access our H-S. Within one or two sessions, when working with clients, I can help them to connect to this profound source of inner wisdom. What is amazing are the insights that are brought to the surface from memories long forgotten. With a little practice we can all learn to link to this inspirational source. The methods for doing this are fully covered in the third section of the book.

Summary

In this chapter we have explored aspects of the personal shadow, looking at its expression through the three modalities of the *negative* shadow, the *positive* shadow and the *malign* shadow. We have also touched on the link to our soul consciousness and our H-S. These elements can be bulleted thus:

- Our negative *shadow* stems from the traumatized aspects of our being which, until helped and healed, reside below the level of the conscious mind.
- Past traumas are held within sub-personalities or ego-states, each of which contains a portion of soul essence or individual consciousness.
- We can become aware of the existence of our negative *shadow* through two primary methods. The first is by monitoring our emotional reactions and the second by seeing how they are projected onto others connected to us.
- Fear and revulsion are the two primary drivers of negative *shadow* experience.
- Negative *shadow* elements will often fall into one of five categories relating to abuse, betrayal, abandonment, denial or rejection.
- Speech will often betray *shadow* elements, in that any statement about oneself or others holds within it the potential of the opposite of what is being declared.
- The positive *shadow* can be consciously helped to manifest by holding a clear thought about its realization. We need to vision our dreams, seeing them as a reality.
- The malign *shadow* operates when we allow our free will to adversely

affect the free will of others, causing them deliberate pain or suffering. These elements generally stem from our deep-seated fears or revulsions.
- Malignant spirit influences can further exaggerate the expression of the malign *shadow.*
- We all have an aspect of our soul consciousness that provides access to our higher-wisdom, which has been referred to here as the Higher-Self (H-S).

Chapter Eight

The Collective Shadow

Art teaches you the philosophy of life, and if you can't learn it from art, you can't learn it at all. It shows you that there is no perfection. There is light, and there is shadow. Everything is in half tint.

William Morris Hunt

In this chapter we will look first at how the *shadow* operates through small groups before considering its impact on the wider collective. To do this we need to be mindful of the salient elements of *shadow* expression. The first is that all things are held together by polarity balances. As soon as a collective stance is taken, something of the opposite is projected onto those perceived to be outside the group. In this process there is a pressure on those linked to the group to conform to the group's ideology or rules. This position is contained within the principle 'united we stand, divided we fall'. Even small societies have rules by which their members need to abide, and when those rules are broken individuals can be expelled from the society.

In past ages, severe retribution and even execution was meted out to those who broke the taboos or mores of specific cultures or societies. This is less prevalent today, particularly within western culture, but it still goes on in different parts of the world. The challenge for any group is how to perceive and deal with those who sit on the opposite side of the fence. This is normally not an issue as long as those twin-forked emotions of fear and hatred do not raise their distorted heads or become part of the group's shadow ethos, but, when they do, more serious polarized positions can occur. The human collective is faced today by ideologies that have these elements woven into them, and our collective challenge is how to bridge some of these divides so that we can operate in a less polarized world.

One of the most pressing areas that society has to face is how to deal with malign *shadow* expressions, both within the collective as well as outside it. The principle of 'no harm to others' needs to be the core of all *shadow* assessments and this should only be broken in extreme cases and with a great deal of caution. At what point is it right to take another's life? As history has demonstrated, this is ever a vexed question. In this chapter we will explore some of these themes, highlighting cases where different elements of the collective *shadow* manifest. I am aware that situations relevant at the time of writing (2015) can be changed by future events and some of the cases shown here may soon become dated or forgotten. What is important to consider is the themes they contain, as these are perennial.

> *Activity 8:1*
>
> Make a list of some of the groups that you are connected to, starting with your family. Do you feel linked to those groups or alienated from them? If the latter, try to identify what it is that creates this feeling of alienation.

The Shadow in Groups

The smallest group we first encounter is that of our immediate family. In most cases, this is our mother, father and siblings, if there are any. As already mentioned, within family constellations the primary group is the triangle of the mother, father and child, which might also be regarded as the smallest possible grouping. Two people do not constitute a group, whilst three do. For the child to survive they have to learn what is expected of them by their parents. This sets the pattern for the child's development, and is likely to have an impact for the rest of their life. For safety and mutual benefit, individual families within the earliest societies would have banded together to create tribal groups and these too would have set down rules for their regulation. In this process, compromises would be made between the full expression of individual free will and that of the collective, particularly in times of crisis or need. This becomes obvious when considering the command structure within military units, which would allow space for a limited amount of individual initiative but still hold it within a tightly controlled hierarchy of authority. Within such a structure the *shadow* is operating both at an individual level in how one might get on with one's fellow colleagues in arms as well as collectively in how those outside the group might be perceived as either friends or enemies.

Whilst a utopian society might conceive of everyone getting along together and working co-operatively without any enforcement of society rules and values, experience has shown that this is not possible at this stage of human development. Society needs laws for it to function and this applies from the smallest unit to the largest. In an ideal world, the greatest amount of free will expression needs to be allowed to individuals because this conforms to the evolutionary impulse, whether we wish to view this scientifically or spiritually. It is an interesting reflection that British common law, based upon precedent, has evolved in a bottom-up approach in which individuals are allowed to express themselves fully unless the law dictates otherwise. In other cases, laws can be imposed from above, such as those that occurred under Napoleonic law which sought to put right some of the mess of the then French legal system. In these cases, individuals can only do what civil law codifies, which is how the Council of Europe operates (SB, 2013).

Another example of a top-down approach is the United Nations Declaration of Human Rights. We can apply the concept of opposites to this declaration to see what the *shadow* elements might be.

Article 1 states: 'All human beings are born free and equal in dignity and rights. They are endowed with reason and conscience and should act towards one another in a spirit of brotherhood.'

The opposite of this statement is that human beings are not born free and equal in dignity and rights, nor are they all endowed with reason and conscience and nor do they act towards another in a spirit of brotherhood. As far as the world collective is concerned, the converse of Article 1 is the truer statement.

Some certainly aspire to these ideals but the majority of human beings do not. We only have to look at what is happening within the so-called enlightened nation states to see how far human beings diverge from these ideals. In recent times, within the British Parliament, a scandal arose because MPs were fiddling their expenses. Were they, as representatives of the people, acting in a spirit of brotherhood or simply looking for what they could get?

Article 3 states: 'Everyone has the right to life, liberty and security of person.'

The opposite of this statement is that 'no one has the right to life, liberty and security of person'.

Sadly, this is again the truer statement when looking at the present world situation, which is why governments resort to guns, bullets and detention when dealing with world situations. The bombing of innocent civilians is seen simply as collateral damage in the 'war on terror'. We live in a world full of insecurity, which some exploit for their own selfish ends. Whilst many individuals might consider themselves free in a theoretical sense, they are generally held in bondage by debts, ideologies or laws that curtail their liberty.

As we can see from these examples, the aspirations of the Declaration of Human Rights are an ideal towards which humanity can strive, yet we also need to be ever-mindful of the opposites. The right to choose one's path in life should be sacrosanct, provided that path does not cause any suffering or adversely affect other human beings or members of society. It is through this process that liberties can be restricted, for balances need to be struck.

For example, in 1983 a law requiring the compulsory wearing of car seatbelts was introduced in the UK. This law clearly impinged on the free will choice of those driving cars, and certainly some objected to this law as an infringement of civil liberty. Parliament, on the other hand, took the view that the interests of society stood above that of the individual. The idea was sold on the view that this law would save lives and prevent severe injuries. The problem here was not so much to do with the effects on those involved in accidents as on the wider ramifications and costs incurred by society by those who had to deal with these injuries and fatalities. In this case, the price to society of not wearing seatbelts outweighed the cost to the individual and most drivers now accept this change without any complaint.

Moving in the other direction, laws from past times, which have been perceived to curtail human freedoms, have been repealed. One area where this is very apparent is society's view on homosexuality, which until fairly recently was considered a crime in the UK. Society, within the UK, has come a long way in accepting differences of sexual expression. Whilst the bulk of the world's population expresses itself heterosexually, it is very important that a good/bad polarity is not projected onto those who express their sexuality differently. It is additionally important that protection against homophobia is available for this minority group, with steps taken to defend individuals against persecution. Yet equally, those who are truly homophobic, like all people with phobias, need help and understanding, not vilification. The so-called hate police reaction can easily become a projection in the other direction by demonizing those who find it difficult, for religious or moral reasons, to accept this aspect of human nature.

Human Development

In looking first at the child, the core principle, in line with the free will concept, would be to allow children to develop in ways that give full expression to their innate self and only to set boundaries when this expression negatively affects other individuals or adversely affects the child. The no-harm principle needs to be paramount both towards other members of society and then ideally towards the self, although in growing towards adulthood this latter element needs to be encouraged rather than enforced. One can argue that all young adults need the freedom, without undue restriction, to explore the world they inhabit.

With these concepts in mind, it then becomes possible to see to what extent the negative *shadow* operates through society. We need to remind ourselves that the twin driving energies of this negative expression are fear and revulsion. Through these twin poles it is possible to criminalize segments of society because they wish to express themselves differently. To reaffirm what has already been stated, the principle of the right to explore our free will gift should be inviolable, provided this does no direct harm to others, except by mutual consent. For example, those participating in competitive sports might inflict pain and suffering on their opponents, such as rugby, American football and boxing. Rules for these sports mean individual participants do not normally suffer serious injury, except by accident. In all cases, individual freedoms of expression should be encouraged, except where these might affect a greater social need, such as the case of the seatbelt law stated above.

One clear example of the infringement of this free will principle is in the area of prostitution. In an ideal world all individuals should be able to find a suitable sexual partner, but in the real world this is not always possible. In line with the principle presented here it can be argued that should a man or a woman choose to use their body to give sexual relief to another human being for a payment then that should be their free will choice and society has no right to interfere.

Prostitution is a complex subject. In ancient times, prostitutes were highly regarded in society, fulfilling the duties of high priestesses as well as their sexual duties (Jacobs, 2015). This is very different from what we witness today, where debates on prostitution generate strong emotion reflecting different moral standards and the projection of personal and collective fears, such as the fear of the moral degeneration of society or the fear that legalized brothels might encourage infidelity. Legalizing this profession would allow women and men to provide their services in a healthier protected environment, whereas criminalizing it encourages the *shadow* expression through the criminal fraternity and potentially gives rise to greater problems of sexual exploitation and abuse. The underlying reason why most men and women resort to prostitution, if they have not been coerced or groomed, is financial gain. A high-class prostitute can earn a substantial sum of money every year (Jacobs, 2015).

It is beyond the comprehension of the larger society of healthy-minded people when the innocence of childhood is abused by sexual predators. In these cases, the full force of the law has every right to step in, because the individual freedoms of those who are being exploited are being abused. Recent investigations, triggered by the Jimmy Savile scandal, are bringing the enormous *shadow* of childhood sexual abuse into the light of a wider social collective, and those institutions that have failed to protect children are rightly being exposed.

What is also important is to try to understand why this aberrant form of human behaviour manifests in the first place. Recent research has shown that paedophiles have an innate sexual attraction that is directed towards young children, whether boys or girls. This research suggests that between 1 and 5 per cent of all males may have this predisposition (Zarembo, 2013). In order to help such individuals, there needs to be a greater awareness of this form of psychological imbalance, so that individuals can be helped before they start physically abusing children. Unfortunately, because of the demonizing of this aspect of human expression, those who participate in psychological studies are often those already incarcerated in prisons. At this point in their life, it is probably already too late to affect any deep-seated change, whereas picking up this tendency earlier might have helped. There have also been suggestions that the intention and influence of malevolent discarnate entities may have a significant part to play in paedophilia, in addition to serial rape and serial murder (Palmer, 2014).

Falling into a similar category of free will expression, although moving closer to the area of self-harm, comes the use of cigarettes, alcohol and drugs. In our hierarchy of *malign* shadow expressions, self-harm falls into the lowest category. Those who take different stimulants, whether by smoking, drinking or injection, could also well argue that the exploration into drug use provides them with some positive psychological benefits. A survey carried out by Opinium Research in July 2014 showed 31 per cent of British society – nearly one third of the population – had taken one or more illegal drugs at some stage in their lives (Huey, 2014). This is the reality of what happens within western society when the pressures of modern living, abuse and trauma are relieved by self-medication or simply perceived as a way of exploring different states of consciousness. One could argue that the use of all addictive substances, including alcohol and tobacco, is a symptom of imbalance and whilst I, as a therapist, might contend that there are other, safer ways to tackle inner problems I do not have the right to condemn or block others from this exploration, nor should society.

As an alternative approach, instead of criminalizing drug use, clinical centres could be established in which these stimulants, properly formulated, would be available for purchase. Such centres could be backed up with medical help to assist habitual addicted individuals to wean themselves off the habit. Ongoing support in the form of therapy is needed in order to assist the sufferer to come to terms with the *shadow* that created the problem in the first place.

If a pragmatic legalized drug approach were to be adopted, as with alcohol and tobacco, it would undermine a large segment of the criminal underworld by bringing it into the light. The cost of not facing and tackling this issue has resulted in trillions of dollars, pounds and euros being spent trying to block drug use, and countless burglaries and personal assaults perpetrated by those desperate to obtain a fix. The financial and human cost equations are immense. For example, the cocaine trade in South and Central America has resulted in an excess of 100,000 'disappearances' and has cost the US more than a trillion dollars in the 'war on drugs' since the 1970s (Huey, 2014).

In Asia, selling poppies for heroin is one way that the poor Afghan farmers are able to eke out a living. During the recent conflict in Afghanistan, western powers had every opportunity to set up a properly managed system to obtain supplies of this narcotic or, if possible, to introduce non-harmful cash crops as alternatives. This system could then have been funnelled through government-managed departments instead of offering the criminal element, such as the Taliban, the opportunity of exploiting this area to fund their activities. Crimes and criminals always sit within the collective negative *shadow* aspects of society. Their activities then move into the *malign* shadow where both fear and greed become deeply entrenched, and where the momentum results in harming the whole of society at every level, from vulnerable individuals to the greater social collective. The ultimate calamity is war with catastrophic consequences, as we have seen in Afghanistan and Colombia.

What emerges from these examples is the way that society's attitudes and prejudices feed into the *negative* projected *shadow* and this in turn can tip over into feeding a criminal element. Put another way, that which we do not face squarely creates another compendium of potentially worse problems, including criminality, huge humanitarian and economic costs and possibly war. This taps into another *shadow* element of the need of the arms trade to generate conflict.

It is right that the young should be protected, as far as possible, from that which could cause them harm. The best way to do this is through wise parenting, education and their being made aware of the physical and psychological dangers of drugs, alcohol and tobacco. Every effort should be made to stop them taking such stimulants before they are sixteen, as we do with smoking, although a case could be made that this threshold should be extended to around twenty-five years for narcotics, because of brain development (Wallis, 2013). In a complementary arena, young people are not allowed to drive cars on the highway until they are seventeen. It can be argued that driving on our roads is no less hazardous for individuals than taking various stimulants. For example, in 2011 just over 1,900 people died in road accidents (GOV.UK, 2015), whilst in the same period some 1,172 people died from different forms of drug abuse, including 287 people on anti-depressants (DrugScope, 2015). We fully accept the consequences of motoring because we consider that the benefits far outweigh the downsides; although we are dealing with an entirely different area of activity in relation to sex and drugs, the same attitude of education and acceptance ought to prevail.

According to the religious teacher J Krishnamurti (1996), all forms of addictive behaviour stem from a desire to escape reality, often because some aspect of life is too painful. Gambling has the potential to be another form of addiction which can sometimes have catastrophic consequences. On the other hand, many people enjoy a 'flutter' on the horses, or buy lottery tickets from time to time and this can be seen as harmless recreation. It is all a question of balance.

Western society has taken a more liberal attitude towards gambling, perhaps because it is seen as a legitimate means of making money, and the negative consequences are less overt than drug addiction. Addiction in different forms can be instrumental in bringing to light many issues for those afflicted, and organizations such as Alcoholics Anonymous (AA) and Gamblers Anonymous (GA) do incredible work in helping those trapped by their compulsions. In recent years some adults and young people have become addicted to Internet gaming, spending many hours hooked into a fantasy world. The long-term effect of this level of engagement with continuous Internet and computer use is not known, as studies cannot yet be made over a long enough time span. The research, such as it is, has shown little damaging effect on brain development since the development of the World Wide Web (Mills, 2014). However, its negative effect in isolating young people who are therefore unable to develop social skills is a worry for many who are concerned with social psychological health. Although the explosion of the World Wide Web has brought many benefits, we still need to recognize the polarizing power of the negative.

The use of the Internet and media generally has given rise to many new outlets for negative *shadow* expressions, and these can cause enormous psychological damage to those who are the recipients of anonymous abusive comments. Persecutory individuals, known as 'trolls', take great delight in using the anonymity of the Internet to project their *shadow* onto others, often in a malign or cruel way. Laws to curtail these hate crimes are necessary, although a better understanding of the origins of the trolls' negative *shadow* would help recipients to deal more easily with their impact. In this area, children are the most vulnerable and need the greatest level of support and protection.

The Shadow within Business

The *shadow* can be found in every strata of society, including the business world, where its lack of recognition can be disastrous for some companies and even, in some cases, for the wider collective. In a fascinating book by Gillian Tett, entitled *The Silo Effect: Why Putting Everything in its Place Isn't Such a Bright Idea* (2015), we learn that the collapse of the financial markets in 2007-8 was not caused by the banking industry per se but by what has now become known as the *shadow* banking system (Wikipedia, 2015).

This stemmed from a natural tendency within human beings to group together in tribal structures, which when transferred into the business world is known as the 'silo' effect. This manifests when different departments or segments of a business are established to perform specific tasks, such as finance or marketing. Within small organizations of less than 150 people, communication between these sectors can be readily maintained. Once businesses become larger, problems can occur if there is not a careful regard for communication between different elements of the organization or company.

There will always be a tendency for the tribal mentality to kick in and if this happens these individual sectors can begin to erect mental and sometimes physical walls around their departments. The tendency then is to create a 'them and us' mindset and not to readily communicate important information across boundaries, thereby creating individual distinct and disconnected 'silos', which look to serve only the interests of their specific group rather than to consider its implications for the organization as a whole. The *shadow* can then become projected onto other departments through rivalry and self-protection. This problem is made worse when some organizations deliberately foster competition between these segments based on the dictate that 'you eat what you kill'. In other words, different profit centres are set up within the organization which then seek to maximize their profits without regard for the greater collective (Tett, 2015).

This is what had happened within the banking world prior to 2007-8. At the periphery of these major global institutions, small individual groups of inventive investors established many different ways to make profits, often wrapping up their operations with technical gobbledegook that the overseeing managers and directors neither understood nor regulated. Effectively a significantly large segment of the industry slipped into the unregulated *shadow* side of these corporations. When the first signs of disaster started to manifest those in control of the institutions were oblivious to what was happening within this *shadow* area. When the subprime mortgage lending within the US started to unravel, many of the larger banks, such as UBS, discovered that they had been seriously exposed, leading to their potential collapse and the need for governments to step in and shore up these vital institutions.

As well as discussing the banking sector, Tett's book highlights a number of different major world corporations, like Sony and Microsoft, where the 'silo' effect has taken root, leading to major problems that have stultified innovation and creativity within these institutions. Some companies like Facebook have taken specific steps to circumvent the 'silo' effect and to ensure that open communication is maintained throughout their organization, allowing for a fertilization of ideas between all segments of the company; in effect, to keep breaking down and challenging any barriers that might occur between the different sectors of the business. As outlined in this book, the simple process of continually turning ideas on their head is one way to re-evaluate a business and thereby maintain a competitive edge. New ideas then need to be able to be disseminated throughout the organization and across all departments for the betterment of the whole organization and not just its one segment.

One such innovative company that has taken this step is the Cleveland Medical Clinic in Ohio. This very successful company, employing some 40,000 staff, was originally structured into different departments based upon the classification of types of doctors, such as surgeons and physicians. In 2004 a new CEO, Toby Cosgrove, took over. Early in his tenure he was confronted by a comment that his clinic, whilst being highly efficient, lacked 'empathy'. This set him thinking and led to the complete reorganization of the company which is now based not on the hierarchy of doctors but on the perceived symptomatic needs of the patients, such as back conditions or cancer treatment. All surgeons, physicians, nurses, dieticians and clinicians were simply labelled 'caregivers'. This led to a greater pooling of resources, where a variety of therapeutic interventions could be drawn upon for the holistic treatment of conditions that included a mental, physical and spiritual component (Tett, 2015:loc 3255).

The Shadow within Nations

As human beings evolved, developed and gathered in groups, specific habits and modes of expression emerged. This eventually led to the creation of nation states and forms of specific identity and culture.

It is beyond the scope of this book to explore in any detail the complex interactive components that contribute to the evolution of nation states and cultures, and to the emergence of powerful empires. History teaches us that many ancient civilizations have risen and fallen, such as the Roman, the ancient Persian and the Ottoman empires. Their collapse, which is generally part of a natural rhythm or cycle, can also be spectacular. Early in the twentieth century, the British Empire extended to nearly one quarter of the Earth's land mass, yet within a few years it was no more, with the different nation states wisely, in this case, being given their independence. These sovereign states now form a collaborative group known as the Commonwealth of Nations (Commonwealth.org, 2015).

We are now moving towards a global culture in which there is a mixing of ideas and identities, at least within the higher echelons or richer elements of society. The development of the exchange of ideas is very positive and healthy because the more we can learn to accept and respect other viewpoints the more balanced we will become as a world society. Sadly, on the other side of the coin, there are still many conflicts taking place across the globe fuelled by different levels of national self-interest and misguided actions. As already stated, as soon as an individual, or a nation state, perceives themselves as the 'good' guys, someone, somewhere, has to be 'bad'. This process was worked out in recent years through the Cold

War, with what was then the USSR and its allies on the one side and the US and its adherents on the other, both with different sets of beliefs which could be expressed as a communist or capitalist system respectively.

As has also been stressed in this book, extremes are always problematic. We sometimes need to explore extremes in order to understand what they might contain. However, the ideal is to try to find a balance between these polarities, for the more that we can try to learn to tread in another's footsteps, to see the opposite viewpoint, then so much the better for society.

Again, I wish to stress the fundamental principle of free will expression, as long as this does not cause harm to others. What is relevant for the individual should also be applicable for the collective. In 2014, Scotland held a referendum on whether it wished to become an independent country. Whilst one might argue about how this was instituted, what was most important was the fact that it espoused the right to choose. Self-determination is an important issue and people need to be offered opportunities to decide how they are governed without resorting to guns or punitive sanctions. We can pick up a few examples from around the world that highlight this principle and how it is either being applied wisely or not.

The first example is to consider what is taking place in present day Ukraine, which originally came under the domination of Moscow as an integrated part of the USSR. It is now an independent state, but has become split between those who hanker after, or more closely identify with, the old Soviet state and those who lean towards Europe and the western ideologies. How can this split be healed? The only balanced way is through dialogue and acceptance. Both sides need to be able to sit down and talk to each other, to listen to each other's viewpoint and try to find some form of rapprochement.

Sadly, both sides appear to be influenced by the conflicting ideological stance between the US and Russia. Both sides consider themselves to be right. Those who favour the western connection in Ukraine, which appears at the time of writing to be the central government, need to take every step to hold out their hands to those who lean towards the east. If this means instituting a form of self-autonomy then so be it, and the western powers ideally should encourage this stance. Every effort needs to be made by both sides for dialogue and openness and to avoid and ignore thoughtless emotive comments (Jones, 2014).

The Ukraine situation is but one of many such scenarios being worked out across this planet. More concerning, and potentially more deadly, is the previously mentioned long-standing clash between Israel and Palestine. It is hard sometimes to step back from the difficult history that lies behind these blood-soaked lands and the suffering that has endured there for so long for both the Jewish and Palestinian people. It is one of those curious facts that Jerusalem is the focus of the three main Abrahamic religions. One of the problems of history is that we can become stuck in a repetitive cycle and this creates many difficult *shadow* issues.

Those of Jewish ideology firmly believe that the land of Israel was ordained for them by God and they have every right to live there. The Palestinian people, on the other hand, maintain that, as occupiers of this area for the past thousand or more years, the land belongs to them. Historical records show that the earliest accounts of the Israeli people, living in the region of modern Palestine, probably date back to the time of the Egyptian king Merneptah, who ruled circa 1209 BCE (Redmount, 2001:58-89). They were not alone because other ethnic groups, such as the Philistines and the Canaanites, also lived there. As a land bridge between Africa, Europe and Asia, this stretch of land has seen many invasive groups passing through and the consequent bloodshed that these have entailed.

Archaeological evidence has revealed that, since the very emergence of organized society or so-called civilization in the Near East from 3500 to 1000 BCE, this area has been a flashpoint between all the four great ancient empires of Egypt, Babylon, Assyria and the Hittites. In Roman times it was contested between Rome and the Phoenicians, and in medieval times it was contested between the Christians and Islam through five great Crusades. The history of conflict in this area of the Middle East includes invasion and occupation by the Mongols, the Seljuk Turks and the Ottoman Empire (Roberts, 1995). It seems almost as if the cradle of western civilization is also the crucible of eternal conflict between religious ideologies or the economic and territorial domination of one ethnic group over another.

Whatever the history, at the time of writing two groups face each other locked into a conflict which many have tried to resolve. Of all the peoples on this planet, the Jewish people are unique in that through their traditions they have maintained a clear sense of their racial identity. Other cultures, when overrun and conquered, would soon have found themselves absorbed into the invasive ethos, or when they settled in new areas would have begun to identify and perceive themselves as natives. The British Isles are full of such assimilations, with the different settled groupings such as the Vikings, Danes, Jutes, Picts, Angles, Saxons, Normans and Huguenots being merged into what we now identify as British culture. The Jewish people stand out, in that despite the length of time that they have resided in these or other lands, for the most part they still maintain their Jewish racial heritage. This can be seen as both a strength and a weakness for, whilst allowing a collective identity, it also singles them out as a distinct group, which creates the polarity of either being Jewish or Gentile.

It could be claimed, with some justification, that the Jewish people have made huge contributions to humanity in many different areas, yet such racial separation has the danger of being influenced by the malign *shadow* for, eventually, such a group will be seen as, or regard themselves as, either 'good' or 'bad'. This can occur when, for political or ideological reasons, the collective wishes to project its *shadow* of oppositeness onto the perceived minority or inferior group. The destruction of the Jews in Nazi Germany was an example of this projection, yet this same persecution mentality may be found within extreme elements of the Israeli people today.

There is also a sense within the Jewish ethos of being God's chosen people. As soon as the psyche takes on this perception, those outside the group are not 'chosen', and at some level are therefore 'inferior'. This *shadow* element becomes a trap which can lead to persecution, paranoia and separation. The ramifications of this are that those who espouse such beliefs will, sooner or later, become either persecutors or victims themselves. History is full of such examples. The early Christian Church drew strength from its martyrs and then, when the tide turned, wished to inflict their ideology onto others. The same is true within Islam, where the extreme elements want to impose a specific set of beliefs on others, regardless of what those individuals might think. Nazi Germany was fuelled by a similar mentality of considering themselves part of the 'superior' Aryan race (Holocaust Encyclopedia, 2015). Assuming the mantle of the Master Race, they considered lesser beings as inferior and deserving of being downtrodden, conquered and killed.

The *shadow* projection in such cases becomes a potent force, sweeping individuals along as though caught in the powerful current of a river. It gives permission for individuals to act in brutal ways that they would not do in other circumstances. In recent times in the Americas, we have witnessed the Jonestown massacre, the Waco Siege, the Rajneesh fiasco in Oregon, and so on. In all these cases, the polarity positions became split, allowing fear and paranoia to become the dominant impulse.

Any and every group, through their free will gift, has the right to establish itself and to explore different elements of life. This can be very positive and creative, leading as it has to the development of many diverse societies across the globe, exploring the world we inhabit from flower arranging to painting; from golf to football; from science to religion or spirituality, and so on. Groups can compete with each other for their self-improvement, which can further insights and abilities, all of which is healthy and balanced. Issues occur when a group begins to perceive itself as different from those around them, the ego becomes inflated and then the negative or possibly malign *shadow* kicks in.

With these thoughts in mind, let us now return to considering what is taking place in Israel and Palestine between the Jews and the Arabs. Of the two groups, the most powerful are the Israelis and it is interesting that, despite their long history of persecution, when the boot is on the other foot they are not averse to being persecutory themselves. Those who feel persecuted will certainly feel aggrieved, which can lead to violent reactions. Sitting on the other side of the divide are the Palestinian people who have been forced from their lands and now harbour feelings of anger and hatred towards their dispossessors. These entrenched attitudes in turn can lead to both sides demonizing each other. The projected *shadow*, in this case, is that neither side trusts the other, with the consequence that every move or step is perceived in a negative light.

In 2009, an embossed book entitled *The King's Torah*, written by Rabbis Yitzhak Shapira and Yosef Elitzur, was widely circulated in Jerusalem. This book suggested that the prohibition of 'Thou shalt not kill' applied solely to Jews killing Jews and that it was quite acceptable to kill non-Jews, including babies, since 'it is clear that they will grow to harm us' (Estrin, 2010). The radical, fear-based views promoted in this book are little different from the extremist elements of Islamic culture which classes non-believers as 'infidels', and therefore to be regarded as individuals who can be murdered without conscience, as has happened with some frequence in recent years.

Clearly people need to be able to defend themselves but this should not be an excuse for an unwillingness to understand the grievances of the other party. One cannot fight terror with terror, for all it does is fuel anger, hatred and the desire for revenge. As the stronger party, the Israelis should go out of their way to help the Palestinians build for themselves a land and society where they can feel free to live in peace and security. A truly balanced, spiritual mindset would perceive every single Palestinian person to be of equal status and value with an Israeli, and for the Jewish people to recognize that when they unleash their weapons of destruction against any individual they are indirectly harming themselves. The wise way forward is to reverse the trend of violence and do all in their power to help those that they perceive to be persecuting them. In this way, the extremist elements on both sides could be challenged in a more compassionate and less antagonistic way. Another very important factor that contributes to the continued conflict in Palestine is the aggressive occupation of Palestinian land and the Israeli persistence in building settlements on it. All the while invaders occupy land considered to have been stolen there will be a tendency towards conflict.

These comments are not intended as an attack on the Jewish people or on Islam but rather an observation on the likely outcomes when a sense of separateness and superiority is maintained. If any should feel offended by what I have written then I apologise unreservedly. The intention here is to highlight imbalances so that they can be tackled. All individuals need to be seen to be of equal worth and importance, whether they are white, black, Jewish, Muslim, and so on. Wise international intervention could and should do far more to help balance self-destructive processes when they occur, because these have the potential to draw in others to further this conflict. Crimes against humanity will only be stemmed when the followers and leaders of all peoples reject notions of superiority for themselves and perceive all life as sacred.

The Falklands and Gibraltar

When looking at what is taking place in our world, very often the approach adopted by governments produces exactly the opposite result

Illuminating the Shadow

to that which is intended. For example, in two anachronistic situations that are the remnants of Britain's empire, we have two settled areas of Gibraltar (1713) and the Falkland Islands (1833), whose right of sovereignty is being disputed by Spain and Argentina respectively. The history behind both of these situations is complex, and undoubtedly Britain, in the past, used its superior military strength and colonial intentions to take control of these areas. However, as has been previously stated, the principle of free will choice needs to apply to the collective as well as the individual. If those living in the Falklands or Gibraltar wish to remain allied to their British roots then that should be their sovereign right, for that is the de facto position regardless of history. Land disputes can be complicated and raise deep-seated passions, as we have seen in Palestine. In most cases, and as a matter of principle, there could be simple ways of settling such disputes internationally. For example, when a group of people has inhabited a land for three generations, say one hundred years, then their rights should override any other claims. Similar laws have been instituted within the borders of sovereign nations to settle land disputes and similar principles could be agreed within the United Nations.

Once this principle has been accepted then should either Spain or Argentina wish to provide or hold some influence over these two areas, the way to go about this would be for both countries to make every effort to be helpful and supportive to these colonial groups, instead of setting up barriers, blockades and restrictions. Adopting such an approach could mean that in time both of these old colonies might see themselves being more allied to, and more co-operative with, the nation states that they border, rather than holding allegiances to their mother land. Effectively, the projection of the *shadow* onto Gibraltar and the Falklands creates the opposite effect to what is the professed desired intent of both Spain and Argentina to have some direct influence in these areas.

Tribal Mentality and the Shadow

Sadly, since the Second World War we have seen many conflicts driven by deep-seated tribal hatreds that sometimes flare up with little effort. In a period in 1994 of approximately 100 days, between 500,000 and 1 million Tutsi and moderate Hutu people were massacred in Rwanda in a planned genocide by the ruling right-wing Hutu elite. The conflict was only brought to a close by an uprising of Tutsi in the north of Rwanda, which eventually led to the capture of Kigali, the capital city. In the aftermath of the war the United Nations and many of the major powers, including the US, Britain, France and Belgium, were criticized heavily for not acting to prevent the massacres.

During the same period the break up of what was then Yugoslavia led to a number of massacres in Bosnia and Kosovo. After the Second World War, Josip Tito unified a number of states including Slovenia, Croatia, Bosnia, Serbia, Montenegro and Macedonia together with Kosovo and Vojvodina under the banner of 'Brotherhood and Unity'. Under Tito's rule, his inclusive policy held the state together in a relatively benign way. After his death, factional interests emerged to tear the state apart. The strongest of these groups were the Serbs under their leader Slobodan Milosevic, who headed a powerful Serbian army. Like Hitler he gained power by inflaming nationalist sentiments and tribal and religious hatreds.

The first of the states to leave the Federation were Slovenia and Croatia. After a brief ten-day war against Slovenia the Serbian army withdrew and focused their attention on Croatia, where there was a sizable Serbian minority. The city of Vukovar was reduced to rubble and hundreds of Croats were subsequently massacred. The western powers did little to intervene. Worse was to follow when Bosnia, a predominantly Muslim country, declared independence. Milosevic now turned his attention to Sarajevo and started to shell the city from the surrounding hills. Throughout this period, despite terrible massacres, there was no military intervention by the European Union or the US. Milosevic, made confident by this supine approach, was supported by his henchmen and continued to inflict terrible suffering on Sarajevo and Kosovo where approaching 200,000 people were said to have been killed.

This war was only brought to an end by the intervention of NATO forces, which led to the defeat of Milosevic and the establishment of a more moderate government in Serbia, which again recognized the rights of the minority groups. These events show how easy it can be to inflame tribal hatred and for the malign *shadow* to take hold. Fired up by their success in the Balkans, the US and UK determined to adopt the same approach in Iraq and Afghanistan, which led to the overthrow of Saddam Hussein in the Iraq War and the initial ejection of the Taliban from Afghanistan. As history has shown, these successes were short-lived, particularly in Iraq where religious intolerances between the Sunni and Shia communities and the partial collapse of Syria have bred an even more ferocious adversary in form of the Isil Caliphate.

From these destructive scenarios it would seem that the foreign policies of the European Union and the US are in a mess because of an inability to consider working, wherever possible, in a co-operative and collaborative way with those they consider their enemies. It is very easy to condemn such leaders as Saddam Hussein, Colonel Gaddafi and President Assad of Syria as the 'bad' guys, without considering the consequences of that projection. There surely have to be other ways to protect civilian populations from oppression, without using guns and bullets, except as a very last resort.

The Collective Shadow Within Religion

We now come to consider how the *shadow* operates within religious belief. Most religions accept the view that some form of afterlife exists. This can range from seeing a complementary hierarchy of experience within a spiritual world where souls go on evolving, to a literal belief in the resurrection of the body on the Day of Judgement, whenever that might be. The belief in an afterlife can help individuals gain meaning in their physical incarnation, which is one of its greatest benefits. However, religious belief can be both a benefit as well as a trap, particularly when the *shadow* elements are ignored.

Religion generally contains three predominant components – the cosmological, the ethical and the spiritual. It could be argued that one of its primary functions is to provide a vehicle for the expression of a person's spirituality. This can be done individually, through personal prayers and meditations. It can also be carried out within a collective structure, where the dynamic of the group can give an added impulse to the experience. A form of group psyche, or collective consciousness, is created when individuals unite or harmonize their thoughts with others. This can occur in forms of crowd hysteria, when individuals are sucked into acting in ways that are uncharacteristic. The collective within religion can give an added boost to that spiritual seeking, which can be very beneficial for its adherents. This is why meditating within a group structure allows for greater depth of experience. Added to this can come the cumulative impulse of all that has gone before. A form of collective power can be generated from those participating in previously enacted rituals, such as within the Christian Mass or Islamic rites. All of this can be to the good and helpful for an individual seeker.

So where does the *shadow* come in? All religious rituals of this ilk are locked, by definition, into previous historical periods and can then easily become stuck there. As science has demonstrated and leading edge spirituality has maintained, evolution sits at the heart of all processes. All religious beliefs and expressions of the spiritual component of human activity need to evolve and keep pace with modern thinking. This is the great strength of the scientific world, where knowledge and understanding are cumulative. When new discoveries are made and affirmed, old ideas are re-examined and modified. Sometimes 'correct' ideas are needlessly jettisoned when new perceptions come along. Material science has done this with 'spirit' and, as a result, the concept of spirit has, to a greater extent, become taboo in the scientific study of human experience. Nevertheless, ultimately that which is true will eventually resurface. This has happened recently with a re-examination of the role of DNA in the latest studies of epigenetics. What was heretical to science in the 1990s is now accepted as fact (Spector, 2013). It is all part of progressive evolution.

The same concept needs to be applied within religious systems, particularly those that stem from the major religions of the planet, including Christianity, Islam, Hinduism, Buddhism and Judaism.

It is very easy for these institutionalized religions to become trapped in their ideologies and for these to fail to keep pace with contemporary thinking, which is why Richard Dawkins and his fellow atheists are able to attack them so readily. Indeed, these religions need to be challenged so that their viewpoints can be brought fully into line with modern thinking and not trapped in the mentality of the Middle Ages or earlier.

For example, one of the fundamental elements within modern culture is recognizing men and women as having equal importance and rights. Both sexes express different aspects of a polarity balance and both hold the same complementary status. At the time of writing, the head of state in the UK is a woman and few would argue against the sense of dedication and commitment shown by the Queen, which undoubtedly is the equal of any male monarch. This same principle needs to be applied within religions, yet how many have fully taken this step? The Anglican Church, after considerable internal wrangling, has finally accepted the concept of women bishops and two appointments have now been made. The next step will be to appoint a woman to the role of archbishop. The Roman Catholic and Eastern Orthodox Churches have still a long way to go in this respect.

A few years ago, I had the opportunity to visit and climb Mount Athos in Greece, which comes under the jurisdiction of twenty monastic communities on the Chalcidice peninsula. It forbids all women to go there, which is strange bearing in mind that the monasteries were founded on the dedication of the Blessed Virgin Mary who is supposed to have set foot on the mountain and consecrated it.

Looking at many other religions, we can also see this same imbalance manifesting to a greater or lesser degree. The males of our species, through their physical strength, often perceive themselves to be superior. However, when considered across a range of human expressions, this is not so; when given the opportunity, women can excel in all areas of life and that is what a balanced society should express. The feminine presence should be given full representation within religious institutions.

The Use of Fear Within Religions

Another *shadow* element, held within many religious ideologies, is the way that fear is used to control and manipulate people's thinking. To reiterate one of the key points made within these pages, fear sits within the malign side of the polarity between light and dark. On the one side of this divide, as an expression of the Divine, sits love, illumination, healing and balance, whilst on the other resides fear, ignorance, hatred and control. Therefore, the use of fear, at any level, is an expression of the malign *shadow* and therefore, per se, anti-God. One can easily ascertain, when looking at the belief structures of different religions, to what extent they have introduced the fear principle, such as the fear of damnation. Fear, in these contexts, is always used to try to control people's thinking.

Fear, in its different forms, is the many-headed Hydra we need to confront. Collectively we should always be on the lookout for when the fear card is being played, whether by governments, businesses, charities or religious institutions. Unfortunately, the fear card can be a very lucrative source of revenue. Businesses use it regularly in their advertising and medical research charities do it by heightening our fear of death. In past times the Vatican sold indulgences to those who wanted their sins mitigated. Islamists are using the same weapon in promoting their ideologies – the fear of not going to heaven if you do not engage in jihad.

All groups on this planet should be open to having their beliefs challenged, for this is how evolution works. Biological organisms are tested by life to go on adapting and improving themselves, and if they do not they ultimately become extinct. Examples of this can be found in the variola virus which causes smallpox. Unable to mutate fast enough to combat a worldwide vaccination programme, this virus has been eradicated from the human population. *Mycobacterium tuberculosis*, on the other hand, has been able to mutate with sufficient rapidity that some strains of it are now drug-resistant. As long as we are open to criticism we are open to change, and therefore can keep pace with evolutionary development.

Fundamentalism

One of the challenges of being in a group is that one can easily be swept along by the group dynamic. This occurred in an extreme form in Nazi Germany, when many found themselves drawn into the fervour of Hitler's rhetoric. It is often easy to go along with a group's identity by default, by not challenging its extreme elements.

In the early years of this present millennium we have seen a re-emergence of the more radical teachings of Islam, where some of the belligerent verses of the Quran are being used as an excuse to carry out barbaric acts against innocent people. The background to this particular version of Islam stemmed from Muhammad Ibn Abd al-Wahhab, an Islamic scholar who lived in the eighteenth century. He spent time conversing with various

Islamic scholars before repudiating what he came to regard as the idolatry in their beliefs. He desired only to follow a very restrictive form of Islam that was based on three pillars: One Ruler, One Authority and One Mosque (Crooke, 2014). These concepts were taken up by a minor prince named Ibn Saud, who saw how the puritanical precepts of Ibn Abd al-Wahhab could be put to good use to serve his own ambitions, and an alliance was forged between the two men. Drawing inspiration from an earlier fourteenth-century hate-filled scholar called Ibn Taymiyyah, Ibn Abd al-Wahhab determined to purge Islam of its heresies and idolatries by creating an extreme form of Islam we now know as Wahhabism or Salafism. Ibn Saud became 'the Ruler', Wahhabism 'the Authority' and the literal version of the Quran became 'the Mosque' (Crooke, 2014).

Ibn Abd al-Wahhab's precept was that Muslims who did not adhere to these views 'should be killed, their wives and daughters violated and their possessions confiscated' (Crooke, 2014). For this stance he could draw inspiration from the hundred or so verses within the Quran which encourage different forms of violence against unbelievers (Roberts, 2014). For example, in Quran 8:12-13 we read (Pickthall, 1938):

> *12 When thy Lord inspired the angels, (saying): I am with you. So make those who believe stand firm. I will throw fear into the hearts of those who disbelieve. Then smite the necks and smite of them each finger.*
>
> *13 That is because they opposed Allah and His messenger. Whoso opposeth Allah and His messenger, (for him) lo! Allah is severe in punishment.*

The development of the Kingdom of Saudi Arabia, with its enormous oil wealth and control of the most important Islamic shrines of Mecca, Medina and Jeddah, has helped to promote Wahhabism at the expense of the more liberal interpretations of the Quran. The Caliphate of Isil has its roots in this doctrine. Some of the doctrines promoted by Mohammed and deemed to be relevant during his life run contrary to all that has been stated here about the Divine, which offers only love, tolerance and understanding. Fortunately, Wahhabism is not the only interpretation of Islam. In 2007 Ani Zonneveld founded an organization called Muslims for Progressive Values, which draws also on Quranic teachings and presents a very different version of Islam, showing how it can be a religion of peace, respect and co-operation (Zonneveld, 2014). It needs all Muslims who stand for peace to speak out vociferously against those who preach hatred and intolerance and, where possible, to forbid their activities within the mosques. The *shadow* trap that undermines such an outcry is posed by the dilemma that if the Quran is literally the word of Allah it cannot be contradicted.

Those who have been engaged with any form of channelling activity, or 'Divine' revelation, know that all information has to come through the agency of the human mind, which is fallible. We do not know the state of consciousness when Mohammed was receiving his revelations but we can be sure that some inaccuracies would occur. Moreover, Mohammed was writing for a particular time, and whilst the broad thrust of his ideas may be correct, changing world situations would make their context very different. Furthermore, as has been argued here, the Creative Intelligence behind the universe is also evolving and growing. Nothing stands still. All ideas, no matter how profound, need to be continually challenged and, where necessary, updated.

In a powerful TV documentary entitled *Exposure: Jihad – A British Story*, shown on ITV in 2015, Deeyah Khan explored the roots of British Islam through the eyes of a number of people who had been radicalized, fought their jihads and then completely rejected this mindset, returning to the ways of peace. It became clear through the film that each of the participants had felt some deep sense of grievance or isolation during their childhood or adolescence and this fuelled their hatred against their perceived enemies. They came to realize, after going down this path, that this journey led only to more destruction. In many cases, instead of defending Muslims they ended up fighting them, just as the Sunnis and Shias are doing to this day. The only way forward was through love and forgiveness. One of the participants stated towards the end of the film that he considered his greatest jihad was coming to terms with himself, which was a journey of realization that he had been on for the past eighteen years.

It is clear that Muslims can find a peaceful, loving and forgiving way to lead their lives as demonstrated by Ani Zonneveld (Muslims for Progressive Values, 2015), whose ten tenets represent an ideal that is fully in accord with the views presented in this book. These voices need to be heard above those that preach violence and hatred. In his website www.thereligionofpeace.com, Glen Roberts highlights, in a factual way, how different elements within Islam use the scriptures as justification for acts of murder and repression. These examples are all too evident in world news at present. Set against this blood-soaked background are those Muslims who shun all violence and point to many verses within the Quran that preach the opposite. These voices can be found at websites like www.islamforpeace.org and the Quilliam Foundation (www.quilliamfoundation.org), which highlight those texts that support a peaceful worldview and challenge all forms of extremist ideology.

The only fundamental principle that needs to be promoted strongly and clearly is that of respect for the rights of every human being to act and believe as he or she chooses, on the proviso that these choices do no harm and do not preach harm to others. On this basis, all human beings need to be regarded as being of equal worth and value. In all other instances, we are not equal but unique individuals with the gift of free will to explore life as we choose.

In past times, Christianity has shown its dark side with the Crusades, the conflicts between Protestant and Catholic ideologies and its persecution of minority views, which continued in Northern Ireland through to the end of the last century. Fortunately, the majority of this Old Testament fundamentalism has been checked and discarded. Religious leaders of good will, in all faiths, are working more co-operatively. However, I still remember many years ago speaking to a group of Christians on the theme of spiritual healing and being heckled off the stage because I did not espouse a solely Christian stance in my approach. The stones we cast at others can come back to haunt us if we are not very careful.

It would be unfair in this short exploration into fundamentalism to target only the Abrahamic religions of Judaism, Christianity and Islam. Fanaticism can be found within all the major world religions and the tenets of their beliefs are easily distorted when specific groups feel threatened. Terrible atrocities were carried out by the Hindus against Muslims during the Partition of India and the massacres at the Golden Temple of Amritsar, first perpetrated by the British in 1919, were replicated in 1984 by the Hindu government against the Sikh minority. Buddhism, with its emphasis on peace, has largely escaped this fanatical brush yet, in recent years, a more extreme version of Buddhism has seen the death of many Muslims in Myanmar (Beech, 2013).

The Malign Shadow in the Collective

Before concluding this chapter, something needs to be said about the manifestation of the malign *shadow*, which has been defined here as those conscious acts that willingly inflict pain and suffering on others. In a broad sense, it can be equated with what are regarded as 'evil' acts. However, the word 'evil' can easily be subverted and projected onto others simply because they have different beliefs. The intention here is to make a clear distinction between conscious deeds and a set of beliefs. The challenge for the collective, within all societies, is to understand the causes that lead to such malign actions and then, when they occur, to consider the steps required to prevent them happening in the future.

As has been highlighted within this chapter, moralistic stances within society can encourage criminal elements. The repressed collective *shadow* will always find an outlet where it can, and if this is not acknowledged and integrated it easily slips into becoming malign. One way to approach this task is to look at all those areas where criminal gangs operate, such as drug trafficking and prostitution which have already been discussed. Both these activities need to be brought under legislative control in the same way that alcohol, tobacco and gambling are legalized.

More serious are those activities which pertain to terrorism. The method for dealing with these extremist elements has to be through a similar process that led eventually to peace in Northern Ireland, in 1998, through the Good Friday Agreement (BBC, 2015). This came about through dialogue with those willing to talk. As a result of such a process, extremist elements can be marginalized. This will only come about by taking positive steps to challenge all forms of radicalism no matter from where they stem. Those in different faith groups who are prepared to actively speak out against the fanatical element within them need to be encouraged and supported by governments, showing clearly that the way forward is through communication, understanding and mutual respect.

The challenge for all 'light workers' is to keep sending thoughts of love, peace and forgiveness to those who wish to commit malign acts, despite the atrocities that they perpetrate. Steps, using measured force, need to be taken to prevent these influences spreading because they can easily take hold when people feel disaffected and alienated. This is when the elements feeding the malign *shadow* come to the surface and need to be cleared and cleansed.

Summary

A collective *shadow* is created whenever any group comes together to express itself in a unique way. The positive element of this *shadow* is the opportunity it offers for that group to go on growing and expanding either through knowledge or insights. The negative and malign element comes about when a sense of separateness and superiority is fostered against those perceived to be outside the group. It might also arise when issues within the group are shunned, ignored or suppressed, such as dissenting voices. In extreme forms, this can lead to the taking of another's life simply because they are not part of the group.

Organizations such as religions and nation states are composed of many people. It is important that individuals personally challenge the negative *shadow* within their group whenever it has a tendency to manifest. This is why a free press is so important. In a truly balanced world, all states, religions and groups, no matter how large or small, should be open to comment and criticism, provided that this does not deliberately incite hatred, fear and intolerance. Yet, it is often easy to persecute those who challenge the collective status quo. This has happened with whistle-blowers, where the group psyche can often persecute them for speaking out. The *shadow* sits in all areas of life and we need to be ever mindful of its expression.

SECTION THREE

*Transmuting and Healing
the Dark Side of the Psyche*

Chapter Nine

The Higher-Self and the Shadow

There is a certain amount of kindness, just as there is a certain amount of light ... We cast a shadow on something wherever we stand, and it is no good moving from place to place to save things; because the shadow follows. Choose a place where you won't do very much harm ... and stand in it for all you are worth, facing the sunshine.

EM Forster, *A Room with a View*

For most people the soul and the Higher-Self (H-S) are vague concepts that would seem to have little direct meaning or relevance to their daily life. This chapter will attempt to show that these twin aspects of the Self can play a valuable and helpful role within the life of any individual. For the majority of people the subtle whisperings from our H-S, soul and *shadow* are transmitted through dreams which, when explored, can be a valuable resource. However, the communication from our H-S does not need to wait until sleep. When working with clients, I have been amazed at how insightful the H-S can be in providing awareness of particular issues and the steps required for their healing. This can take many forms, such as bringing up memories of specific traumas as well as the process needed for their resolution. This chapter will explore these different elements and includes a number of exercises for both accessing the wisdom of the H-S as well as healing the negative *shadow*.

The role of the H-S, as a fundamental component of the psyche, was recorded by psychiatrist Dr Ralph Allison (1974), who used hypnotherapeutic techniques to assist clients suffering from multiple personality disorders. In one of his regression sessions he stumbled across an inner character who appeared to have a very different level of awareness from the other sub-personalities he had previously encountered. This personality seemed to be cognisant of the other elements of the psyche, in all their complexity, and knew what needed to be done to heal the wounded mental, emotional and psychologically damaged parts of the individual. Allison went on to discover a similar character in all his clients. Unaware of the term 'H-S', he called this aspect the 'Inner Self Helper' or ISH. In an online article on the Dissociation.com website (Allison, 2014), the characteristics of the ISH are outlined, and I paraphrase them here:

- The main function of the ISH is to help the individual fulfil his or her 'life plan' and to protect the life of the person, at all costs, doing everything to prevent suicide or life-threatening events when these contradict the life plan.
- The ISH is present from the moment the soul enters the body and remains for the duration of the life.
- Stemming from the Divine, the ISH can only express love and is incapable of hatred.
- Being part of the cosmic impulse, the ISH has an awareness of the Creative Intelligence behind the universe and through that contact can access the highest wisdom and understanding that can be drawn upon to help an individual lead a balanced, fruitful life.
- The ISH is able to work co-creatively with a therapist in bringing forward insights and understanding to help resolve inner issues, including healing damaged sub-personalities.
- The ISH has full access to the history of a patient both from the context of the present life as well as past lives and can predict the short-term future.
- The ISH possesses no personal sense of gender identity but can assume any form that the therapist accepts.
- The ISH will communicate dispassionately rather than emotionally,

basing comments on spiritual concepts such as the need to express forgiveness and humility.
- It avoids using slang and never engages in put-downs or guilt trips.

This clearly defined list encapsulates the qualities of the H-S, which was a term brought to western attention through the writings of AP Sinnett and Madame Blavatsky of the Theosophical Society. In Blavatsky's book *The Key to Theosophy*, citing Sinnett (1889:173-4), she says:

The Spiritual realm would all the while be the proper habitat of the Soul, which would never entirely quit it; and that non-materializable portion of the Soul which abides permanently on the spiritual plane may fitly, perhaps, be spoken of as the HIGHER-SELF.

The term 'H-S' is also used by Dr Tom Zinser in his therapeutic work and collaboration with his spiritual guide Gerod. Of the H-S, Zinser explains (2011:150):

The more I learned about the Higher-Self over the months, the more its abilities and characteristics resembled those of the inner self helper. I don't recall the moment, but at some point I realized that the inner self helper I knew from psychology and the Higher Self I was investigating with Gerod were the same phenomenon.

The Higher-Self

Over the many years that I have been practising as a therapist the H-S has been central to my healing work. I have utilized many different techniques to help clients access this aspect of their psyche, with profound results. Indeed, going one stage further, I believe that we all have the ability to access this phenomenal inner resource if we give it space to inform our lives.

This insight emerged when I first started to explore, through meditation, my own inner nature and the spiritual dimension in which we reside. From reading many different books, I had the perception that it was going to take me many years of inner work before I could communicate with my higher-wisdom. I read that enlightenment only came about through dedicated spiritual study. However, I was also aware, from a young age, that there was some aspect of inner guidance that I could readily access. This 'intelligence' informed me about significant elements that I needed to address or, when they arose, how to deal with specific problems. This seemed at odds with what I had studied. I eventually came to realize that if I believed that accessing this higher-wisdom would take a lifetime, then indeed it would take that time. However, if I believed I could do this instantly then that would be the case. In other words, we can all connect to a profound source of inner wisdom simply by intent, provided we apply a little effort to the process. The only limitation lies in our own minds.

My H-S, your H-S is a fundamental aspect of our being that has complete oversight of our lives and all of the facets that make us who and what we are. It has direct communication with the spiritual realm and therefore has access to all the wisdom of the universe. Additionally, it can draw upon the power of 'the Creator' to clear any blockages that may be residing within. It knows the blueprint of our life and, if we engage with it, can steer us towards the fulfilment of our life-plan. What it will not do is interfere with our free will, or the free will of any aspect of our being, such as our sub-personalities. As already stated, the free will gift we all enjoy is sacrosanct and your H-S cannot and will not override any decisions you have made. In this sense, it is limited by cosmic law, although in all other areas its powers would appear to be limitless.

> *Activity 9:1*
>
> Theme: *Connecting to your H-S – the first steps*
>
> Duration: *5 minutes*
>
> 1. Sit quietly, take a few deep breaths and close your eyes; then imagine an aspect of your being (your H-S) that has unlimited power and is overseeing your life. You might like to perceive this as your God part.
> 2. Ask your H-S to begin to communicate its messages to you, either through feelings, images, words or sensations. What do you experience?
> 3. Bring yourself back to full waking consciousness, open your eyes and write down your experiences.

In this chapter, we will look at other exercises that you can do to help you connect to this aspect of higher inner wisdom and support. For now, it is enough to have a sense that this part exists and that it can be readily accessed by requesting its help and assistance.

The Higher-Self, the Soul and the Spirit

When reading books on these topics you will come across terminology that is nuanced in slightly different ways. The terms 'soul' and 'spirit' can sometimes seem interchangeable. Many years ago, to iron out these confusions, I asked for clarification from my own inner guidance on the terms 'spirit', 'soul' and the 'H-S' and the following definitions emerged. I later confirmed these with a number of other mediumistic colleagues. These definitions might slightly differ from other writings you have accessed but they are given here to clarify the terminology being used:

The Spirit

Your spirit defines your primary life force energy that has within it a seed of God consciousness. It is infused with the sum total of all of your experiences, both from within your physical incarnation as well as its sojourn in the spiritual realms in the periods between lives. The accumulation of these experiences leads to wisdom. All spirits contain an inbuilt programme that awakens a desire to go on evolving until they reach a level of being whereby they can rejoin the Creator, thus bringing with them their unique understanding and adding to this infinite level of consciousness. Spirits do this through the accumulation of experiences and the process of distilled wisdom and understanding in the utilization of their free will gift. The higher spiritual planes are far removed from what is experienced here on the earth.

The Soul

Your soul is the aspect of your spirit that is put down into the physical body to provide its life force energy for this current, or any, incarnation. One might imagine it like a pie chart, where the circle of the chart represents your spirit and a 10-15 per cent segment is the part that enters into physical life. Effectively, with most individuals, the majority of their spirit continues to reside in the spiritual realm during the course of their incarnation, providing the access into spiritual sources of knowledge and understanding. For a healthy fulfilled life, the soul needs to be properly anchored within the body. However, it can sometimes be partly disconnected or dissociated, which can lead to psychological issues and problems. The soul also retains all the memories of a particular life and feeds these back into the database of the spirit during the course of an incarnation.

The Higher-Self

Your H-S acts as a bridge between the spirit, soul and conscious mind. It is always present, monitoring what is happening to you, and will do everything in its power to protect your life against 'accidents' or life-threatening situations that are not part of your karma. It will not interfere with your free will and accepts that you have the choice to access this part of your being or not. It therefore needs to be specifically engaged in the healing process for its wisdom to be tapped. Additionally, it will not override any sub-personality aspects of your psyche, as these also have free will. Nevertheless, it will allow you to identify them and connect to them. Once these parts are open to receiving the help and healing from the H-S it will then step in to effect the necessary changes. It can also remove any psychic intrusions from within your energy field.

Representations of the Higher-Self

When working with clients, assistance from the H-S can be elicited by simply requesting its help and support in the therapeutic process. This approach is also applicable when working on one's own. For example, you could inwardly say 'I request the insight of my H-S to help me understand my anger.' Or, 'I request the support of my H-S to help me heal my inner fears.' The key element here is to recognize that the H-S will not take away or change the outer experience if that is part of your learning process, or if there is some aspect of spiritual growth that needs to be understood and integrated. The best way therefore in approaching the H-S is to keep requesting insight and help to resolve the cause of the problem.

Normally the H-S is perceived as either a wise being or a source of pure light, like the light of the sun or a star. In practice, it is happy to present itself in any guise that you choose. Within Alcoholics Anonymous (AA), it is referred to as a 'higher power' and that higher power can be conceptualized in the way that makes sense to you. The primary aspect to be remembered is that this is *your* H-S and it has the specific task of assisting you through your life. It should be your first point of call for any other level of spiritual support.

The H-S can be perceived as sitting within the core of your being or, alternatively, above you, where it can be accessed through the crown of your head. In Vedic tradition, the crown chakric point is known as the Sahasrara chakra and is symbolized as a thousand-petalled lotus. The light of the H-S can be drawn through the lotus into the body and from there to infuse the rest of your chakric system. When working with clients I will often get them to work with the sun as a symbol of the H-S, drawing on the light to clear and cleanse any blockages or elements that are impeding the healing process. To start the journey of connecting with the H-S I normally take my clients through a simple relaxation or self-awareness exercise.

To utilize fully these inner exercises I would suggest that you record them as a voice message into your computer, phone or other recording device and then play them back to yourself whilst doing the exercise. You can add any words that seem relevant and set the pace of the recording to suit yourself. Eventually you will get to the point where you can remember the words entirely and then you will not need these prompts.

Symbols of Light

Before starting the exercises, something must be said about light, which is a term often used here. There are many natural sources of physical light in this world, such as the light of a fire and the light of the Sun, Moon and stars. Physical light travels at an astonishing 186,000 miles per second. Yet if the universe is a mental construct, as quantum mechanics suggests, then thought must be quicker, for as soon as I think about something I interact with it. The farthest reaches of the universe, light years away, are available to my consciousness the moment I peer down my telescope to view them. I may be witnessing an object from the past, because of the amount of time that light has taken to travel to the Earth, yet my contemplation is in present time and therefore my connection is in the now. Effectively, thought travels faster than light. On this basis, the concept of the light from one's H-S or the light from the Divine transcends physical light. Put another way, we can postulate a spiritual light which is non-physical and has the potential to carry the highest levels of spirit that travel instantaneously across the universe.

Nevertheless, physical light can be used as a symbol of this higher spiritual light. When working with clients who are confronting difficult psychological conditions stemming from their *shadow* self I will often get them to imagine themselves in a beautiful place filled with sunlight. In these cases I can ask them to use the symbol of the sun as a representation of their H-S, to good effect. The sun is the primary source of light and life for this solar system and, at a physical level, we are all the children of the sun for without it we would not be here. The sun, in mythology and spiritual tradition, is also associated with the Divine, and in linking to this source of light we are aligning ourselves to the highest level of spirit.

However, we should be clear that the sun is not our H-S and we can also work with other sources of light, such as individual stars or simply by connecting to whatever we perceive as the Divine. From experience, I would caution against using the light of the Moon because, as a reflected light, I have found that *shadow* entities will sometimes hide themselves in this light and manipulate it deviously.

Activity 9:2

Theme: *Relaxation and body consciousness exercise*

Duration: *5-10 minutes*

1. Sit in a chair with a straight back, close your eyes and focus initially on your breathing. By observing your inward and outward breaths you can make them slightly deeper and slower.
2. Next, bring your attention down to your toes and feet and consciously relax them. In the process feel the link to the ground and the earth through your feet.
3. Move up to your legs, slightly tensing the muscles and then relaxing them.
4. Become aware of your back and spine. Sense that there is a smooth flow of energy along your back and spine and relax any tension there.
5. Become aware of your breathing again and with every outward breath feel that you are accessing a deeper level of your being.
6. Become aware of your fingers and hands and feel that these are relaxed.
7. Become aware of your arms and shoulders and consciously relax the muscles, especially letting go of any tension in your shoulders.
8. Become aware of your neck, jaw and face and then let your attention come to rest at a point between and slightly above your eyes. You might like to imagine that you are looking inwardly at this brow point.
9. From there send a thought of healing and balance to the whole of your physical body.

10. Then imagine that there is a light within your heart area that represents your inner core self. Connect to this light in your mind and imagine that its luminance is radiating through every cell of your physical body and then extending out around you so that you are surrounded in a halo of its light. (If you find it difficult to imagine a light within yourself, you could try using a symbol such as a white equidistant cross within a circle.)
11. Finally, slowly bring yourself back to full waking consciousness and reaffirm your link through your feet to the ground.

Once the process of the above exercise has been mastered then the next step of linking to your H-S can be carried out, which can be done as follows:

Activity 9:3

Theme: *Accessing your Higher-Self (H-S)*

Duration: *5-10 minutes*

Close your eyes and then carry out the Body Consciousness Exercise (Activity 9:2, see page 204).

1. Imagine that your H-S is above you and there is a beam of light coming down from your H-S and linking to the core soul light within you.
2. Ask your H-S to oversee the following exercise.
3. Imagine that you are standing in a beautiful scene in nature. This scene can be any place that you know or imagine.
4. Perceive yourself as barefooted and become conscious of the ground beneath your feet. Which sensations do you experience?
5. Look around your scene to see what you aware of, such as any trees, flowers or distant views.
6. Listen out for any sounds that you can hear, such as the hum of bees or birdsong.

7. When you have surveyed your scene, become conscious of the sun shining in the sky and turn to face it, feeling its warmth on your body.
8. Feel the rays of the sun healing your body and filling it with light.
9. Request the sun to send you a representation of your H-S to which you can easily connect. This might just be the sun itself, a star or you might become aware of a being of light, an animal or symbol. See this representation coming down from the sun and standing with you.
10. Connect to that aspect and sense its presence linking to and overlighting your body. What do you experience? Does it communicate anything specifically to you?
11. Thank your H-S and acknowledge that some aspect of it is always with you and that this part can communicate with you when you reach out to it.
12. Slowly bring yourself back to full waking consciousness by counting down from ten.

This exercise, if practised correctly, will allow you to begin to connect directly with the power of your H-S. It does take a little patience and effort but the rewards can be immense. Your link to your H-S is the single most important step on your journey towards wholeness. Once this link is in place then you can begin the process of tackling any negative *shadow* elements of your psyche.

The Higher-Self and the Safe Space

Once you have mastered the link to your H-S you will be in a position to tackle any specific issues and problems that may be besetting your life. When I first explored my inner world with the support of my H-S and guides, I was encouraged to create an inner safe space within natural surroundings. This was very easy to do and I chose to imagine a beautiful circular temple within an open area and surrounded by woodland. My inner temple contains a fountain, colours and beautiful columns and is a place of sanctuary and inner holiness which I enter whenever I wish to access the higher-dimensional aspects of my being. I also use the temple to explore my *shadow* self, whether this is my negative or positive *shadow*. With a little practice, you can imagine yourself within your inner safe space even with your eyes open. It is as though the mind and consciousness can be in two places, or states of reality, at the same time.

Your inner sanctuary can be any place that you wish it to be, whether you create this in a normal waking state or through meditation. Mine is a circular Greek-style temple but yours could be a church, synagogue or mosque. Some individuals, preferring a link with nature, have worked with a stone circle or simply a clearing in a forest, whilst others, coming from a more secular perspective, have created a house or a castle. What is important is that it reflects your inner requirements. If you have created your safe space using the rational and logical part of your mind I would recommend that you ask your H-S to modify this imagined space to suit your particular needs. Over a period, both my temple and its surroundings changed and developed as I grew in understanding, awareness and confidence.

If you are not good at imagining or seeing things with your inner eyes, you can create such a sanctuary by first drawing it on a piece of paper. You might then like to place the sanctuary in one of your favourite places in nature, or indeed in any such place, by visiting that site and taking photos of it. There are endless different possibilities here but the significant part is that you establish a place in which you can feel safe and secure. Once the sanctuary has been created you are then in a position to explore different aspects of your positive and negative *shadow*. The following exercise shows how this can be done.

> Activity 9:4
>
> Theme: *Creating an inner world sanctuary*
>
> Duration: *5-10 minutes*
>
> 1. Close your eyes and then carry out the Body Consciousness Exercise (Activity 9:2, see page 204).
> 2. Connect to your H-S and imagine that you are stepping into a scene in nature. This can either be an imaginary place or somewhere you know.
> 3. Ask your H-S to help you create an inner world sanctuary for exploring your *shadow* self and allow whatever elements you need to come forward in your mind.
> 4. When your sanctuary has been completed, enter into it and then ask your H-S to help you ground and establish it in the most suitable form for you.
> 5. Thank your H-S and bring yourself back to full waking reality, making sure that you feel grounded through your feet into the earth.

The Higher-Self and the Shadow

Once you have created your inner sanctuary you can embark on the process of illuminating your positive or negative *shadow*. Remember that your positive *shadow* contains all of those elements to which you aspire. For example, if you are studying for an exam, your positive *shadow* holds the final realization of this aspiration. You can help to manifest this future state by seeing in your mind's eye, or imagination, this goal being achieved. If the exam is for a university degree, you can imagine or visualize yourself on stage receiving your award. The trick of this process is to keep affirming this potential reality. Whatever you can dream of, you can become. Some people continually set themselves specific targets to which they aspire but all you really need to do is to keep perceiving or seeing yourself achieving your maximum potential in a happy and fulfilled way.

Your negative *shadow* contains all the elements that get in the way of the fulfilment of your aspiration. You may discover one or several *shadow* characters that prevent, or even seem deliberately to block, this realization. Your H-S knows what they are and can help you to become aware of them. In practice, we all have specific character traits, stemming either from our current life or from previous lives, that can undermine us. They manifest in different ways. For example, we may be successful in business but not so good in relationships, or gifted linguistically but hopeless at maths, and so on. Activity 7.6 on page 145 in Chapter 7, which helps you to assess how you perceive your positive and negative qualities, will give you some idea of this process.

The steps to achieve our goals are really quite simple. On the one hand we need to keep holding on to the thought of the goal's realization and on the other we need to keep asking our H-S to bring to the surface any element that gets in the way. Even if there are two dozen factors or mountains that need to be climbed or resolved, this can be accomplished.

Activity 9:5

Theme: *Accomplishment of your goals and aspirations*

Duration: *5-10 minutes*

1. Write down the goal you wish to achieve.
2. Imagine, visualize or see yourself achieving that goal.
3. Connect to your H-S and request help in achieving your ambition.
4. Request that your H-S highlights for you any part of your being that is getting in the way of the goal's realization and then request help to tackle each element in turn.

Higher-Self and the Negative Shadow

Having set the goal, the next task is to tackle any character or sub-personality within your psyche that might impede the realization of your aim. Achieving our ambitions often requires dedicated hard work and effort and this needs to be part of the process. However, there might also be some fear, or rejected aspect of the self, that continually undermines your goal's fulfilment. These negative elements need to be flushed out, balanced and healed. There are different ways of achieving this but one of the most effective is by working with the H-S in conjunction with your inner sanctuary.

The next exercise shows how this can be done.

Activity 9:6

Theme: *Discovering your shadow elements*

Duration: *5-10 minutes*

1. Close your eyes and then carry out the Body Consciousness Exercise (Activity 9:2, see page 204).
2. Imagine your inner world sanctuary and step into it.
3. In your imagination turn and face the Sun as a symbol of your H-S and feel that you are drinking in its vitality and energy.
4. Request your H-S to help you face and deal with any aspect of yourself that is preventing you achieving the goal that you have set yourself.
5. Next, turn with your back to the Sun, seeing the *shadow* of your inner self cast on the ground in front of you. You will now feel the warmth of the H-S supporting you from behind. Acknowledge that support and help.

> 6. Request that any *shadow* element that you need to address comes into view outside your sanctuary. You might see this as an object, a creature or sub-personality, or simply as a feeling of something being present.
> 7. Connect to your H-S and send light to whatever is there in your *shadow*, requesting your H-S help you to heal and balance what emerges.
> 8. When you have done this, thank your H-S and bring yourself back to full waking consciousness.

What appears within the *shadow* part of your being can be very individual. Sometimes it is not clear and in these cases you can request your H-S for help in clarifying what needs to be worked on. Even if it appears as just a vague shape or outline, you can send it acknowledgement and a thought of light and healing. I have worked with many clients using this simple process; it has proven effective in clearing the blocks within the psyche that need to be addressed. Those cases that carry difficult or challenging aspects within the self, such as extreme fears or repressed elements, can always be tackled with the help of a therapist who can then work with you in a supportive role. By requesting your H-S to bring only to your attention those aspects that you can readily resolve, you will ensure that you will not be confronted by that which is outside of your current ability. This is a growing process and, with practice and time, you can develop the necessary skill to deal with personal issues that are more complex. Once the process has been started the H-S will bring these *shadow* elements to your consciousness through the characters in your dream world. These characters, when identified, can be worked with from the safety of your inner temple.

The Healing Process

The first part of the healing process has begun as soon as the *shadow* element has been brought into the light of your consciousness. The instant it is perceived I would recommend that you send a thought of love, light, healing and balance to it by channelling the energy from your H-S. Remember, there will be a tendency to be frightened of, or to feel repugnance for, any sub-personality aspect of your negative *shadow* because these characters, or aspects of the self, were created by the psyche in response to a traumatic experience. The methods for working more directly with sub-personalities will be tackled fully in the next chapter. At this stage, all that is required is to be aware of the emotional content that they carry. They will always be stuck in time, locked into the trauma that brought them into being. The inner child, terrified after being bitten by a dog, sits anxiously within the adult psyche, monitoring when any dogs come into view. It will provoke a sense fear as soon as a dog is spotted.

These characters have minds of their own. They need to be loved, helped and accepted back into the sanctuary of the self, free of their terror. By connecting to your H-S you can gain the insight that they need for their healing. The best way to do this is to keep working with them until they take on a form that appears to be whole and balanced. They can then be integrated within the self or released back into the H-S. This work can take two forms: the *shadow* that stems from fear and the *shadow* that stems from revulsion.

Fear-based Shadows

The *shadow* parts that stem from fear will generally take on frightening forms. Remember that you are working through this process with your H-S and from within the safety of your inner sanctuary, therefore there is nothing to be frightened about. The fear stems from the past and not your present reality. It may be that the sub-personality carries the memory of being abused as a child or being led away to be executed in a former life, when the fear would have had some validity. However, this is not what is happening within the present time. You are working to bring all of these elements into 'now' time with the awareness of what is needed to heal and balance these inner characters.

These inner world characters can appear in two distinct forms. The first is the actual character that experienced the trauma, such as the child. The second is the emotional charge that is wrapped around the incident, which can also appear as a character. The latter will often carry distorted images and appear as monsters or demons. Both of these parts can be tackled either together or independently, according to what seems appropriate. Sometimes the 'demon' is hiding or disguising the inner character. These overlays need to be dissolved to reveal the true character within.

Once you have begun to discern the part that requires healing you can request your H-S to bring it to a size that you can readily tackle. Large, imposing monsters can be reduced immediately, through the power of your mind, to something small and manageable. For example, on one of my inner journeys I was confronted by a giant figure, dressed like Darth Vader wielding his light-sabre, who was blocking my path. Such an image might appear terrifying but in connecting to my H-S I was told that I needed to imagine him as being much smaller, which is what I did. He became toy-sized, so I sent him healing, then put him into my pocket and continued on my way! This process has worked very well with many clients, where large monsters have been reduced and tamed. Remember the story of Admetus in Chapter 4, who was able to tame two wild beasts to pull his chariot, with the help of the sun god Apollo.

Once the monster has been reduced in size you can then ask your H-S for further insight into what is needed for its full healing and redemption. I always remind the characters, however they appear, that they too have a source of light (soul essence) within them and that they too can have the help and support from the H-S if they wish. In most cases, they respond well to this approach and the H-S can then take over. Some parts, once they are sufficiently healed, will wish to rejoin the H-S and you can imagine that you are lifting them into the light. Others will want to be accepted back into your inner sanctuary, which you can then do by allowing them to be reintegrated within your soul essence.

The only other element that is important with *shadow* aspects is to ascertain whether these are part of your psyche or separate beings or entities. In other words, they might be a split-off part of someone else's psyche or soul essence. In the course of our current life and in previous lives we can sometimes pick up stragglers or hangers-on that have hitched a ride. More often than not, these are just lost soul fragments, but occasionally they can hold some malign element. You can request your H-S to indicate whether these sub-personality characters are part of you or something that is separate from you. If separate from you, they need to be helped back to their own source, which you can do by requesting your H-S to connect to a healing guide to help them back to where they need to be. You might like to imagine an angel is coming to collect them.

You can use this method to deal with known fears, such as agoraphobia. Once you have created your temple and carried out the *shadow* exercise you can ask your H-S to bring to you the part or parts that hold the specific fear. Once they appear, send them healing, as already suggested, and help them to be in touch with the H-S by making them aware of their own inner light. You can then ask them to reveal to you the source of the fear, which will relate to a specific event. You do not need to relive the event, simply to be aware of its origin. These parts are stuck in the past and locked into the trauma that brought them into being. When brought into present time, or just acknowledged, their energy can be released.

Revulsion-based Shadows

From long experience working with many clients I have found that reviled *shadow* sub-personalities are often more difficult or problematic for the individual to heal. The general immediate response is to reject what is being presented on the basis that this cannot be part of them and therefore has to be something separate. As already mentioned, we can occasionally pick up interlopers on our journey and these need to be sent back to their own H-S source. However, because something appears ugly and not a character that you can easily accept does not mean that it is not an aspect of your being.

Many years ago, when working with a client, she saw a hideous slug-like character on a stage in front of her. When questioned, this creature called itself 'sloth and envy'. The immediate response was that this could not be anything to do with her, but the creature assured her that it was and then proceeded to inform her of the many times that it had operated through her life. This recognition was the start of her healing process.

We need to learn to love and accept all of the ugly parts of who and what we are, because they can then be redeemed. Whatever appears when carrying out the *shadow* exercise, always send it a thought of love, light, healing and balance. This is the first step that can then lead to its full redemption and integration within the psyche. In the greater scheme of things, all aspects of humanity are part of us, even the most debased and hideous. By loving and healing these corresponding parts, we also help to heal them for the collective.

For example, the media might wish us to demonize the Osama Bin Ladens or Jimmy Saviles of this world, but in doing so we only reinforce the rejection of the corresponding parts within our own being. If I reject my own internal terrorist or paedophile, who is going to carry that energy for me? Someone in life will pick up this quality and act it out. If, on the other hand, I can learn to love, understand, accept and integrate these parts within me, they no longer pose any threat. That is the personal challenge that faces humanity. By integrating and balancing our own negative *shadow* selves, we can actively help to heal world situations.

Once the healing of the sub-personality has been completed, you can request your H-S to bring forward any other characters that hold similar energies. A person who has been abused as a child will often have several dozen such characters that need help. I have found when working with many abused clients, whether the abuse was sexual, physical, mental or emotional, that healing of their inner worlds can take considerable time. Each trauma will effectively generate its own sub-personality that ultimately needs to be acknowledged, healed and integrated. In a normal one-hour therapeutic session, depending upon the complexity, a client might deal with only two or three such inner characters before needing to finish the session. Their energies need to be assimilated back within the psyche, which can take a number of days, sometimes bringing to the surface different emotional reactions. The key here is to be loving and gentle on oneself; to take each step in turn and to know that as these characters are healed, balanced and integrated within the self that you are furthering your own evolution and sense of well-being and happiness. When you have tackled one or two characters in your own self-healing process, you can bring yourself back to full waking consciousness.

The Soul, Higher-Self and the Body

The next element that needs to be acknowledged and understood is the role of the soul or life force essence within our life. There are differences of opinion about when the soul enters the developing foetus. The studies on twins mentioned in Chapter 6 suggest this happens quite early in the gestation period, whilst the channelled guidance from H-A indicated that it was at conception (H-A, 1975:25). As soon as the connection is made, a two-way process begins of both recording the life experiences as well as motivating the individual in their journey through life. According to Newton, souls incarnate with a basic script, or life plan, which will have some details mapped out but also allows free choices to be made (Newton, 1994:213). As soon as the spirit splits off part of itself to create a soul, that soul is imbued with its individual free will. Under cosmic law, the H-S cannot then step in to override that free will element, except in extreme cases to protect the life of that individual. Just as our children, when grown to adulthood, make their own choices, so too do the split-off parts of our spirit. Your spirit has effectively separated part of itself and sent the soul as a probe into the material world to explore physical incarnation. Your soul has absolute free will within the terms of conditions that it has chosen to take on. In other words, the free will is only limited by the original choices that you have made, such as whether to be born a man or woman and the country and genetic background that is part of that specific journey.

The first task of the soul, when entering an incarnation, is to take control of the body. In normal circumstances this is an ongoing process right through to full adulthood, which might not be until the mid to late twenties. The soul will link with the mind and emotions to gain some measure of control over these elements. At the start of this journey, some of the memory banks of the soul are anaesthetised, so that there is generally no recollection of any past lives or the spiritual domain from which it has just left. There are two good reasons why this spiritual amnesia occurs. As already stated, if it were not so then the pull to return back to the spiritual realm could be overwhelming, particularly if the current life is full of challenges. Those who attempt or actually do commit suicide can driven by this feeling. Secondly, a trauma in, or particular outcome of, a previous life could seriously skew the present incarnation (see Chapter 6).

The soul, or life force energy, is most closely identified with the heart, although the ego mind is generally the dominant part of the psyche. This latter aspect is another layer of the onion of the self. Often, the primary ego can be at odds with the intentions of the soul plan, causing inner issues and conflicts. If, at end of life, the ego self has completely dominated the soul or heart self, the individual can find themselves becoming trapped or earthbound close to the physical plane. They effectively become stuck in the first stage of the Near Death Experience, when they realize they do not have a physical body but have not transited back to the spiritual realm. These lost souls will often attach to an incarnate person and, as already mentioned, they can become unwelcome guests within the residency of a particular physical body, especially if the tenant of that body has not assumed full executive control. It can be rather like the individual who owns a two-storey home but chooses to live only on the upper floor, not bothering to close the doors and windows on the floor below them. This leaves the way open for all sorts of lost souls, or soul fragments, to wander in. Once these lost souls have taken up residency, they generally need the help of the owner's H-S to see them on their way.

Because of all of these factors, one of the important first stages is to get your H-S to assist in the process of anchoring your soul fully within your body. Ideally, its source of focus should be located somewhere within the middle of the chest, in the region of the heart. The following exercise will assist this process.

Activity 9:7

Theme: *Anchoring the soul within the self*

Duration: *5-10 minutes*

1. Close your eyes and then carry out the Body Consciousness Exercise (Activity 9:2, see page 204).
2. Connect to your H-S and request your H-S to help you fully anchor your soul essence within your physical body and then help you to see or imagine this light located within the middle of your chest area. If you perceive the light to be in any other part, such as the head, request your H-S to assist in relocating it as indicated.
3. When you can sense, feel or imagine that your soul is centred within your heart area, imagine or affirm that you are bringing down a beam of light from your H-S and connecting it to the light within you. In this process you are effectively relinking two sources of light – your H-S and your soul essence.
4. When this linking process has been completed and your soul essence is located in the area of your heart, imagine you are now bringing the light from your H-S further down your body, through your legs and anchoring it into the earth, in a similar way to how a tree puts down its roots. In this case, your roots are roots of light, not physical roots. You can then imagine you are drawing up energy from the earth into your being.
5. The next step is to imagine this light radiating out around you, creating a protective shield like that of the Earth's atmosphere.
6. Finally, thank your H-S and any other guides and slowly bring yourself back to full waking consciousness.

The Balance between the Higher-Self, the Soul and the Ego Mind

For the majority of people the dynamic energies of the soul and the H-S sit below the level of the conscious mind and they are not aware, except through dreams, of the impact these elements have within their daily life. The process that Jung called individuation requires these elements be made conscious (Stein, 2006). In other words, we need to move them from our *shadow* self into the light of full awareness. When reviewing the lives of significant historical individuals it is clear that the connection to a personal higher power was understood in past times. For example, the ancient Greek philosopher Socrates had his daemon, which guided his actions. In Plato's *Apology* (Jowett, 1871), Socrates states:

> *You have heard me speak at sundry times and in divers places of an oracle or sign which comes to me, and is the divinity which Meletus ridicules in the indictment. This sign, which is a kind of voice, first began to come to me when I was a child; it always forbids but never commands me to do anything which I am going to do. This is what deters me from being a politician. And rightly, as I think.*

Although Socrates alludes to it as his daemon, this inner voice can readily be identified with the H-S, as its connection and involvement with Socrates' life would seem very similar to what we have already described. Joan of Arc had her voices which communicated information, letting her know about key moments in her life and guiding her to take the actions she did. Amongst other distinguished hearers of the inner voice we can include Winston Churchill, Mahatma Ghandi, Anthony Hopkins and Zoë Wanamaker. The key component of this guidance is that it is informative without being imposing, except in extreme circumstances.

A close friend of my mine refers to her H-S as her angel. It makes suggestions, in the form of inner promptings, on what would be most helpful, without wishing to take over. Only when there is something of prime importance to the life do these whisperings feel like a prime command. Winston Churchill narrowly avoided being injured in a bomb explosion whilst out one night in the Blitz. When about to step into his usual seat in his chauffer-driven car, he unexpectedly stopped, then went round and got into the seat on the opposite side of the car. On the way home, his vehicle was nearly turned over by a bomb blast. Churchill joked afterwards that it must have been his counterbalancing weight which kept it from tipping. When asked by his wife Clementine why he chose to change seats he stated that his inner guidance had insisted that he sit in the other seat (Khatri, 2008:45).

> *In my own life, this guidance comes through in a variety of different ways. Sometimes I have intuitive feelings, sometimes I hear words within my head and sometimes I see clairvoyant images in my mind's eye. The times that I am most in touch with my H-S is when working with clients, when sending healing to specific situations and when I am writing. The steps you can take to assist this level of connection can be found within my book Develop Your Intuition and Psychic Powers (Furlong, 2008).*

When individuals first begin to connect to this profound part of their being there can be a tendency to want to relegate all ego responsibility to this wiser part of the self. However, this can create its own set of problems. The ego self through its connection to the physical body is locked in time and space. The H-S, on the other hand, through its link to the spiritual realm, is outside the space-time continuum. Because of this, there can sometimes be misunderstanding or confusion when requesting the H-S to take over the life because its guidance can be unrealistic or misinterpreted. Additionally, it is very easy to project our ego wishes on to the information that the H-S provides and thereby distort its guidance. The H-S has a tendency to see always the bigger picture – a whole forest, rather than the individual trees in the wood. Physical incarnation offers a unique opportunity to explore both. It is also important to realize why an individual might wish to relinquish to the H-S the decisions of their normal conscious self. This is usually because of life choices in the past that have appeared to go wrong. Decisions that end up causing pain and suffering can lead one to becoming fearful of the ability to judge or assess situations. When this occurs, there can be a tendency to want to hand over all responsibility to the H-S, often perceived in these cases as God. However, this is not balanced because the cause of the indecision is fear-based and not anchored in love.

Remember also that God, or the Creator, is not interested in running your life for you because, if He/She did, the whole of Creation would be pointless. Our *spirit* has been given life and the gift of free will to experience and grow for ourselves and that is what we need to do. We can draw upon the support and help of the Creator in that process, but we cannot hand over the task to the Almighty for, as hard as this task may feel, the Divine will not comply.

In extreme cases, individuals can be so paralysed by fear that they will not make any decision without the sanction of the H-S. If one thinks about this issue from the perspective of considering child development, it would be as though the young adult refuses to make any choices without parental sanction. We know from experience that this is not a healthy state. With the exception of those suffering true mental incapacity, our children need to learn to take decisions for themselves, to accept responsibility for their choices. In the greater scheme of our life journey, there is no such thing as a wrong decision, for all decisions create experience from which we grow. Whilst in a physical body we need to accept the limitations of our life and to work with them, without trying to get the H-S to take over the task for us. Ultimately, there has to be a balance in which all elements can work together in mutual co-operation. It is important that we affirm our link with the H-S, but we should not expect it to make our daily life choices. It will always inform us if we need to be aware of anything that is an important part of our karmic journey.

The *soul* is most closely linked to the energies of the heart and this should be the primary point of balance within the psyche. This was perceived intuitively, or through higher guidance, in ancient Egypt, where the heart was considered to be the most important organ of the body. In the *Halls of Judgement* at the end of a life the most significant question, posed to the *soul*, was whether they had been 'true of heart' throughout their life. Anchoring our point of balance within our heart is becoming one of the prime directives within the leading edge of spiritual thinking, as exemplified by the HeartMath Institute (HeartMath, 2014).

The following activity will help with this balancing process.

Activity 9:8

Theme: *Balancing the link between the H-S, the soul and the ego mind*

Duration: *5-10 minutes*

1. Close your eyes and then carry out the Body Consciousness Exercise (Activity 9:2, see page 204).
2. Link to your soul centre by feeling the connection to your heart, then feel a link through to your H-S.
3. In your imagination move this vertical linking to perceive your H-S standing on the right side of your body and your ego mind on the left. This sometimes requires a little creative imagination and practice.

4. Sense the point of balance anchored within your heart centre and sense from this place that the other two elements of your psyche are linked into you in a balanced way. You can immediately tell whether this is so by imagining a pair of scales in front of you and seeing whether they are balanced.
5. If the scales do not appear balanced, request your soul essence to help you balance these two elements within your psyche.
6. Finally, thank all of these elements for the part they play in your life and bring yourself back to full waking consciousness.

Summary

In this chapter we have looked at the relationship between the H-S and other aspects of the self, such as the *soul* and the *spirit*, and at the important role of the H-S within the drama of your life. This aspect of the *self* sits within your positive *shadow*, until such times as you take the necessary steps to link to its wisdom. Once this has been achieved, the process of working with other elements of your *shadow*, such as the sub-personality parts of your psyche, can be facilitated. This ongoing process can continue through the whole of your life. Your soul-essence also needs to be properly anchored within you, which can be achieved through the help of your H-S. Finally, there needs to be a working balance between these different elements of your being, so that each plays a part within your life.

Chapter Ten

Sub-Personalities, Archetypes and the Shadow

I will give you three days to seek your shadow. Return to me in the course of that time with a well-fitted shadow, and you shall receive a hearty welcome; otherwise, on the fourth day – remember, on the fourth day – my daughter becomes the wife of another.

Adelbert von Chamisso

In this chapter, we will look at the characters that reside within us, highlighting the complexity of our inner world. For most of us, these characters sit beneath the level of the conscious mind, within our *shadow*, seamlessly moving in and out of assuming executive control in response to different situations. Some of these characters hold traumas from the early stages of our life or even from past lives, whilst others carry positive elements that we can draw upon to help us through different situations. This work is about first bringing these different elements into the light of consciousness. As part of this process, we will look both at the diverse methods for healing the damaged elements of the psyche as well as at the methods for accessing our superheroic self, which can take us to new levels of awareness and skill.

The Characters Within

Our inner world has the potential to be as vast as the outer world we inhabit, filled with multitudes of beings. However, as in our own real-life situations, only a few characters really stand out and have direct influence upon us. A study report in the online BBC Magazine suggested that we might have up to five core friends and a further ten close friends. Beyond that, there is another layer of around thirty-five people where there are some close connections, and further sub-groups of up to one hundred acquaintances (Geoghegan, 2009). Not all those who interact with us would be classed as friends. Some people, such as work colleagues, we might detest or might cause us a great deal of upset.

For each of these outer-world connections, there has to be an inner-world correspondence, which is why our inner world can be quite complex. In practice, the key characters in our life have the most impact upon us and the same is true of our inner world. We can class these into three distinct groups:

- Daily Life Characters
- Traumatized Characters
- Heroic or Admired Characters

Daily Life Characters are created as we move through life and acquire specific sets of skills. These characters reflect the different personas we portray in response to varying situations. For example, in thinking of myself I can easily identify 'the healer', 'the teacher', 'the father', 'the lover', 'the friend', 'the explorer', and so on. Whilst we might not immediately recognize these qualities as individual characters, with a little inner exploration they soon emerge. Some assume masculine forms, others feminine, regardless of which sex we might be. With a small amount of effort, one can discover at least a dozen such characters residing within one's psychic space. They can take on various forms, whether contemporary or ancient, and each will appear to have its own individuality and consciousness. They are also held in a polarity balance and sometimes these polarities become split into two distinct characters. For example, 'the warrior' and 'the wimp' might be held within one character or split into two separate characters. The latter often arises out of a trauma, although it might be generated when there is a specific lesson that needs to be learnt or understood.

To start accessing these fun characters you first need to identify the different elements that make up your psyche, such 'lover', 'parent', 'boss', 'joker', and so on. The following activity shows how this can be done.

> *Activity 10:1*
>
> Theme: *Discovering your inner characters – first steps*
>
> Duration: *15 minutes*
>
> 1. Write down eight different aspects of your personality, such as 'lover', 'parent', and so on, which operate at specific times. When the list is complete, you might like to consider how often these aspects come to prominence. Some qualities will be more dominant than others. When the list is complete, put them in their order of hierarchy.
> 2. Now think about the list from an emotional perspective. Which predominant feelings do you ascribe to each aspect? You might like to note down two or three for each one. For example, for 'parent' (father or mother), you could be happy and contented or, alternatively, frustrated and angry. You might discover that this 'parent' quality can be expressed quite differently, depending upon which of your children you are dealing with.
> 3. When you have completed Step 2 to the best of your ability, select one of these personality aspects. With your eyes either open or closed, try to imagine a character that represents this dynamic for you. What sort of character do you imagine? How do you feel in their company? Do they say anything to you?

> 4. Before finishing you might like to consider whether any of your colleagues, family members or acquaintances reflect this character. There is always a correlation between our inner and outer worlds.
> 5. When you have completed Step 5 you could go back to Step 3 and repeat the process if you wish.
> 6. Finally, thank the character or characters for the part they play in your life and bring yourself back to full waking consciousness.

When this list is complete, you will have eight characters. You can then begin to interact with them and find out what they might need from you or how you can help each other.

Traumatized Characters or Negative Sub-Personalities

The traumatized characters are part of our negative *shadow* and are created in response to specific distressing situations in the past. In this process, the soul infuses part of itself into the character or sub-personality and this is then locked into its own space and time within the psyche. These characters can hold a lot of emotion in the form of fear, pain, hatred or self-loathing. They are often deeply buried or hidden away and, on occasions, can even be ejected from the psyche. When this occurs, they can sometimes seem like possessing or attacking spirit entities. These characters have little free will. Generally, they are locked into a past-time scenario correlated to the moment when the original trauma occurred. However, although the past-time event is sealed into them, they are also aware of present-time situations and are continually on the lookout for any event that might reactivate or aggravate the trauma. In this way, they can also act as triggers or magnets that draw similar experiences back into the psyche. For example, the inner child that has been severely punished by the mother will be very wary of some aspects of the feminine and might even invoke a partner or friend to act aggressively towards them. This can occur with men when a wife or partner shifts from being a lover to being a mother figure. The fear of being punished invokes punishment, which is then acted out in adult life. Our fears, which stem from specific events, are an expression of these characters.

As previously stated, these characters can sometimes appear in forms that are not human, such as animals, monsters or ogres. When initially contacted, traumas from childhood will generally show themselves as children who are locked into their pain in a confused, frightened and untrusting state. However, if this child then takes over the psyche it will project a monster onto what it feels is assailing it. In this case, we are dealing with two separate elements – the pain and suffering of the child and the fear projection that it carries.

With a little effort, or when working with a therapist, one can become aware of the actual event that triggered the trauma and the emotion that it held. Our daily life experiences will often trigger emotional responses that relate to past traumas, which is why being in touch with one's emotions is so important. Because we do not like pain, we will often try to block off our emotional responses by creating barriers around our self, or by deliberately blocking our feelings. The litmus test on whether any traumatized sub-personalities reside within you is your emotional response to different situations. When your emotions are triggered in a negative way, whether by fear, anger or tears, then you can be sure that you still hold traumatized sub-personalities.

Most of us are unaware of these characters and can work to heal and balance them in an unconscious way by simply dealing with the outer issue they hold. For example, when you overcome specific fears you can help the corresponding sub-personality move into a different state of awareness. However, I have never been sure whether the use of hypnotism to block the fear state heals the sub-personality or simply stops it manifesting so easily. It would be better if the hypnotherapeutic process also dealt with the corresponding sub-personality.

These emotional responses can also stimulate physical sensations such as nausea, heart pain, breathlessness, choking, headaches, numbness, and so on. When working with clients, the H-S will bring forward the relevant sub-personality to be healed. This can initially take the form of being aware of the event or the character that stems from the event. For example, if we take the case of a ten-year-old child that has been locked away, as punishment, in a darkened cellar, the first awareness in a therapeutic session might just be a fear of the dark. Once this fear has been identified, I will then get my client to try to locate this fear in their body, such as nausea in the stomach. When this has been achieved, a process of objectifying the fear can be started by seeing it as a colour and shape and then perceiving it as being outside the body. From there can sometimes come the awareness of the actual incident that caused the trauma. Conversely, a client might immediately remember the incident, even though they would not have otherwise made the association, and the healing process can begin. The method for healing these situations will be covered in greater depth later in this chapter.

Activity 10:2

Theme: *Uncovering your traumatized characters or sub-personalities – first steps*

Duration: *20 minutes*

1. Draw a column in the centre of a piece of paper or on a computer document. In the left-hand column make a list of your known fears, such as heights, spiders, and so on. Once this list is complete, write down in the right-hand column when this fear started. This might be obvious or it might not. If there are gaps, they do not matter at this stage.

2. On a separate sheet of paper or computer document make a list of any incidents when your negative emotions were triggered during the past week, or month, according to whichever seems most appropriate. Negative emotions can include the following: fear, anger, hatred, loathing, jealousy, irritation, suicidal thoughts, depression, sadness, grief, despair, shame and frustration. You might come up with more but the above list should serve well.
3. When this list is complete see if any emotion correlates with any of the items listed in Step 1. If they do, make a special note of the fear and the incident when this occurred.
4. Return to the list in Step 2 and note the number of times when these feelings were experienced. For example, you may have felt irritated for several days during the week or month but sad only once. Remember that in this process you need to include everything that triggered a strong emotion, which might occur when reading a book, seeing a film or TV show, as well as when dealing with interpersonal relationships.
5. From these lists see whether you can begin to identify any themes or patterns that run through you. Try to identify just one of these events and see if you can imagine a character that might carry this quality. What sort of individual might they be?

Through this process we can begin to build up a list of those characters within that might hold trauma. You might also discover that some situations arise on a regular basis, which for women may link to their monthly cycle when there are hormonal changes within the body. This raises one of those interesting chicken and egg situations in posing the question of whether the hormones generated the emotion, or whether the slight imbalances within the body allowed space for the emotion or psychological state to emerge.

Heroes and Heroines

In addition to the healthy inner characters, we all have access to a higher level of their potential. This concept was first explored in Chapter 7 when discussing the personal *shadow*. In this section, we will consider this idea in greater depth, looking at how we call upon heroes and heroines for help and support. These characters can be invoked when we have specific tasks we wish to perform, such as for healing, teaching, artistic endeavours and inventions. Superheroes can appear in many different guises. During the space of my life, I have worked with mythological creatures like the white winged horse Pegasus, and famous people from the past, such as different saints, as well as angelic or semi-divine presences. These characters have their own life energy and dynamic. They never seem to be constructs of my psyche; rather, they appear as independent beings and I have always worked with them in that way.

Sometimes they appear spontaneously, like the Egyptian god Thoth, who turned up in my bedroom one Sunday morning, many years ago, and told me that I needed to start to run courses on healing and meditation. This was back in the mid-1970s, before any training for healers in the UK, at least, was generally available. A few colleagues and I went on to start the first training courses in healing, which ultimately manifested many years later in setting up the College of Healing, which is still going strong today (College of Healing, 2015). I would add here that the manifestation of Thoth was not a flesh and blood character but, rather, perceived within my imagination. What is salient is that the information relayed was pertinent to my life then.

On other occasions, these characters come in response to a specific request for help. They are always supportive and co-operative but they will not take on the task for themselves or rather they make sure that we carry our share of the burden of responsibility because that is how we grow and learn. Working with these heroic characters can be enormous fun and very revealing. They highlight for us the potential to which we might aspire.

Although I have used the term 'superhero' or 'superheroine', one of my colleagues much prefers the term 'Team', such as in 'Team David' or 'Team Sarah', to denote the group of intelligences that can support your work and activities. This idea is grounded in that it helps place the individual at the centre of the experience, rather than perhaps feeling somewhat overawed by the concept of superheroes working for you. It is important to find the most appropriate vehicle for this idea that suits your psychological make-up.

> *Activity 10:3*
>
> Theme: *Connecting to your heroes or heroines to create your inner support team*
>
> Duration: *20 minutes*
>
> 1. Draw up a list of eight characters, either male or female, which you would like to meet. The list can include religious as well as secular figures or, indeed, mythological characters. I suggest that you make the list equal with regard to gender, i.e. four females and four males. However, if you wish to slant the listing towards one gender then I recommend that you do this on a 5:3 ratio. As an example, here is my list: Jesus of Nazareth, the pharaoh Akhenaten, Pegasus, Thoth, the White Owl, the Lady of the Lake, Kwan Yin and Hathor[1]. If I were to limit my list to known historical characters that I have connected to, or worked with, at different stages of my life, as well as Jesus and Akhenaten the list would include Lao Tzu, Pythagoras, St Francis of Assisi, Florence Nightingale, the Madonna and Elizabeth I.
> 2. Select one of your characters and close your eyes, connect to your H-S (Activity 9:3, see page 205) and then imagine the character coming and standing next to you. What do they have to say to you? What do they communicate? How can they help you in your everyday life? Make a note of anything that happens and allow your imagination full rein in this exercise.

3. Think of a situation in your life where having the support of one of these superheroes might be helpful for you. For example, if you wish to clinch a business deal, who represents the ideal business executive (man or woman) that could assist you? If you are a teacher, who would you perceive as the ideal teacher? Having identified the character, you can imagine they are always with you in the classroom.
4. Before finishing any such exercise, always thank the character for their support, wisdom and help.

Exercises for Working with Your Inner Characters

The following exercises are designed to help you connect to, and work with, your inner characters in a creative and insightful way. These characters reflect aspects of your present personality as it now stands and therefore, like you, these characters will grow, develop and transform themselves. They all have a polarity balance, or twin aspect, and the more extreme the character the greater will be its polar opposite. For example, a very wealthy executive could have the polarity of a pauper. The trick in this process is to discover where the pauper resides within you because it might be reflected in another aspect of your character. By engaging with these inner characters, we can gain insight into ourselves as well as find a level of humility and balance

There are several ways to discover these characters. The first is purely intuitive by going within your psyche to locate and discover the characters that reside there. Another way is by making a list of the qualities that reflect your nature as you did in Activity 10:1 on page 227. You can expand this list to include many more facets of your make-up but always remember to include the polarity of what you noted down. For example, if your list includes being happy, fun-loving and optimistic, the polarities might be sadness, seriousness and pessimism. You will find that there will be an inner character who reflects each of these qualities. By connecting to these characters, you can gain insight into how they operate within your psyche and the function they fulfil. You can then balance these characters by linking them up or getting them to meet each other and seeing how they respond to one another.

The final way that you can discover your inner characters is by considering how they are reflected out into the world around you. This can be your immediate world of friends, neighbours, colleagues and family or through the wider collective world of individuals within society. A simple way to approach this is to draw up a list, noting down those individuals that you enjoy being with, those that you have ambivalence about and those that you actively dislike. Each of these people will reflect one or other of your inner characters and your challenge is to get to know them and to integrate their qualities within you. Naturally, the hardest reflections come from the individuals that you detest or despise because these often relate to deeply buried components of your negative *shadow*.

The following three exercises explore each of these approaches. The first stems from our dream world, where we can find ourselves on forms of transport, such as planes, cars, coaches or buses, together with other people whom we may or may not know. These characters in the dream world are reflections of our own sub-personalities, even if we know them as real people.

Activity 10:4

Theme: *Intuitive connection to your sub-personalities*

Duration: *10 minutes*

1. Sit quietly and close your eyes. Carry out the Body Consciousness Exercise (Activity 9:2, see page 204).
2. Connect to your H-S and request its assistance in carrying out this exercise.

3. Imagine that you are on a form of transport such as a bus, coach or train. Your H-S is the driver and each passenger is one of your sub-personalities.
4. Ask the driver to set you down at the most appropriate place and request the relevant sub-personality to get off with you. Have a look at your surroundings and then find somewhere where you can communicate with this character.
5. Some people have a very good visual sense, others operate at a more auditory level. Whichever is your favoured modality, with a little practice you should be able to describe the sub-personality character. The sort of questions you can ask your self are:
    a. Is this character male or female?
    b. How old are they?
    c. How are they dressed?
    d. What do they say to me?
    e. What function do they play in my life?
6. Try to give them a name that reflects something of their character, such as 'Busty Bertha' or 'Ginger Gerald', which is an idea suggested by Debbie Ford (Ford, 2001). A character that I connect to when writing is called 'Learned Lenny', who is tall, thin, wears glasses and enjoys being in a library. He researches information for me, which I can ask him to do at any time.
7. When you have connected sufficiently with the character and established where they reside within your inner world, it is then possible to access them whenever you need help.
8. When you have spent sufficient time with the character, allow them to remain in their space (in Lenny's case it is the library) and then return to the bus and repeat the process.
9. I suggest that you do not try to connect to more than two characters during any visit so you can give yourself plenty of time to get to know them.
10. When you have completed the exercise, thank your H-S and bring yourself back to full waking consciousness.

Illuminating the Shadow

This exercise can be carried out dozens of times, so that your inner world begins to have a greater reality and structure. The next exercise is a development of the first.

> *Activity 10:5*
>
> Theme: *Connecting to those sub-personalities that relate to qualities*
>
> Duration: *10 minutes*
>
> 1. Study the list that you made in Activity 10:1 (see page 227) and select one of the qualities or attributes along with its polarity.
> 2. Carry out the Body Consciousness Exercise (Activity 9:2, see page 204) and link to your H-S.
> 3. Ask your H-S to bring you to the place where the quality resides. For example, when I first did this exercise I chose 'anger' and 'serenity' as my two qualities.
> 4. Ask the first quality to take the form of a character and see where this is located.
> 5. Communicate with the character to see whether it is happy, and if not what needs to change. If you are unsure, connect with your H-S to request help.
> 6. If the sub-personality seems distressed, send it healing by imagining a beam of light coming down from your H-S and being sent to the character. This will normally bring about transformation.
> 7. When one side of the polarity is sufficiently balanced, connect with the other side and repeat the process.
> 8. You will now have two sides of polarity balance. See if you can bring them into a single space where they can reside together. You may need to request further help from your H-S to achieve this objective.
> 9. Finally, thank the characters and your H-S and then bring yourself back to full waking consciousness.

When I first did this exercise and asked my H-S to take me to the place where my anger resided I found it locked up in a small prison and feeling very disgruntled. Clearly, it needed more space and freedom to express itself but not in a way that caused problems for others or myself. By bringing it into a place of healing and balance, it now provides a considerable amount of energy for my projects. Serenity, on the other hand, was fast asleep in a bedroom. Clearly, I could be serene at night-time but perhaps not at other times. It proved very helpful to bringing both 'Serene Salome' and 'Angry Algernon' into the same space where they could communicate with each other in a more balanced way. When I contact these characters now I normally find them walking hand in hand in the countryside.

Sub-Personalities that Reflect People

The next exercise entails working with sub-personalities that reflect real people within your life. These can fall into two categories, in the form of those that you get along with and those that cause you some form of issue. In the following exercise, we will tackle the latter example, as these sub-personalities will often be the most problematic and pressing. Technically speaking, they will often relate to aspects of your *negative* shadow. The first step is to recognize that there are two component sub-personalities involved here. There will be the sub-personality that represents the persecutor or protagonist and there will be the part that corresponds with the victim. We will normally relate more closely with the victim sub-personality than the persecutor, because the victim carries the pain. The trick in this exercise is to separate yourself from the victim and to create a triangle between yourself and these other two parts. Effectively, you need to assume the role of rescuer or healer to these inner traumatized aspects.

Exercise 10:6

Theme: *Connecting to sub-personalities that relate to real people where there are issues between you and them*

Duration: *10 minutes*

1. Consider the names of those individuals with whom these issues arise and select one of them.
2. Close your eyes, carry out the Body Consciousness Exercise (Activity 9:2, see page 204), then link to your H-S and request it to bring to your attention the two sub-personalities that represent both this individual as well as the part of you that feels hurt.
3. Imagine yourself on your preferred mode of transport from Activity 10:1 (see page 227). When it stops, get off with at least two characters (there may be more). In some cases, you will actually see the person who has caused the issues or they may have morphed into another character entirely.
4. Be aware of the scene that you find yourself in when you alight. Consider what is happening between the two characters.
5. You now need to request assistance from your H-S and, additionally, one or more of your superheroes to help you heal this relationship within your internal world. If the two characters are in conflict, or one is beating up the other, you will first have to separate them.
6. Now send a thought of love and light, no matter how difficult this might seem, to both characters. Tell them that you want to help them to understand what is going on between them and how they can be brought back into a balance within you.
7. The next step can vary depending upon what is happening but the process entails getting into dialogue with both sets of characters to understand what they require from you and what needs to be done to bring them both into a space of wholeness and balance. To achieve this you might also have to call upon both your H-S and your superheroes for support and help.

8. One way to begin would be to ask each character why it has come into your life and what is the learning that you need to work through for this character to be healed.
9. In this process, it can be valuable to sense what is going on within the protagonist, to imagine what he or she might feel like and express when acting in this role.
10. Working through this process entails both sets of characters becoming friends and acknowledging each other.
11. Finally, thank your H-S and any superhero who has helped and then bring yourself back to full waking consciousness.

This exercise may need to be carried out on a number of occasions before resolution. Its most interesting aspect is monitoring what happens in your outer world because of these internal changes. In some cases this can be dramatic, in others subtle, for the process involves internal change. When this occurs your outer world will be modified to reflect your inner, for both are held together by resonance. As you change within so your outer world also must shift and develop.

Healing Exercises for Traumatized Sub-Personalities

The next two exercises relate to those sub-personalities in which trauma resides. These are the most difficult to tackle on one's own and may need help from a therapist, particularly if there has been a great deal of childhood trauma. Some clients need regular sessions over a long period when confronting deep-seated issues that might perhaps have been repeated over a number of lifetimes. Occasionally, the process might entail dealing with intruder spirits or sub-personalities from others that have become entangled within the psyche.

In using the metaphor of a house, with the primary occupants being your ego self and your sub-personalities, you can sometimes find additional characters that are not part of you taking up residence in the form of lodgers, intruders or invaders. These can be tricky to deal with, as sometimes there are levels of collusion going on. One part of you might want to eject them, whilst another sub-personality might wish them to remain.

Even though tricky situations are best dealt with by working with a therapist there is still much we can do for our own internal healing. The following exercise demonstrates this process.

Activity 10:7

Theme: *Healing traumatized sub-personalities*

Duration: *10 minutes*

1. Carry out the Body Consciousness Exercise (Activity 9:2, see page 204) and connect to your H-S.
2. Enter into your sacred safe space and request your H-S to bring towards you the sub-personality that needs healing. You can do this using the visualization given in Activity 9:4.
3. Once you have become aware of the sub-personality or character you will next need to enter into dialogue with it to understand what it needs to be healed. This can take effort and time and entails bringing a great deal of light, love, forgiveness and balance to the situation where the trauma occurred.
4. Once the sub-personality has been contacted, always remind it that it has its own focus of inner light (a fragment of your soul essence). It needs to know that it too can be in contact with the H-S and receive healing directly from that source of higher power or light.

> 5. Each sub-personality will be holding an emotional charge of pain. This will need to be acknowledged and released.
> 6. When healed, the sub-personality can be brought inside your inner sanctuary and thereby integrated within you.
> 7. Occasionally sub-personalities which have been severely traumatized will need to go back to the H-S for full healing. I have found this to be particularly so in cases which have entailed past-life deaths. Once accessed, acknowledged and healed, the sub-personality can be lifted into the sunlight, requesting the H-S to take over.
> 8. When complete, thank your H-S. Then sense yourself aligned and balanced, bringing yourself back to full waking consciousness.

Re-framing the Past

From a normal world perspective, time flows in a linear way from the past to the future. Normally, we have the view that events, once they have occurred, are fixed and immutable. If I had a car crash yesterday that event has already happened and as much as I would like to change it I cannot. What is interesting about our inner world is that it is not quite so compartmentalized and fixed. At any moment a number of different possibilities could occur. Instead of crashing, I might have swerved just in time to avoid the accident or even have slowed down earlier so that I was not present when the accident would have occurred. It is always fascinating reading or hearing the stories of those who avoided being caught up in major catastrophes, such as the Twin Towers, when they should normally have been present. Whilst our outer world seems fixed and rigid, our inner world is fluid and open to many different possibilities. Events from the past can be reframed quite easily with enormously powerful effects.

The process entails going back to the original scene of the trauma and then changing the dynamics of what was perceived to have happened. The following, which occurred recently in a therapeutic session, is an example of this approach. The client became aware of a ten-year-old part that experienced great upset and unhappiness from a school situation which involved a particular teacher. The child wanted to leave the school and go to another one, where she felt she would have had better teaching and appreciation of her skills. The adult self of the client could fully recognize that the teacher had been completely out of order in the way that she dealt with the child and that the new school would be better for her. In the original incident, the child had pleaded with her mother to move schools but this had been ignored, so the child continued to experience the trauma with the thought that her needs would never be acknowledged. Put another way, she was still stuck in the classroom, experiencing the trauma, with the feeling of abandonment to her real needs.

The healing process entailed the adult first making contact with the inner child, still stuck in the classroom with an unsympathetic teacher, and then stepping into the scene as though re-enacting the drama. Then, in her imagination, she told the child that she had now come to rescue her and that she was going to take her to a new school where she would be happy. After telling the teacher that her actions were inappropriate, she took the child to the new school, making sure that she had suitable teachers, and installed her there in such a way that the teachers fully supported the child in her development.

In this way, the traumatized sub-personality was moved out of its stuck state into a more wholesome place where she could receive help and healing. Ultimately, these traumatized childhood parts need to be reintegrated within our psyches into inner places where they can feel happy and secure. For this process to be complete, the adult self needs to acknowledge the emotional or physical pain and then to release the child from the need to carry the trauma by bringing them into a happy state within the psyche.

Through this simple process, we can reframe the traumas that have beset our life or lives. When working with clients there have been many instances when they become aware of a traumatic death in a past life, either on a battlefield or through execution such as hanging. In these cases, the sub-personality involved is still stuck in the trauma. It can be rescued and brought to an inner place of healing for the pain to be released. One approach that works well is to reframe the situation so that instead of dying a horrible death, a new scenario is created in which the sub-personality is liberated or escapes. When dealing with traumas that stem from past lives, I normally request the H-S to bring them back into the spiritual plane, whilst current life traumas can be reintegrated back within the self in a balanced way.

Reframing situations is not new and can be considered in a variety of different ways. An approach adopted in Neuro-Linguistic Programming (NLP) practice is to look at the positive learning outcomes from any negative situation. This can be valuable from an adult perspective. In other words, the adult within us can go back to our original painful memories and re-evaluate them, looking to see the experience from a positive rather than a negative perspective. One can ask simple questions like, 'What did this experience teach me?' or 'How can I see this experience in a positive light?' When linked to the H-S an overlighting wisdom can be brought to bear on the incident. This approach certainly will help to ameliorate the trauma. Nonetheless, I would still bring the traumatized sub-personality into a new situation.

This process was highlighted in Michael Newton's book *Destiny of Souls* where an individual, who had suicidal tendencies, was regressed to a former life where she had committed suicide. She had been a farmer's daughter and had fallen in love with a local thatcher, which ended with her becoming pregnant. However, before they could marry, her lover had died tragically when falling from a roof and she was now alone. She was terrified about what might happen to her and her unborn child. She feared that she would be driven from her home and would then end up in the slums of London, living as a prostitute. This thought was so overwhelming that she chose, instead, to drown herself in a millpond (Newton, 2002:156).

When reviewing her life, in the between-life state, she was shown that there were a number of different options open to her, one of which did entail the tragic end that she had tried to avoid. Others were much more hopeful and allowed both her and her child to live in relative peace and happiness. When reflecting on this particular case and what might be the determining factor for a particular life outcome my H-S came forward with one simple word – 'fear'. In other words, that which we fear will pursue us. The challenge we face is the need to move through our fears into a place of wholeness. I recognize that this is sometimes not an easy process. We need to keep asking for help from our H-S and our superheroes, to strengthen our resolve to face the fear and move through it.

The following exercise looks at the process of reframing the past.

Activity 10:8

Theme: *Reframing the past*

Duration: *10-15 minutes*

1. Reflect on any incident from the past that you would like to change, particularly one that relates to your childhood, although it could be an event that was more recent.
2. Carry out the Body Consciousness Exercise (Activity 9:2, see page 204) and then link to your H-S and request help with this reframing.
3. Ask your H-S to help you link to the part of you that holds the trauma. This may be obvious but can sometimes be subtle and less distinct. Remember, your H-S knows the situation intimately and can direct your thoughts to whichever aspect requires help.

> 4. Send a thought of love, healing and balance to the part that holds the pain and ask your H-S to help heal and balance the energy. See that part moving into a new place of understanding.
> 5. Reframe the situation into a form that suits you better, envisioning a different outcome and scenario. Remember we sometimes have to live through an experience in order to see how we might like to change it.
> 6. Finally, thank your H-S and bring yourself back to full consciousness, affirming the change within yourself.

Situations that stem from childhood or earlier can easily be reframed through this method. Experiences that are more recent can require a greater flexibility in approach. For example, in the case of a recent marriage break-up, the events and emotional reactions can be quite raw. The challenge here is to be able to identify the aspect that holds the pain in a dissociative rather than associative way. In other words, to see the part of you that holds the pain as being a separate character, within your psyche, rather than the whole of you. You can then send healing to this part, requesting your H-S for help to balance this aspect of your psyche and release any of the trauma that it holds. You now need to focus on positive outcomes, seeing these as part of your current reality. Whilst there may be a desire for revenge when a marriage breaks up, this is not helpful for long-term well-being. The ideal is for both partners to move forward in their life and to find a measure of happiness and fulfilment. You cannot predict this for your ex-partner but you can, at least, manifest this for yourself by seeing the best possible outcome.

Exercises with your Superheroes

Superheroes can be any inner world character that inspires you to greater things within your life. They are all teachers at some level, through either courage or wisdom. We can create many such characters to assist us in different stages of our life. The following exercise will help you to connect with one or more of the characters drawn from Activity 10.3 (see page 233).

> Exercise 10:9
>
> Theme: *Connecting to your superheroes*
>
> Duration: *10-15 minutes*
>
> 1. Consider which particular character you would like to meet from the list you produced in Activity 10.3 (see page 233).
> 2. Carry out the Body Consciousness Exercise (Activity 9:2, see page 204) and connect to your H-S.
> 3. Link to your inner safe space and then turn to face your inner sun or star.
> 4. Imagine that your character is coming down a beam of light into your sanctuary. Go up to them and communicate with them. What do they share with you? What feelings do they bring forth? What can they teach you and how do they inspire you?
> 5. Ask the character to show you how they can help you in your life.
> 6. Finally, thank them and your H-S and bring yourself back to normal waking consciousness.

Many years ago, when working on a project which involved co-operating with a number of other people, my inner teacher suggested that I bring the relevant archetype or superhero into the room with me. I was generally the ideas man of the venture, and new concepts would often be blocked by the fears or prejudices of my colleagues. I was informed that if the archetype character felt that the new idea was important then this would bring an added dimension to the table and would go a long way to ensuring that the idea would become acceptable. I have followed this advice since, through most of my life, to good effect. Once the link is made, you only need to imagine that the character is with you in whichever situation is relevant.

Summary

In this chapter we have looked at ways to connect to our sub-personalities or inner characters. These characters are created in response to different life situations and are imbued with consciousness by our own soul fragments. Those that hold trauma can be helped, healed and brought back into a place of balance and wholeness. A higher level of these characters offers a potential to what we might become. We can draw upon reflections of these characters as superheroes, who can then assist us generally in our daily lives or help us to tackle specific situations. Those who pray to saints and deities are working with this principle. In summary:

- Our inner world can be as vast as the world outside, peopled with all sorts of characters.
- These characters are generally known as sub-personalities or ego states.
- Some of these characters were created in response to trauma and then become locked in their own space-time continuum. They need help and healing if they are to be released from their stuck position.
- Some of our inner characters reflect outer world individuals. Therapists are often aware of the way that their clients mirror their own issues.
- Our inner world characters are evolving. They all have the potential to grow into something much greater than they are. Connecting to our superheroes helps this process because it provides an example of what we might become.

Chapter Eleven

Soul Wounds and the Shadow

We're often afraid of looking at our shadow because we want to avoid the shame or embarrassment that comes along with admitting mistakes.

Marianne Williamson

The concept of soul wounds was originally introduced to me in the mid-1990s by my good friend Annie Davison, whose first book *The Wise Virgin* (under the pen-name of Annie Wilson) was regarded as a seminal work in the field of Transpersonal Psychology (Wilson, 1979). The idea had been relayed to her from one of her spirit guides and I found the inspiration captivating. Since then I have been able to verify its tenets, in part at least, with many of my clients over the past twenty years.

The idea, touched on in Chapter 7, is very simple. It suggests that we each hold one of five soul wounds that sits within our *shadow*. This wound then tracks through a number of incarnations until it is resolved. Whilst it is impossible to be sure of any past-life manifestation of these wounds, I can certainly vouch for the fact that they appear to be evident when assessing the patterns that are inherent in the current lives of my clients. Parenting certainly plays a part in how these patterns are formulated but appears not to be the main or sole factor. Even in cases where there has been a relatively happy childhood, issues can emerge which then come to the surface in therapy.

Individuals can generally identify their own wound when given time to reflect on their lives, although in some cases more than one wound stands out. The original list of five wounds is as follows:

- Rejection
- Abandonment
- Abuse
- Betrayal
- Denial

> *Activity 11:1*
>
> *Initially assessing your particular soul wound*
>
> Consider each of the five wounds above and think of any traumas that come into each category. Can you spot any themes that best describe a pattern in your life? For example, you might remember a situation in which you felt betrayed. Have there been other incidents when betrayal has occurred, particularly in childhood?

The psychological states associated with each of these wounds and the steps leading out of them are not unique and have been covered in other books and scholarly articles. What is original is the concept that during the course of our life we need to work with the dynamics of just one of these wounds as an inherent part of our soul's journey and that this process entails working with its polarities. In other words, if *abandonment* is your wound, you will need to heal those sub-personality aspects of the psyche that have been abandoned, as well as consider all that you abandon. We will look in depth at how these wounds can be healed but, at this stage, it is worth describing them briefly to give an overview of the concept.

Rejection

My particular soul wound is *rejection,* so I am going to start with this one as I can best illustrate it with examples from my own life.

When people first consider this idea, they are often aware that more than one deep-seated wound has operated within their life. For example, they may have felt at one time abused and at another abandoned. In the gamut of our life journey, we probably experience each of these wounds at different times. I know that I certainly have. There have been moments when I have felt betrayed, abandoned, abused and denied. Yet, when I come to look in depth at my life, *rejection* touches the core of my being in a way that the other experiences do not. I sometimes imagine this part of me is like a sea anemone that instantly clams up as soon as it is prodded. It is as though I have a super-sensitive sixth sense that is continually on the lookout for *rejection*. I can feel, or I used to feel, mortified when I felt rejected by someone or by a group. The fascinating and challenging dynamic of life is that we attract to our self those elements that we need to address and I can recall many situations when the *rejection* button was pressed within me. Therefore, the first part of the process is to consider your emotional responses to people and situations. What presses your buttons?

The second part of my own process in looking at the *rejection* wound was to consider, as its complement, all of the things I have rejected. My partner sometimes jokingly says to me that my initial response to any of her spontaneous ideas is to say 'no' – *rejection*! This shows how unconscious these aspects can be within our psyche unless we start to make them conscious, which is why the soul wounds, as patterns, sit within our *shadow*. I have had to think consciously about a number of elements in my life to do with *rejection* and in this process to ask myself 'Who have I rejected and what have I rejected, both within myself and others?' These questions can be painful, for they mean stripping away the veneer of how we would like to be perceived. If you think about the journey you have been on through this book, if *rejection* is your soul wound you will spot many examples where it has come to the fore.

The process of healing soul wounds entails looking first at those situations when a specific wound manifested strongly within your life, when you were in the victim position. In other words, if *rejection* is your wound, you must look at those times when you felt rejected, either by an individual such as a parent, or by a group, when you have felt blackballed for something you may or may not have done. The early exposure to this wound can manifest in early childhood, when the primary caregivers reject the child for some misdemeanour or action that is perceived to go against the caregivers' wishes. Comments like 'I don't love you any more' can strengthen this patterning. These patterns can then be further reinforced in schooling by being excluded from different groups or gangs.

As human beings, we struggle with two different innate impulses. The first is to comply with and be part of a group, because in the earlier stages of human development co-operation was an important ingredient for survival. The second element is to be able to assert one's individuality, because the gift of free will empowers this sense. At times, these two dynamics can be at odds with each other because the group dynamic might not suit the individual. One way that the group can punish those who step out of line with the group's dictates is through *rejection*. Being 'sent to Coventry' is an example. The emotional pain this causes often crushes any individualism, ensuring that the collective will is maintained. When individuals do strike out on their own a great deal of conflict can arise, sometimes causing societies to become split. History attests to the number of people who have been martyred for their beliefs, which is a dramatic expression of the *rejection* wound.

As adults seeking to balance our inner world, we first need to address the primary source of our particular wound and its subsequent manifestation at different times in our life. Once these moments have been healed, the next step entails looking closely at the instances when we operated as the persecutor, either against others or against our self. This second step is often the harder of the two to discover, because we are less conscious when it kicks in. My 'sea anemone' immediately responds when I feel rejected but it is much less aware when I am doing the rejecting. With practice and patience, we can begin to resolve these patterns within us and then, hopefully, they will not come to dominate our lives in the future. The spiritual challenge of this wound is how to be able to assert one's individuality yet at the same time blend it into society with as little conflict as possible.

Abandonment

Those individuals whose wound is *abandonment* will often carry a great deal of emotional pain. These situations generally start in early childhood, with the loss of the mother or father from death or divorce. It is dependent upon an emotional connection being made at an early stage of life to a primary caregiver, who then, for various reasons, abandons the child. These situations can be temporary or permanent, and always cause a considerable amount of inner distress and emotional pain. The psyche very often is then locked in a process of expectation that this type of experience is going to happen again, and steps need to be taken, at all costs, to avoid this trauma.

We all, at different times, will have experienced being temporarily abandoned, such as our first day at school when we leave our mother's care. If we have been used to leaving our parents from time to time this will probably not be problematic, but for someone who bonded very strongly with their mother and were then wrenched away, the trauma can be immense and cause a great deal of inner confusion and suffering. Such situations can occur when young children are forcibly separated from their primary caregivers through illness or tragedy. For example, a child may need to spend time in hospital. If their mother, or primary caregiver, does not stay with them when they are confronted by the illness, the feeling of *abandonment* is further reinforced by being linked to physical suffering.

Such cases are not so prevalent in hospitals in the UK in today's society but they certainly occurred in the past.

These situations highlight the commonality of potential *abandonment* problems, which sit in addition to the more obvious cases of children being put up for adoption because of genuine cases of abuse or neglect, or one or other of their parents leaving at an early stage of their life. The trauma generated seems to tap into a visceral response within the psyche which the ego self immediately takes steps to protect against. At an early age, children can learn that adults cannot be trusted to care for their primary emotional needs and defence mechanisms need to be put into place to guard against such situations happening in the future. As we have seen, the psyche creates sub-personalities or ego states to hold these traumas, and once in place they can become self-perpetuating. To be in control the psyche can trigger a response that provokes other individuals to abandon them. I have known a number of adults with *abandonment* issues who have undermined their relationships by being provocative. Eventually, the recipient of these attacks leaves their partner, thus completing the self-fulfilling prophecy with a self-reinforcing repetitive cycle that can continue right through an entire life.

The other way that the psyche deals with these issues is by learning to abandon a situation or partner before the critical pain threshold is reached. Such individuals will often find it hard to sustain meaningful relationships because they will not want to stay around long enough to form a strong emotional bond for fear of being hurt again. Additionally, they will often be open to abandoning many different elements within their life so that 'stickability' – the process of seeing something through to the end – becomes an issue for them. One finds such individuals starting and then dropping out of many different courses or situations. They can prove difficult clients for therapists because they often will not complete the therapeutic process.

If *abandonment* is your soul wound then you will need to address not only the original feelings of *abandonment* and the sub-personalities involved but also your tendency to abandon. This is often the trickiest element for the psyche to address. The spiritual challenge of *abandonment* is the completion of those projects and goals that you have set yourself and overcoming any adversity or hardship set against you.

Abuse

Like *abandonment*, *abuse* can start very early on in a child's development. In my own case, with a little delving beneath the surface, I realized that I had been a clock-fed, bottle-fed baby. If I woke up and was hungry or wanted comfort, my mother, through the best of intentions, would not feed me unless the clock agreed. Additionally, at the appointed hour I would be woken up if I happened to be fast asleep and given a feed which I might not then have wanted. All very subtle, yet I became aware in later life of the pattern that this had set within me and I then needed to take steps to clear or deal with this unwelcome intrusion.

Although no one at the time would have regarded this as *abuse*, to the tiny infant the feelings of discomfort can create trauma. In most cases, the loving care of the mother can help assuage these feelings unless they are reinforced by a continued pattern of deliberate *abuse* or neglect. Once this happens an expectation is set up within the psyche that tends to perpetuate the normality of *abuse* and this can then follow through into later childhood and adolescence, when *abuse* is experienced physically, emotionally and sexually. With the many different clients that I have worked with in my life, those who have been continually abused tend to be the most fractured individuals. The ego shell is so broken down that they become susceptible to many different psychological conditions and even to spirit possession or attachment. Such cases can also tip over into self-abuse in all of its many forms, such as addictions, mutilations and eating disorders like anorexia and bulimia.

Healing an abusive wound is not an easy task and requires a great deal of inner therapeutic work to restore the ego boundaries and to help the many sub-personalities back into a place of wholeness. The power that comes forward from the H-S is most important in this type of case. The spiritual challenge of this wound is learning to be loving and forgiving, both to oneself and to others.

Betrayal

Betrayal is a more subtle wound in that it requires a degree of self-awareness before it can be properly recognized and understood. It occurs in childhood when there is an expectation of something happening, as part of a special event or a routine, which is then dramatically reversed. This generally occurs when promises are made and then broken. Instead of the primary caregiver disappearing or walking away, as with *abandonment* issues, in *betrayal* the child can be assaulted emotionally and sometimes physically, generally without warning. Expectations are first raised and then dashed, which causes great instability within the psyche because the tendency then is to learn not to fully trust individuals, particularly those who are close. As with *abuse* and *abandonment,* the inner anticipation becomes one of expecting to be deliberately hurt at some stage.

A typical example from my clients can be those who have experienced an absent parent, often a father, promising to come to take them out for a treat and then failing to turn up. The expectation of some special treat is first raised and then squashed. In one particular case, a daughter was promised by her father, who was about to leave home prior to divorce, that he would always be there for her. He assured her that she could rely on him to help her through whatever situation might arise, only to be told a few months later that he would have nothing more to do with her because she had not given up a boyfriend to whom he objected. For two years, he never spoke to her despite her frequent attempts to contact him.

Such situations create great scarring on the psyche and set a pattern of instability for the ensuing life.

Individuals that I have worked with who carry this wound are often super-sensitive, which can manifest in a multitude of ways. They can be mortified by any criticism and the natural response is to immediately attack back, which can lead to them betraying before they themselves are betrayed. They do not like allowing anybody to be too close, preferring to keep individuals at arm's length. The spiritual challenge of this wound is learning how to balance expectations and to forgive those who cause you pain.

Denial

Those who have *denial* as a soul wound are often the hardest to help because their defence mechanisms are based largely on fear. They emerge from two forms of childhood upbringing. The first is where the emotional elements of the child are denied and repressed on the basis that they do not occur in 'normal' people or they do not meet the expectations of the parent. When the child steps out of line some form of retribution is meted out to them, so they learn to hide or distort their emotions and, additionally, to create a form of fantasy world where they are in control. They effectively choose not to accept normal reality because it is too frightening but distort the world to suit their own inner perceptions of how it should be rather than how it is. In this process they can become very good liars, both to themselves and others.

One of the themes of the Robin Williams film *Dead Poets Society* (1989) involves a pupil called Neil Perry discovering his desire to act, which his authoritarian father does everything to suppress, wanting him to go to a military academy and then Harvard. This results in Neil committing suicide rather than abandon his passion for acting. This level of repression is common in households where *denial* is prevalent. Parental control ensures that children in such households become confused and emotionally blocked because they are not allowed to express their feelings naturally.

The second way that *denial* comes out is where parents refuse to accept their role as parents and thereby fail to set clear boundaries for the developing child. This also creates a great deal of uncertainty within the child, although in these cases individual children might respond differently, depending upon their particular soul wound.

Those with *denial* as their soul wound are frightened of accepting the world as it is because, for all manner of reasons, it is too terrifying. They therefore create an artificial worldview that might be a long way from what is the truth of a situation. The fear keeps them locked into specific perspectives, which become very stuck and difficult to remove. Individuals in the victim mode of *denial* might find themselves in abusive or destructive relationships, yet always make out that everything is really OK or make excuses for the behaviour of others. Those who are protagonists will deny the consequences of their own behaviour on others, such as the effect that gamblers or alcoholics might have on their families. They effectively make good excuses for their actions, choosing to blame others for what they have or have not done.

I find those that have *denial* as their soul wound are some of the hardest clients to help because they do not wish to accept any perspective other than that which they espouse. An example of this was an ex-nun who I worked with many years ago, who was convinced that she was the Devil incarnate and the epitome of evil because she had ambivalent feelings towards her mother. This happened to contravene the biblical command of honouring one's parents. Her mother was clearly abusive towards her but no amount of explanation or reason would shift my client's entrenched belief.

The spiritual challenge of this wound is to conquer fear by facing it and to espouse the truth of any situation by seeing its reflection not only within oneself but also through the eyes of others.

Summary of Soul Wounds

As can be seen from these five wounds, their source or origin could be explained in terms of parental upbringing although I am more inclined to believe that the pattern lies deeper within the psyche and the childhood simply reflected or drew out the specific wound. Although I have never worked with siblings from the same family and therefore have not been able to compare their experiences, the explanations from my clients about their families suggest that either other siblings responded in very different ways to their upbringing or, alternatively, the parents responded to them in different ways. In the case, already mentioned, of the woman who felt betrayed by her father, it would appear that only she had been singled out for this treatment and her other siblings were still on good terms with him, prior to his death.

In the next section we will go through each of the different wounds in turn with a series of exercises to help their healing. These exercises will first look at the steps required to heal the various moments in your life when you suffered as the *victim* of the wound and the second set will explore those areas where you might be considered the *perpetrator*.

Healing the Wound of Rejection

As already mentioned, those who carry *rejection* as their wound will feel deeply hurt whenever they have been rejected, and in some cases this can lead to the creation of traumatized sub-personalities. The following exercise will show the steps necessary for healing. This exercise is an adaption of the exercise in Chapter 10 (Activity 10:7, see page 241) for healing sub-personalities. It entails a slightly different, and more direct, approach.

Activity 11:2

Theme: *Healing the rejection wound – part 1*

Duration: *10-15 minutes*

1. Find a comfortable chair and then carry out the Body Consciousness Exercise (Activity 9:2, see page 204). Connect to your inner soul essence and then link to your H-S.
2. Ask your H-S to help you remember or recall an instance in your life when you have felt rejected or when your *rejection* wound was activated.
3. Now imagine that the 'you' of today is stepping back into the past to connect with the 'you' of your memory, whatever the age you were at the time.
4. Ask your H-S to help this part and together with your H-S send it a thought of love, light, healing and balance.
5. Remind this sub-personality (S-P) that it has a beautiful light within it (a fragment of your soul consciousness) and that it can have the support and help of your H-S for its healing. Once this part is open to receiving healing, request your H-S, along with your healing guides, to bring it healing.
6. Send and request forgiveness for any aspect of the situation that is relevant. In other words, forgive those who have rejected you and ask for forgiveness for any occasion when you have rejected them.
7. Whatever the scene, change the scenario so that the S-P is brought into a new situation that reverses the original picture, as suggested in the Reframing the Past Exercise (Activity 10:8, see page 245).
8. Once healed, your H-S will allow this part to be reintegrated into your inner soul essence or to return to the H-S.

> 9. When the S-P has been reintegrated or returned to the H-S, ask your H-S to fill all of that part of yourself where the memory resided with a new energy of love, light, healing and balance and to close and seal any doors, openings or windows within your psyche that relate to that situation.
> 10. Lift the whole scene up into the sunlight, requesting that all elements are healed and forgiven.
> 11. Thank your H-S and healing guides and bring yourself back to full waking consciousness.

In the duration of our lives, there could have been a number of incidents when sub-personalities would have been created through the activation of our soul-wound. You may therefore need to carry out the above exercise a dozen times or more to clear all of this wounding. I find in my life now that this trigger is rarely activated but, whenever it is, I request my H-S to highlight the source of the problem, which might be a childhood or past-life situation. I then go through the process of healing the relevant part of myself. This form of healing can then become an ongoing process that is worked through whenever the situation demands. You can always tell when your *rejection* button is being pressed by your emotional triggers to any situation.

Although it is easy to know when we feel rejected, it is often harder to spot when we might be rejecting. Remember this can apply across the whole gamut of one's life. It is not just who we reject but what we reject, such as new ideas, belief systems or ways of doing things. We all, at times, will reject that which does not fit our worldview, yet in this process we should remember the importance of polarities. As soon as I reject something, its opposite polarity becomes part of me, sitting within my *shadow* self. If I do not accept its potential it is then projected onto others. This can be very subtle, causing the stunting of our progress in many different ways. Our H-S is the holder of our life-plan and knows intimately the different elements that we wish to accomplish as part of the current incarnation. By being open and requesting help from your H-S you can fulfil your karmic plan, allowing your guides to engineer the circumstances to bring this about.

The following exercise involves requesting your H-S for specific insight into situations that you might be rejecting.

> Activity 11:3
>
> Theme: *Healing the rejection wound – part 2*
>
> Duration: *10-15 minutes*
>
> 1. Carry out the Body Consciousness Exercise (Activity 9:2, see page 204) and then link to your H-S.
> 2. Request insight and help from your H-S and guides to uncover that which you reject in your life. This can relate to parts of the self as well as to people, ideas and opportunities.
> 3. When the H-S brings forth any insights, which it will inevitably do if you are being honest with yourself, request help to heal and balance the aspect of yourself that is generating the problem. You might be given perceptions about what needs to be done to change this behaviour.
> 4. Make a contract with yourself to begin this process and make a request to your H-S to support you in this.
> 5. Thank your H-S and bring yourself back to full waking consciousness, making sure that you are grounded fully within your body.
> 6. Write down on a piece of paper or type into your computer the steps you need to remember or activate. You can also make an affirmation in line with this perception such as 'I affirm my intention not to reject out of hand any ideas put forward by X'.
> 7. Monitor your progress in line with this intention and try to ensure that it is embedded within you.

In summary, if *rejection* is your soul wound, you will need to keep working on the elements of your psyche that feel rejected as well those that are doing the rejecting. The concept of this being a very deep-seated part of our consciousness suggests that this is likely to be an ongoing process that will continue for the majority of your life. That these elements might continue to return should therefore not be perceived as a surprise or any failure but rather as an aspect of your particular journey.

Healing the Wound of Abandonment

If *abandonment* is your wound, you will probably already be aware of those situations when you have felt abandoned. It is probably worth drawing up a list of those times, arranged either chronologically or in their degree of severity, that you are aware of, such as being abandoned as a child. The next step in the healing process is to connect to each of the sub-personalities that are carrying the wound and to bring them into a place of consciousness. You can then carry out the exercise given in Activity 11.1 (see page 250), replacing the word '*rejection*' with '*abandonment*'.

Two elements should be remembered in this process. The first is that the traumatized sub-personality needs to be brought into a place where it no longer feels abandoned. Effectively you are venturing within to rescue this part of your being and to bring it into a safe and loving space. Secondly, it needs to be reminded that it too has its own inner light and a connection to the H-S. This allows the H-S to connect to the sub-personality and to bring it further healing, rebalancing and enlightenment. Ultimately, this part will either need to be reabsorbed within the soul essence or to return to the H-S if the trauma has been overwhelming. Once the part has been healed, you can then move on to the next remembered event. Eventually, when you have completed all of the remembered moments, you can ask your H-S to bring forward any other situation that you might have forgotten. I have been amazed when working with clients by how often deeply buried memories have come to the surface once the H-S has engaged in the process.

Having completed those areas where trauma resides, the next step entails looking closely at all the times and situations when you have been the protagonist and either have abandoned others or sometimes have needlessly given up projects, plans or ideas. This requires stripping away all of the veneers and beliefs we hold about ourselves and then looking closely at how we operate in the world. Sometimes this needs the help of others, such as a therapist, to reflect back to us those parts of our psyche to which we are blind.

I have found those that hold this wound will frequently start projects and then abandon them partway through. Naturally, there will be times when we need to assess a situation to see whether we like it before making a decision about it. This is very different from the *abandonment* process where there is often an initial enthusiasm for a project or person before it is abandoned just before completion. In extreme cases, most suicides could be seen as an *abandonment* issue. Life gets difficult, so the easiest way of dealing with the problem is to opt out. As with *rejection*, the exercise given in Activity 11:2 (see page 260) will help you to deal with this wound. However, it is important to remember that all these situations need to be anchored in the physical world. If you have embarked on a project and are contemplating giving it up, you will need to think carefully before you act. To heal this wound, we sometimes have to see things through to the end, despite the adversities that get in the way.

Healing the Wound of Abuse

Depending upon your childhood, *abuse* can be one of the hardest of the soul wounds to work through and overcome. Whilst it would be untrue to say that every child born into an abusive family environment will have *abuse* as their soul wound, the two often go together. When this happens the psyche can end up being highly fractured, with a multitude of split-off soul fragments holding the pain and trauma of specific events. When reaching adulthood, individuals who have gone through such traumas will generally find their lives moving into *self-abuse* (drugs, alcohol and other addictions) or abusive relationships. Sometimes this leads to abusing others, such as children. These are not easy issues to deal with and require a great deal of inner healing work to resolve. Of all the soul wounds, the abusive wound requires the greatest level of therapeutic support and help.

For healing to be truly effective, the soul needs to be properly anchored within the body. This is generally focused in the area of the heart. This point of stability allows the soul both to deal with, as well as to integrate, the different fragmentary parts of itself that have become split off into sub-personalities. In *abuse* wounds, the soul, through fear of trauma, generally finds it easier to remain slightly disconnected from the body in a dissociated state. This creates an issue when trying to centre the sub-personalities within the soul essence, as they can end up not being grounded properly within the body. Drug and alcohol addictions only add to these problems.

Healing such cases requires time, patience and effort. Once the core self is balanced within the psyche the process can then be quickened, with the ego boundaries being strengthened and levels of fear reduced. In some cases, it can take a considerable time to reach this threshold, such is the level of trauma. What has proved most helpful in such situations is carrying out regular mindfulness meditation (Williams and Penman, 2011).

Those who have slipped over into being the protagonist in abusive situations are also not easy to help, as the psyche has hardened itself against being hurt and then gains a form of perverted satisfaction in harming others. Such individuals can often find themselves on the wrong side of the law and will not normally desist unless caught. Perhaps, in time, society will be better prepared to spot the potential for *abuse* in childhood and adolescence and then be able to take steps to help such individuals work through their wound before it is expressed in a destructive way towards others.

Research also suggests there might be a genetic component in those who have psychopathic tendencies and that child development is likely to determine whether someone turns out to be an abuser (Blonigen et al, 2005). This area of research is still in its infancy, and genetic and epigenetic patterns may have a part to play. Mainstream psychology and psychiatry are continually searching for solutions to such difficult problems through the fields of genetics, epigenetics and neuro-biology, thereby discounting, or at least ignoring, the spiritual dimension. Past-life patterns or spirit attachment might be involved here.

If you suspect that *abuse* is your wound then using the Activities 11:1 (see page 250) and 11:2 (see page 260) will help, although as these situations begin to come back into full awareness, forgiveness will also be an important part of the process.

Healing the Wound of Betrayal

As with the other soul wounds, the first step is healing those situations where *betrayal* has been felt most keenly. Like *abandonment* issues, these will often stand out in the memory like beacons, full of pain and suffering. They may take the form of one major incident although normally, with a little introspection, many smaller *betrayals* will become apparent. *Betrayal* often feels like a knife in the heart (or back), where all of one's hopes and expectations have been first stored up and then dashed. The pain can be intense because it is often so unexpected. In the process, the heart can become calloused with what is sometimes a powerful urge to get revenge. It is worth reminding ourselves that Dante regarded *betrayal* or treachery as the most serious of crimes and therefore worthy of being placed in the lowest depths of hell (see Chapter 3). In such cases it becomes very easy to identify with the emotions of being betrayed but much harder to ever consider the complementary Judas part of our own psyche that betrays others.

Illuminating the Shadow

Those who have *betrayal* as their soul wound will often need to work extensively on forgiveness as part of the process of balancing these issues. Many years ago, one of my first spirit release clients was a woman who had felt betrayed by her husband. He had unexpectedly left her to live with a younger woman. This had all happened some twelve months prior to her coming to see me. In her case, her murderous rage towards her husband was so intense that she had split off part of her psyche to hold the energy, which now took the form of the spirit of a man dressed all in black who was trying to murder her. The healing of this *shadow* wound necessitated owning this dissociated part and then working fully with forgiveness, which the following exercise encapsulates.

Activity 11:4

Theme: *Forgiveness exercise*

Duration: *10-15 minutes*

1. Light a candle and place it in front of you.
2. Carry out the Body Consciousness Exercise (Activity 9:2, see page 204) and then link to your H-S.
3. Think of the person with whom you wish to work through the forgiveness exercise and ask your H-S to help you link to their H-S.
4. Request the support of your guides, helpers and the Lords of Karma. Invoke the assistance of any other being or deity that you feel might be helpful.
5. Open your eyes and say out loud the following words:
6. 'In the name of the Father/Mother God and the Lords of Karma, I send out forgiveness to [name of person] for the hurt or harm at any level that [he/she] has caused me in this current life and in all previous lives. I release them fully from any negativity ties or bonds to me. Additionally, I revoke fully and completely any curses that I might have laid against [name of person]. So be it, so be it, so be it.'

7. 'In the name of the Father/Mother God and the Lords of Karma, I request forgiveness from [name of person] for any hurt or harm that I have inflicted on [him/her] in this life or any previous life, either consciously or unconsciously and at any level. I request that I be released from any negative ties or bonds to them. I also request that any curse that has been levelled against me, either in this life or any previous life, from [name of person] be now lifted and its energy dissipated. So be it, so be it, so be it.'

8. 'In the name of the Father/Mother God and the Lords of Karma, I request forgiveness from [name of person] for any hurt or harm that I have inflicted on [him/her] in this life or any previous life, either consciously or unconsciously and at any level. I request that I be released from any negative ties or bonds to them. I also request that any curse that has been levelled against me, either in this life or any previous life, from [name of person] be now lifted and its energy dissipated. So be it, so be it, so be it.'

9. 'In the name of the Father/Mother God and the Lords of Karma, I request and send forgiveness to myself, for the hurt or harm at any level that I caused [name of person] in this current life and in all previous lives. I request that this forgiveness flows to all parts of my being. So be it, so be it, so be it.'

10. When the forgiveness words have been spoken, finish by cleansing and clearing your aura using a symbolic flaming sword or any other cleansing symbol, such as a smudge stick, to wash through your aura. You can do this in your imagination by sensing you are sweeping through your auric energy field three times with your chosen symbol. Finally, blow out the candle and thank your H-S, guides and the Lords of Karma for their support.

Because of its emotional intensity it is often hard for those with this soul wound to acknowledge or accept the responsibility for those times and situations when they are the betrayers. In some cases, it might be done as a deliberate act of revenge but often it sits beneath the radar of the mind, seeping out in all sorts of subtle ways. We can betray trust by breaking agreements or confidences and we can betray ourselves when we go against our moral compass or deliberately self-sabotage a project. If you feel that *betrayal* is your soul wound then it is very important to remember that this will never be one-sided, with just you being the victim. The challenge for you is to examine closely all the elements of your life to see where *betrayal* might have operated. If you are unsure, you will need to check this out with your H-S. The key to healing the *betrayal* wound is forgiveness and acknowledging the propensity of the inner opposites of victim and persecutor. We need to learn to stand within the third leg of this triangle as rescuer or healer.

Whilst *betrayal*, in the sense of first building and then dashing expectation, generally starts at some point in childhood, major *betrayals* will often occur in adolescence or adulthood. People whose soul wound is not *betrayal* might experience similar events very differently. An example is the recent case in the UK of teenage girls being groomed for sex, in which a collective *betrayal* was perpetrated by the police and social services by not acting sooner, whilst the betrayed victims would have more likely experienced these acts as *abuse* (Laville, 2015). In this example, it is possible to see how these wounds can also infect groups as well as individuals. Gang rapes are an example of collective *abuse*. This touches on the concept that soul wounds can also infect the collective psyche or zeitgeist of different groups or even nation states.

Healing the Wound of Denial

As already mentioned, this is probably the most challenging of the soul wounds to acknowledge as well as heal. In the case of the sexually exploited children, mentioned above, we can see both *betrayal* and *denial* being perpetrated by different members of the police, social services and councils. It is interesting to speculate on how this might have originated in their lives because, of all the soul wounds, those with *denial* as their primary wound will be driven most by fear. One can see a certain logic to this as a learned response in childhood. If frightened of being caught out for some misdemeanour a child might resort to denying that they had anything to do with the offence and discover that they can get away with it more often than not.

These learned habits can become ingrained so that there is always a tendency within an individual to distort or misrepresent the truth. Effectively the process reinforces the sense of denying the reality of any situation, which can create issues for those who are close to the person, such as colleagues and family members. Their own sense of reality can then feel compromised. The difficulty with this wound is that the immediate response from the denier would be 'What wound?' For those with alcohol problems, the AA programmes encourage individuals to acknowledge first that they have a problem and this is not easy for those with the wound of *denial*. The innate propensity is to bat the ball straight back using a variety of psychological methods.

The power of this wound lies in the fear that first brought it into being. If this is truly a soul wound, that fear will sit in the heart of the person's being, creating its own form of inner paralysis. This may be overt and recognized but, more often than not, it sits well below the surface of the psyche, not daring to be acknowledged or accessed because there is a sense that what lies within is too terrifying to be acknowledged.

If you have read about the five soul wounds but none of them sticks out for you then you might like to consider whether *denial* is your wound. The first step in this process is to consider how you deal with the situations that reflect back on you; in other words, when you are put under the spotlight. Do you own up to the possibility of the reflection, or do you immediately deny it being an aspect of you? Think about the exercise in considering opposites (Activity 7:6, see page 145) – how did you deal with the characteristics you listed in the right-hand column of the table? Were there any times when your initial response was to deny that they could be part of you?

Illuminating the Shadow

When on the receiving end of *denial*, individuals with this wound will often have experienced aspects of their nature being denied in childhood because they have been forced into a particular box of their parents' construction. The spontaneous, carefree child can find itself being regimented by an authoritarian outlook that blocks their ability to relate. They often become introverted and emotionally blocked, finding it hard to make good and lasting relationships. The first stage in the healing process is to work with those incidents that have particularly stood out in childhood as causing a problem – this can be done using Activity 11:1 (see page 250). Once these different periods are healed then the process can begin of looking at how fear seeps through the current life.

Denial as a self-imposed wound places barriers and restrictions around many facets of a life. For instance, the person might feel that they are not worthy to be whole and balanced or do not deserve to be happy, which can impose a terrible burden. These situations are not easy to overcome and often entail a great deal of therapy once an individual has awoken to the fact that they need help. If the *denial* wound is projected onto others there is little hope of any change, unless there can be some self-reflective element.

Ultimately, all wounds stand as a spur to change and growth. It is when we are in the victim position that the greatest insights and propulsion to change can emerge. During these periods our inner demons can surface to haunt as well as taunt us. The repressed elements of the psyche might then emerge with rage and fury about being ignored and blocked. I suspect that many people who feel they are influenced or possessed by spirits have *denial* as their wound.

General Self-help Tips

In the course of our life we normally endure at least one major traumatic incident relating to our soul wound. These situations can be extremely painful and create a great deal of internal stress and disorientation. They can sometimes seem like cataclysmic life-shattering events from which we will never recover, rather like Miss Havisham in Dickens's novel *Great Expectations*. These events challenge us to look deep within to face our internal demons and transform them. In this process we can recover from them, taking many positives from the experience. The following ideas can be helpful in dealing with all major adult trauma incidents relating to the soul wounds:

- Remind yourself that no matter how painful the experience you will get through it in a strengthened way. I have seen many clients achieve amazing things after such traumatic experiences and have gone on to state that this was the making of them. Time is the healer here if opportunities for change are grasped.
- Engage in some physical activity or sport that is new to you, such as jogging, going to the gym, dancing or hill-walking. Many different outlets are available for the more adventurous. The trick here is to push yourself out of your comfort zone and extend the boundaries of what you thought you could achieve.
- Learn to love and accept yourself for who and what you are, and above all learn to acknowledge and sit with your feelings, no matter how scary or disturbing they might be. To truly heal we need to unblock our emotions and allow ourselves to experience them fully. I normally tell my clients to 'feel the feelings', acknowledge them fully, breathe into them, express them and then, and only then, they can breathe them out and let them go by breathing in the opposite emotion. You can do this using colour. If I perceived my rejected feeling as being grey and my feeling of love and acceptance as rosy pink, I can imagine I am breathing out the grey and breathing in the rosy pink to replace it.
- Learn to focus outside yourself by helping others or attending to their needs in whatever way you can. Research has shown that people who volunteer to help others are happier people (Moeller, 2012).
- Write down one thing each day for which you are grateful, no matter

how simple, such as a beautiful sunset. Research has shown that when we do this our happiness indicator is improved by up to 25 per cent (Emmons, 2007).
- Learn something new by taking up a training course in a new field of activity. This might be something you have thought about doing but have never actually done before. Such a step helps you to break out of your current situation and meet new people.
- Try to make sure that you have a good diet by seeing a nutritionist. Psychological trauma causes physical changes in body chemistry. We need to correct imbalances by making sure that we have enough vitamins, minerals and other trace elements in our body.

Summary

In this chapter we have explored the concepts of soul wounds and how these might impact upon our psyche. Clearly, there are different ways that we can categorize or partition the different elements of the self. The concept of soul wounds was new to me when I first heard about them. When I have spoken of this in the classes that I have taught, others have responded to the idea. They have intuitively felt 'a rightness' about it, as I did myself. It has not been possible to validate the concept completely in the sense of being able to track this perceived deep-seated patterning through numerous incarnations. Another possible explanation is that the spirit, prior to incarnation, determines the particular soul wound to explore within the context of that lifetime, with a different wound being selected each time. That it sits within the core of the being within this current lifetime I can validate both from personal experience and through the mindsets of the many clients I have worked with therapeutically.

Certainly, these patterns are reinforced in childhood. When considering the stories relayed to me from my clients it would appear that their siblings responded differently to them and were not afflicted by the same set of issues or problems. In some cases, the parents appeared to behave differently towards each of their children, not just because of their sex but perhaps because they were responding to some deeper pattern, either from past-life karmic interaction or some other innate quality held within. We are complex beings who incarnate into families with their own sets of ancestral patterns. These patterns can hold their own traumas and I have found that specific wounds, such as *abandonment*, can be tracked through the different generations. In these cases, souls perhaps choose to be born into families that mirror their own wounding. Nevertheless, not all siblings or subsequent generations go on repeating these patterns, suggesting that they stick to some but not to others.

In time, further research and insights will either amend or add to these ideas. I know the concept has been helpful in identifying my own wounds and has given me insights into myself and the steps I need to take to heal my inner world. It helped me to realize what I was experiencing when I felt rejected and then to become aware of all that I have rejected. The same is also true with many clients who I have worked with therapeutically over a number of sessions. If you readily identify your wound then I would suggest working with it to see where it leads you.

To sum up:

- Soul wound theory suggests that we each have a specific deep-seated wound that tracks down through a number of incarnations. These can be identified as follows:
  Abandonment, abuse, betrayal, denial and *rejection*.
- When we have identified our own particular wounding we need to consider both its influence within our victim position as well as when we are the persecutor or prosecutor of the wound. In other words, if *betrayal* is your wound, you need to assess and heal those situations where you have felt betrayed as well as those times when you have betrayed either others or yourself.

- Soul wounds generally start to emerge in early childhood but it is unclear whether these patterns continue through a number of incarnations. Dealing with the problems they cause within the current life would appear to be the most beneficial approach to tackling the inner issues that these patterns raise within us.

Chapter Twelve

Into the Light

Hope is like the sun, which, as we journey toward it, casts the shadow of our burden behind us.

Samuel Smiles

Throughout the course of this book we have explored many of the elements that sit within our *shadow*. The intention has been to consider how to bring the *shadow* into the light of consciousness, to see how it operates both in this world and within us. We have explored its expression through literature, film, myth and fairy tale before looking in detail at how it functions. We have then looked at how we can individually work with our own negative *shadow* to heal its imbalances.

It is a journey that has highlighted a number of patterns that flow through the world we inhabit to give us new insight into the meaning of life. A purely mechanistic perception of reality sets limitations on our understanding of the universe, which cannot account for the full range of human experience that embraces a spiritual component to life. A wider theoretical framework than the purely mechanistic one is needed if we are going to construct a model that encompasses all human experience, which is what this book attempts to do.

This work also contests the concept of a static Deity that created the Earth and the universe in a deterministic way, such as the one described in Creationist theories. Effectively, this challenges the viewpoint held by most religions and particularly those of Abrahamic descent relating to Judaism,

Christianity and Islam. In its place it espouses a view of the universe that attempts to see all of the discoveries of science and the scientific method as part of an unfolding drama based on the evolution of consciousness. In this cosmic play all consciousness continues to exist beyond the death of the physical form, experiencing it in what might loosely be defined as a spiritual dimension. In this concluding chapter, we will draw these threads together so they can be identified as a coherent whole.

Free Will and the Experience of Life

When we sit in our garden or in some beautiful part of nature and reflect on what we observe around us we are likely to become aware of a multitude of different forms: the flowers, shrubs, trees, birds and insects each doing their own thing. They are all a beautiful portrayal of the uniqueness and complexity of life. Yet what we see with our physical eyes is but a tiny fragment of the physical life that is within a few feet of us. With the aid of modern technology, science can now discern microbial activity at a microscopic level. It has been estimated that there are around 10,000 distinct bacterial species in a gram of soil (Gans et al, 2005). We might fruitfully and humbly contemplate how many tonnes of earth lie beneath us, and then consider the vastness of life that is all around.

The website Gut Microbiota Worldwatch, which is the public information service of The European Society of Neurogastroenterology and Motility, states that there are tens of trillions of bacteria in our gut – more than ten times the number of cells in the human body. Additionally there are more than '3 million microbial genes in our gut microbiota – 150 times more genes than in the human genome' (ESNM, 2015). The website goes on to outline the evolution of these microbes and the valuable part they play in our life. More significantly, these microbes are not mechanically programmed, as a machine might be, but have an ability to adapt and change according to their circumstances. In other words, they hold a limited free will expression. This is fully in line with the Darwinian model that sees evolution as a fundamental component of the biological world.

With this supporting evidence, this work suggests that the gift of free will is a fundamental component of life and that this concept can be applied to all expressions of human experience. We might then consider all life that we perceive around us as part of a giant computer-like program that continually adds depth and meaning to the universe we inhabit. The one distinction made here is that this program only really makes sense if consciousness itself survives the death of the physical body.

In the already mentioned Douglas Adams' imaginative and humorous novel *The Hitchhiker's Guide to the Galaxy*, we learn that Planet Earth has been deliberately created to discover the 'meaning of life, the universe and everything'. In this tale, in an ironic and comical twist we find out that World, along with its the 3.5 billion-year-old computer program, is mindlessly destroyed to make way for a space superhighway, just a few minutes before the program is completed (Adams, 1995).

Although we are now sending probes to other planets and even contemplating setting up colonies on Mars, it is not beyond the bounds of possibility that the Earth could be destroyed, either by ourselves or by some cataclysmic event before we have moved beyond its sphere. If the mechanistic paradigm is correct and if such an event were to occur, all evolutionary experience would be lost forever. If, on the other hand, all consciousness continues beyond the death of the physical form, then nothing would be lost, only the outer structures changed. As James Lovelock has suggested in his Gaia hypothesis (1989), we might even consider the Earth and all that it contains to be a single conscious organism.

Our planet has undergone a number of extinctions in previous epochs that have seen many species disappear, most notable of which were the dinosaurs. According to MacLeod (2015), some 1000 to 3000 million species are thought to have inhabited this planet in the past, of which only 12.5 million exist today. Extinction of physical types, it would seem, is as natural as evolution. What we now know is that life has the ability to continually adapt whatever environmental challenges it faces. If suitable mutations cannot occur quickly enough, then the particular species will become extinct. This raises the question of whether all mutation is random or whether it has some form of conscious intent behind it.

A number of anomalies in Neo-Darwinism suggest that this might indeed be the case and that random mutations might not quite be random. This was first spotted by Cairns et al (1988) in his experiments with lactose-intolerant bacteria. Cairns went on to state 'We describe here experiments and some circumstantial evidence suggesting that bacteria can choose which mutations they should produce.' This concept was further developed in an article by Goswami and Todd (1997), in which they provided an argument for some of the mechanisms within the quantum realm which might allow this to occur. They concluded their article with the statement, 'The genetic engineer not only requires the toolbox but also consciousness.' The stress here needs to be put on the word 'consciousness'.

In some impressive research into plants and plant adaption, Dr Monica Gagliano and her colleagues from the University of Western Australia, have shown that plants have 'memory'. Working with the mimosa plant she was able to demonstrate that the plant habituated quickly to induced changes in its environment and could then 'remember' the changes more than one month after the original adaption. In a paper in the online journal *Oecologia* (Gagliano et al, 2014) they stated:

> *Plants may lack brains and neural tissues but they do possess a sophisticated calcium-based signalling network in their cells similar to animals' memory processes.*

The significance of this research and similar studies carried out by Gagliano is that it challenges the notion that consciousness requires a 'brain'. Plants do not have brains and yet they display similar abilities to animals in their learned responses and their ability to consciously adapt to their environment.

Several scientific institutions are exploring consciousness in an open way, such as the Rhine at Duke University, the Institute of Noetic Sciences and, in the UK, the University of Northampton. Nevertheless, science as a whole does not yet accept that consciousness can exist independently of the body, which is the case argued here. However, the extinction of a species would cease to be any problem if consciousness is not limited to the body, for the consciousness could adapt into different forms. Within such a paradigm, the life essence of your pet cat could have been a sabre-toothed tiger in a previous existence.

In the age of the dinosaurs, size generally meant everything, with larger and larger species coming into existence. This has provided endless fascination for youngsters contemplating the world in which these giants roamed. Interestingly, since their destruction, new species have not continued to grow bigger, excepting perhaps the great whales, and most species today would be dwarfed by their dinosaur ancestors. I have never found a satisfactory answer to why this might be but perhaps one explanation could be that the consciousness of the Earth learned that size might be a problem in the light of a cataclysm and that in this case 'small' might indeed be beautiful.

Whilst value and meaning can be found in the nihilistic atheistic perspective, its main flaw is that this limited view of life does not embrace all of human experience but denies a significant part of it. The vast majority of people on this planet continue to have, and believe in, meaningful spiritual experiences. What the atheist mindset generally challenges is the outmoded concept of a single Deity that controls and dominates this world. Such a view has every reason to be challenged because many of the tenets of religion are stuck in modes of thinking that are hundreds or thousands of years old. In this process, human beings have projected onto the Creator their own shortcomings and fallibilities, much as the ancient Greeks did with their gods and goddesses.

There is no evidence from modern explorations into the spiritual realm, through hypnosis and direct revelation, that the Divine is anything other than benign. The Creative force from this dimension would appear to be based on light and love. Punishment has no part in this process, only compassion, encouragement, forgiveness and understanding. Religious leaders need to re-evaluate their pronouncements in the light of these findings. Scientists in turn need to take on board the evidence from consciousness studies, such as NDEs and OOBEs, which indicate that consciousness itself can exist independently of the body. For the moment both sides are stuck in their dogmas yet hopefully, in time, bridges can be made between them. If the programme inherent in all life expressions is to go on evolving both within and without the physical body then there is no limit to where this might take us.

If this assumption is correct it explains why the Creative impulse does not, and never will, interfere directly in the world we inhabit. All life is an expression of this impulse and has the free will choice to grow and develop as it so chooses. What I have found from direct experience, working with many clients, is that there is a 'higher dimensional' aspect of our own consciousness that will step in to help when requested. This part appears to have a direct connection with the positive creative impulses of the spiritual world and can bring forward support and help to resolve specific situations. In other words, help is always available when requested although that help does not simply take away a problem if that problem is there for our own learning and understanding. What it will do is help us to work through the issue towards healing and balance.

The expression of the free will gift, no matter how limited it might be, within the evolution of most species has come to the realization that co-operation and symbiosis work much better than conflict and competition. If all systems were continually competing with each other, then life would become an impossibility. Symbiotic collaboration between species is essential for the smooth running of this planet. Think for a moment of all of those microbes working collaboratively within your digestive system. Human beings need to learn to work in mutually beneficial ways with all aspects of Creation and only interfere when the free will gift is misused to the detriment of other individuals or species (Spangler, 2003). As long as its expression does no intrinsic harm to others then it should not be inhibited. Sadly, we humans often fall short of this ideal, both in our conflicts with each other as well as through the mindless destruction of eco systems as a result of many different forms of pollutant, of which plastics are the most insidious.

Working with Polarities

This work has also postulated the concept that polarity is a fundamental component of the universe, suggesting that its expression can be seen in all areas of life. The idea was first proposed by the Chinese sages of old who perceived the world as being held together by two complementary principles known and yang and yin, which are light and darkness respectively. The exploration of these ideas gives both insight and meaning as to why events happen and how easily, at times, we can be pulled from one polarity into another. In practical terms, as soon as we make statements about ourselves, such as 'I am honest', the opposite concept is dynamically held within it. If we do not recognize or accept this, it is projected onto other people and they will carry the projection for us. Effectively, those who cannot acknowledge the part of themselves that is dishonest will be surrounded by people acting in a deceitful way towards them. By working to balance the polarities within us, our psyche eventually reaches a position where there is no need to affirm one polarity or another, but simply to state 'I am', or 'I am, that I am'. We need to learn to understand how polarities operate within our nature by recognizing how they manifest both consciously as well as unconsciously. Into this area comes the *shadow*, which I have defined as having three different modes of expression.

The Shadow

The first definition of the *shadow* is that it is everything that holds our potential for whatever we might become as a seed of unique consciousness that continues to grow through different lives and forms. This is initially limited to the physical realm and then later, if higher inspiration and guidance are to be believed, within states of pure consciousness. In this sense light and dark might be understood as essential components of an evolving universe, where the dark is always the container into which the light grows. In this sense the dark does not represent that which is malign, only that which has not yet come into consciousness.

The second definition of the *shadow* relates to all of those components of our life journey that we have repressed through *fear*, *rejection*, *abuse*, *abandonment*, *betrayal* or *denial*. These elements have generally arisen through trauma and, as part of the journey towards wholeness and balance, we need to bring them into the light of consciousness for healing and redemption. This element of *shadow* work can be very challenging as it entails digging deep into the psyche to understand who and what we are on all levels. Fortunately, life has a way of highlighting these elements for us, through projection and reflection. In the words of Thackeray's *Vanity Fair*:

> *The world is a looking-glass, and gives back to every man the reflection of his own face. Frown at it, and it will in turn look sourly upon you; laugh at it and with it, and it is a jolly kind companion; and so let all young persons take their choice.*

That which is part of our own *shadow* will have a way of seeping out and reflecting back to us those areas still in need of understanding and balance. The way to recognize when things are amiss is by paying attention to our emotions, for these suppressed parts will always hold an emotional charge. When we experience negative emotions such as anger, irritation, hatred and fear, we can be fairly sure that a suppressed sub-personality sits behind them. We need to bring these aspects into the light of full consciousness to be examined, explored and healed.

The last expression of the *shadow* is through all of those elements that we might define as malign or evil. These deliberately go against the flow of the cosmos, at the heart of which, as has been suggested, sits light, love and free will. These three components may be regarded as the 'Holy Trinity' of Creation. The polarity of this trinity is darkness (fear), hate and control. Within the context of the human world we can see examples of good and evil operating in many different areas of the globe. In the twentieth century, the collective impulses of Nazi Germany could be regarded as an explicit manifestation of the malign *shadow* energies. In today's world, some of the extreme elements of Islam express them most fully. However, most governments are not averse to becoming victim to these *shadow* elements and often fall into the trap of projecting onto others what they cannot reconcile within themselves. As soon as I consider myself to be superior to, or better than, another person, then there is a potential for the malign *shadow* to gain a hold. What is relevant for the individual becomes more potent within the collective. Groups that strongly believe themselves to be right will find adversaries in those they consider to be wrong. The challenge we each face is how best to deal with this destructive influence when it expresses itself fully.

The main problem posed by those who wish to collectively give full expression to their *malign shadows* is that such groups generally wish to impose their will on those who reject their ethos. Hitler's regime was not interested in only ruling Germany but wished to inflict its ideologies on others through warfare. The same is true of Isil, which does not appear to want to maintain a status quo within the borders of Syria but to export terror to other lands. Dealing with such a challenge is not an easy task for the United Nations or world governments, which need to work co-operatively to resolve these issues. All sides need to be 'on board' and collective agreements made.

The 'outcomes' of the *malign shadow*, when expressed through individuals in criminal activity, can be tackled through efficient policing. The spiritual, mental and emotional causes could be better understood through the insights that stem from the way the *shadow* moves through us. Additionally, as we have seen, the incitement to hatred and intolerance can also have a corrosive effect on some people and therefore such attempts need to be curtailed. Unfortunately, some religions do not help this process because elements of superiority and separateness are woven into them. We need to remember that all concepts which espouse creativity, compassion and tolerance flow with the cosmic impulses, whilst that which tries to control through fear, hatred and intolerance runs counter to them. Collectively and individually, we need to promote the former over the latter, yet also acknowledge and balance these latter elements as potentials within us. To remember the maxim 'There but for the grace of God go I' and to recognize that in another life and another time we could have been rapists, murderers or tyrants.

The sole reason to inhibit the free will gift should be when it is being used to suppress and control the freedom of others, to prevent all people from leading fruitful and productive lives. Whenever possible, diplomacy and negotiation need to be used, with force only resorted to when there is no other alternative. Those who attack or harm others need to be stopped, to have their weapons removed and to be held until they have been helped to understand the implications of their ways. One of the *shadow* problems that the world confronts is the free supply of guns and bombs by manufacturers whose economic rationale is to sell more of what they have produced.

Through working with my clients I have come to realize that those who have caused others pain in one life have come back into a current life full of suffering. This has been done as a method of expiation for their misdemeanours as well as a recognition that it is when we are in the role of the victim that we can begin to learn true compassion. In all of the cases that I have worked with in this context, nobody felt that it was God who judged them. Quite the reverse; they recognized that they had judged themselves. Christ indicated this principle when he stated 'all who draw the sword will die by the sword' (Matthew 26:52). One might add, 'if not in this life then in another'. Armed force, when used to defend rights and freedoms in the current world, has legitimacy; when used to coerce others it does not.

To give further classification of these three expressions of the *shadow* I have defined them as:

- The *positive shadow*, which is the container of all that we might become
- The *negative shadow*, which holds all that we suppress within our unconscious
- The *malign shadow*, when we operate through fear, ego-inflation and repressive control to inflict pain and suffering on others

These elements, or their potential, sit within all of us. As long as I acknowledge these potentials within me I am not enslaved by them. Christ did not try to destroy the Devil but simply stated, 'Get thee behind me, Satan' (Matthew 16:23). Ultimately, the only way that the *malign shadow* can be transformed within humanity is by each individual learning to acknowledge and embrace that potential within themselves and not to reject it.

The New Directive

In the light of all that has been suggested here we can now consider the ideal of how our lives can be run. The essential element is the need to respect and value the rights of men and women to lead their lives fully and fruitfully, in whatever way they so choose, as long as this does no harm to others. Many of these ideas have already been woven into the rights and freedoms of human laws. The only caveat or restriction should be where there is a greater collective case to be made for a curtailment of this freedom and in these cases the implications need to be thought through carefully. Whilst freedom of speech is important, we also need to be very mindful of how it can be used to incite hatred and intolerance, of which the Nuremberg rallies are a good example. The use of the Internet and global communication has made these aspects more challenging but it should not be beyond the wit and skill of governments to counter such destructive ideas.

Fear, as stated here, sits firmly in the *shadow* side of our being and we all need to take steps to move through and beyond that which causes us fear. It is a great trap and one that can curtail us in so many different ways. Dealing with personal fear is never an easy task because the aspects of ourselves that hold these patterns are stuck in their terror. As part of our own journey to redemption, we need to learn to connect to these elements and bring them into the light of consciousness to be helped and healed.

Despite all that is going on in the world today I am a firm believer that we can move into a place of peaceful and co-operative coexistence, one where we have resolved our negative *shadow* issues and the malign *shadow* is held largely in check. In this process, we also need to learn to love and respect all aspects of Creation, seeking to work with the natural world wherever possible. I acknowledge this is a utopian view, yet not beyond the bounds of possibility if people can awaken to the way that the *shadow* operates through them. It may be that our planet will need to endure further destruction or cataclysm before this state is reached. It may be that we will subject ourselves to more wars before we, as a species, awaken to how we are operating on the Earth. Ultimately, all steps start at an individual level. If I can work to get my house in order there is a hope that my neighbour can do the same. There is an amazing amount of goodwill and courage within humanity that works tirelessly for a better world. Therein lies the hope for the future.

Conclusion

There are dark shadows on the earth, but its lights are stronger in contrast.

Charles Darwin

I would like to finish with a poem I wrote called 'Loving Opposites', which captures the theme of this book.

Loving Opposites

Can we awake from the madness
That divides this world in two?
Can we set free our 'rightness'
To a different point of view?

Free will as a gift has been given
As a sacred God-given right
To all of life's diverse species
That we might grow to the Light.

Yet that which contains no shadows
Remains forever unknown.

Illuminating the Shadow

For contrast gives depth and meaning
Through light and shade and tone.

This gift we all have been given
Is a wondrous two-edged sword,
For we can explore the darkness
Where hatred and fear are stored.

Can the light exist without darkness
Or the day be complete without night?
For opposites balance the fulcrum
In all that is wrong or right.

If a fool persists in his folly
Eventually he will be wise
To the pattern of God's creation
Where awareness has to arise.

For the pain we inflict on others
Will certainly haunt us again
As part of the path to perfection
Where all is held as the same.

If I only accept my light side,
Who carries my fear and shame?
If I only walk on my 'right' side
I must for certain be lame.

If I see myself as a 'good' guy,
Who then do I see as the 'bad'?
If I hold to one thought or system,
Then someone will see me as mad.

Illuminating the Shadow

Our thoughts and our words condemn us
In all that we say or we do.
Whenever I make a statement
The opposite also is true.

Can we find the way to redemption
In this world with its shade and hue?
For tyrant sits within us,
If we but only knew.

My fanatic sits within me,
Waving his rifle and sword.
My dictator stands beside him,
Condemning my every word.

And how do I deal with these monsters
That generate hatred and fear?
Can I learn to love and accept them
As a part of all I hold dear?

When I love my inner traitor,
My terrorist and my thief,
I can find a place for us to live
In harmony and in peace.

When we come to know that opposites
In all of us have to dwell,
We can find a place of balance
In the space 'tween heaven and hell.

When we stop projecting our shadow
Onto those we know must be wrong,

Illuminating the Shadow

We will find the path to redemption
Where all of us can belong.

Can we awake from the madness
That tears this world in two
By pitting us against ourselves
With different points of view?

Light sits within the darkness
And there's darkness in the light.
By dancing with these opposites
We move from wrong and right.

We can awake from the madness
That splits this world in two,
By walking in the shoes of those
With different points of view.

References and Bibliography

Chapter One

- Cameron, B, 2014. *Dr Quantum – Double Slit Experiment*. YouTube. Video. Available from: https://www.youtube.com/watch?v=DfPeprQ7oGcment [Accessed 22 August 2014].
- Casement, A, 2006. The Shadow. In: Papadoulos, R. ed. *The Handbook of Jungian Psychology*. London: Routledge, 94-112.
- Faye, J, 2014. Copenhagen Interpretation of Quantum Mechanics. *The Stanford Encyclopedia of Philosophy*, Fall 2014. Available from: http://plato.stanford.edu/archives/fall2014/entries/qm-copenhagen/ [Accessed 22 August 2014].
- Ford, D, 2001. *The Dark Side of the Light Chasers*. London: Hodder & Stoughton.
- Geddes & Grossett, 2001. *Ancient Egypt Myth and History*. New Lanark: Gresham.
- Johnson, RA, 1993. *Owning Your Own Shadow*. New York: Harper Collins.
- Katie, B, 2002. *Loving What Is*. London: Rider.
- Lao Tzu, 2015. *The Tao*. Based on a translation available from: http://www.thetao.info/english/page2.htm [Accessed 6 October 2015].
- Liu, Z and Liu, L, 2010. *The Essentials of Chinese Medicine, Vol 2*. Springer. Available from: http://books.google.co.uk/books?isbn=1848821123 [Accessed 22 August 2014].
- Marlowe, C, 2009. *The Tragical History of the Life and Death of Doctor Faustus*. Dyce, A. (ed.). Salt Lake City: Gutenberg. Available from: http://www.gutenberg.org/ebooks/779 [Accessed 3 September 2015].
- Penrose, R, 1989. *The Emperor's New Mind*. Oxford: Oxford University Press.

- St John of the Cross, 2003. *Dark Night of the Soul*. Mineola: Dover Thrift Editions.
- *The Bible, King James Version*, 1932. London: Oldhams.
- Williamson, M, 1996. *A Return to Love: Reflections on the Principles of A Course in Miracles*. London: Thorsons.
- Zinser, T, 2011. *Soul-Centered Healing*. Grand Rapids: Union Street Press.
- Zweig, C and Abrams, J, 1991. *Meeting the Shadow*. New York: Tarcher.

Chapter Two

- *Avatar*, 2009. Film. Directed by James Cameron. US: Twentieth Century Fox.
- *E.T. the Extra Terrestrial*, 1982. Film. Directed by Steven Spielberg. US: Universal Pictures.
- Hoffman, M & Critchley, A, (1994). *Swindler's Mist: Spielberg's Fraud in Schindler's List*. York: CODOH. Available from: http://codoh.com/library/document/488/ [Accessed 21 October 2015].
- *It's a Wonderful Life*, 1946. Film. Directed by Frank Capra. US: RKO Radio Pictures.
- Keneally, T, 2006. *Schindler's Ark*. London: Sceptre.
- *Maleficent*, 2014. Film. Directed by Robert Stromberg. US: Walt Disney Studios.
- *Pirates of the Caribbean: The Curse of the Black Pearl*, 2003. Film. Directed by Gore Verbinski. US: Walt Disney Studios.
- *Pirates of the Caribbean: Dead Man's Chest*, 2006. Film. Directed by Gore Verbinski. US: Walt Disney Studios.
- *Pirates of the Caribbean: At World's End*, 2007. Film. Directed by Gore Verbinski. US: Walt Disney Studios.
- *Pirates of the Caribbean: On Stranger Tides*, 2011. Film. Directed by Rob Marshall. US: Walt Disney Studios.
- Rogers, S, 2012. *Census 2011: How Many Jedi Knights are There in England & Wales?* London: *The Guardian*, 11 December 2012. Available from: http://www.theguardian.com/uk/datablog/interactive/2012/dec/11/census-religion [Accessed 9 July 2015].
- *Schindler's List*, 1993. Film. Directed by Steven Spielberg. US: Universal Pictures.
- *Spider-Man 3*, 2007. Film. Directed by Sam Raimi. US: Columbia Pictures.
- *Star Wars: Episode IV: A New Hope*, 1977. Film. Directed by George

Lucas. US: Twentieth Century Fox.
- *Star Wars: Episode V: The Empire Strikes Back*, 1980. Film. Directed by George Lucas. US: Twentieth Century Fox.
- *Star Wars: Episode VI: The Return of the Jedi*, 1983. Film. Directed by George Lucas. US: Twentieth Century Fox.
- *The Avengers*, 2012. Film. Directed by Joss Whedon. US: Walt Disney Studios.
- *The Pianist*, 2002. Film. Directed by Roman Polanski. Distributed by Focus Features.
- *Wife Swap*, 2003-2009. TV. Created by Stephen Lambert, Channel 4.
- Wikiquote, 2015. *Talmud*. San Francisco: Wikiquote. Available from: https://en.wikiquote.org/wiki/Talmud [Accessed 21 October 2015].

Chapter Three

- Brown, D, 2014. *Inferno*. London: Corgi.
- Coleridge, ST, 2014. *The Rime of the Ancient Mariner*. London: Vintage Classics.
- Dante, A, 1883. *The Inferno of Dante*. Translated by Wright, I. Google Books.
- de Beaumont, J-M, 2008. *Beauty and the Beast*. London: Forgotten Books.
- Huxley, A, 1977. *Brave New World*. London: Flamingo.
- Marlowe, C, 2009. *The Tragical History of the Life and Death of Doctor Faustus*. Dyce, A (ed.). Salt Lake City: Gutenberg. Available from: http://www.gutenberg.org/ebooks/779 [Accessed 3 September 2015].
- Orwell, G, 1983. *Nineteen Eighty-Four*. London: Penguin.
- Rostand, E, 1957. *Cyrano de Bergerac*. London: Heinemann.
- Rowling, JK, 1997. *Harry Potter and the Philosopher's Stone*. London: Bloomsbury.
- Rowling, JK, 2007. *Harry Potter and the Deathly Hallows*. London: Bloomsbury.
- Shelley, M, 2003. *Frankenstein*. London: Penguin.
- Stevenson, R, 2012. *The Strange Case of Dr Jekyll and Mr Hyde*. London: Penguin.
- *The Bible, King James Version*, 1932. London: Oldhams.
- *The Lord of the Rings: The Fellowship of the Ring*, 2001. Film. Directed by Peter Jackson. US: New Line Cinema.
- *The Lord of the Rings: The Two Towers*, 2002. Film. Directed by Peter Jackson. US: New Line Cinema.
- *The Lord of the Rings: The Return of the King*, 2003. Film. Directed by Peter Jackson. US: New Line Cinema.
- Tolkien, JRR, 1970. *The Lord of the Rings*. London: Allen & Unwin.
- Tolkien, JRR, 1970. *The Hobbit*. London: Allen & Unwin.

Chapter Four

- Cotterell, A, 1989. *Illustrated Encyclopedia of Myths and Legends*. London: Marshall Editions.
- Delahunty, A and Dignen, S, 2014. *The Oxford Dictionary of Reference and Allusion* (3rd ed.). Oxford: Oxford Reference. Available from: http://www.oxfordreference.com/view/10.1093/acref/9780199567454.001.0001/acref-9780199567454 [Accessed 17 September 2014].
- Esonet, 2015. *The 12 Labors of Hercules and the Path of the Zodiac*. Available from: http://www.esonet.com/News-file-article-sid-175.html [Accessed 14 October 2015].
- Esposito, J, 2014. *The Oxford Dictionary of Islam*. Oxford: Oxford Reference. Available from: http://www.oxfordreference.com/view/10.1093/acref/9780195125580.001.0001/acref-9780195125580 [Accessed 17 September 2014].
- Geddes & Grossett, 1997, *Ancient Egypt: Myth and History*. Geddes and Grossett.
- Goodrich, N, 1994. *Heroines*. London: HarperCollins.
- Graves, R, 1960. *Greek Myths, Vol. 1*. London: Penguin.
- Guirand, F, 1994. *New Larousse Encyclopedia of Mythology*. London: Hamlyn.
- Heaney, S, 2004. *Antigone*. Kindle Edition.
- Jebb, R, 1902. *Antigone by Sophocles*. Cambridge: Cambridge University Press. Available from: http://sacred-texts.com/cla/soph/antigone.htm [Accessed 19 October 2015].
- Masson-Oursel & Morin, 1994. In: Guirand, F. ed. *New Larousse Encyclopedia of Mythology*. London: Hamlyn.
- Mavromataki, M, 1997. *Greek Mythology and Religion*. Chaitali.
- Oxford Dictionaries, 2015. *Myth*. Oxford: Oxford University Press. Available from: http://www.oxforddictionaries.com/definition/english/myth [Accessed 27 October 2015].

- Norwich, J of, 1998. *Revelations of Divine Love*. London: Penguin.
- Tarmio, H, 1985. *Kalevala: The National Epic of Finland*. Werner, Söderström, Osakeyhtiö Publishers.
- *The Bible, King James Version*, 1932. London: Oldhams.
- Tonnelat, E, 1994. Teutonic Mythology. In: *New Larousse Encyclopedia of Mythology*. London: Hamlyn.
- Wilkinson, R, 2003. *The Complete Gods and Goddesses of Ancient Egypt*. London: Thames and Hudson.
- Wolkstein and Kramer, 1983. *Inanna: Queen of Heaven and Earth*. New York: Harper and Row.
- Zinser, T, 2011. *Soul-Centered Healing*. Grand Rapids: Union Street Press.

Chapter Five

- Almond, J and Seddon, K, 1991. *Understanding Tarot*. London: Thorsons.
- Andersen, HC, 2012. *Fairy Tales*. The Planet.
- de Beaumont, J-M, 2008. *Beauty and the Beast*. London: Forgotten Books.
- Furlong, D, 2008. *Develop Your Intuition and Psychic Powers*. Malvern: Atlanta.
- Giles, C, 1993. *Tarot: The Complete Guide*. London: Robert Hale.
- Grimm, J and Grimm, W, 1983. *The Frog Prince*. London: Anderson.
- Legge, J, 1899. *Sacred Books of the East Vol. 16*. Oxford: Oxford University Press. Available from: http://www.sacred-texts.com/ich/ic39.htm [Accessed 12 October 2015].
- McGoldrick, M and Gerson, R, 1985. *Genograms in Family Assessment*. New York: Norton.
- Marshall, S, 2002. *The Mandate of Heaven: The Hidden History of the I Ching*. New York: Columbia University Press.
- Matthews, C, 1869. *The Indian Fairy Book*. New York: Allen.
- Sherrill, W and Chu, WK, 1977. *An Anthology of the I Ching*. London: Routledge & Kegan Paul.
- Wilhelm, R, 1968. *I Ching: Book of Changes*. London: Routledge & Kegan Paul.
- Willis, S, 1991. *Discover the Tarot*. London: Blandford.

Chapter Six

- Adams, D, 1995. *The Hitchhiker's Guide to the Galaxy*. London: Heinemann.
- Alexander, E, 2014. *What Heaven's Really Like*. London: *Daily Mail Online*. Available from: http://www.dailymail.co.uk/sciencetech/article-2797764/what-heaven-s-really-like-leading-brain-surgeon-says-s-read-testimony-scoff-just-shake-beliefs.html [Accessed 1 September 2015].
- Blavatsky, H, 1877. *Isis Unveiled*. Bouton.
- Casement, A, 2006. The Shadow. In: Papadoulos, R. ed. *The Handbook of Jungian Psychology*. London: Routledge.
- Crombie, R, 1976. *The Findhorn Garden*. London: Turnstone Books.
- Dawkins, R, 2007. *The God Delusion*. London: Black Swan.
- de Chardin, P, 2008. *The Phenomenon of Man*. London: Harper Perennial.
- Efstathiou, G, 2103. *Planck Captures Portrait of the Young Universe, Revealing Earliest Light*. Cambridge: University of Cambridge. Available from: http://www.cam.ac.uk/research/news/planck-captures-portrait-of-the-young-universe-revealing-earliest-light [Accessed 29 October 2014].
- Ellenberger, H, 1981. *The Discovery of the Unconscious: The History and Evolution of Dynamic Psychiatry*. Basic Books; Reprint edition.
- Furey, R, 1993. *The Joy of Kindness*. Crossroads Publishing.
- H-A, 1972. *Cosmic Law and the World Today*. Atlanteans Association Ltd.
- H-A, 1976. *Spirit Evolution*. Atlanteans Association Ltd.
- Henry, R, 2005. The Mental Universe. *Nature*, 436:29. Available from: http://henry.pha.jhu.edu/the.mental.universe.pdf [Accessed 26 March 2015].
- Jeans, J, 1930. *The Mysterious Universe*. Cambridge: Cambridge University Press.
- Kardec, A, 2012. *The Spirit's Book*. Spastic Cat Press.

- Kim, J, 1995. Mind-Body Problem. In: Ted Honderich ed. *Oxford Companion to Philosophy*. Oxford: Oxford University Press.
- Moody, R, 1975. *Life After Life*. Mockingbird Books.
- Myers, F, 1903. *Human Personality and Its Survival of Bodily Death*. London: Longmans.
- Newton, M, 1994. *Journey of Souls: Case Studies of Life Between Lives*. St Paul: Llewellyn.
- Newton, M, 2002. *Destiny of Souls: New Case Studies of Life Between Lives*. St Paul: Llewellyn.
- Newton, M, 2004. *Life Between Lives: Hypnotherapy for Spiritual Regression*. St Paul: Llewellyn.
- Palmer, T, 2014. *The Science of Spirit Possession*. Cambridge Scholars Publishing.
- Sartori, P, 2014. *Wisdom of Near Death Experiences: How Understanding of NDEs Can Help Us Live More Fully*. London: Watkins.
- Spector, T, 2012. *Identically Different: Why You Can Change Your Genes*. Kindle Edition.
- Wilkinson, R, 2003. *The Complete Gods and Goddesses of Ancient Egypt*. London: Thames and Hudson.
- Zinser, T, 2011. *Soul-Centered Healing*. Grand Rapids: Union Street Press.

Chapter Seven

- Boffey, D, 2014. Revealed: How Jimmy Savile Abused up to 1,000 victims on BBC premises. London: *The Guardian*. Available from: http://www.theguardian.com/media/2014/jan/18/jimmy-savile-abused-1000-victims-bbc [Accessed: 19 October 2015].
- Bradshaw, J, 1995. *Family Secrets*. London: Piatkus.
- Brooke, C, Tozer, J and Bentley, P, 2014. Why was Killer Even in School? London: *Mail Online*. Available from: http://www.dailymail.co.uk/news/article-2819529/Why-killer-school-Boy-15-stabbed-teacher-death-classroom-posted-repeated-Facebook-threats-murder-her.html [Accessed 10 November 2014].
- Crone, J, 2014. Anne Maguire's Schoolboy Killer. London: *Mail Online*. Available from: http://www.dailymail.co.uk/news/article-2827271/Ann-Maguire-s-schoolboy-killer-tried-talk-girlfriend-Natural-Born-Killers-style-murder-spree.html#ixzz3IdTS0Nc6 [Accessed 8 November 2014].
- Hill, N, 2014. *Think and Grow Rich*. Ebooksoneverything.com. Available from: http://ebooksoneverything.com/wealth/ThinkandGrowRich.pdf [Accessed 14 November 2014].
- Janet, P, 1976. *Psychological Healing: A Historical and Clinical Study*. New York: Arno Press.
- Newton, M, 1994. *Journey of Souls*. St Paul: Llewellyn.
- Newton, M, 2002. *Destiny of Souls*. St Paul: Llewellyn.
- Palmer, T, 2014. *The Science of Spirit Possession*. Cambridge Scholars Publishing.
- Ronson, J, 2014. Could Will Cornick's psychopathic tendencies have been identified before he killed? London: *The Guardian*. Available from: http://www.theguardian.com/society/2014/nov/07/psychopath-test-will-cornick-rurik-jutting [Accessed 10 November 2014].

- Shakespeare, W, 2014. *Hamlet*. eNotes. Available from: http://shakespeare.mit.edu/hamlet/hamlet.3.2.html [Accessed 14 November 2014].
- Steiner, R, 2015. *The Shaping of Human Form Out of Earthly and Cosmic Forces*. Rudolf Steiner Archive. Available from: http://wn.rsarchive.org/Lectures/19201126p01.html [Accessed 17 November 2014].
- Verny, T and Kelly, J, 1982. *The Secret Life of the Unborn Child*. London: Sphere.
- Wallis, L, 2013. *Is 25 the New Cut-off Point for Adulthood?* BBC News Online. Available from: http://www.bbc.co.uk/news/magazine-24173194 [Accessed 8 November 2014].
- Zinser, T, 2011. *Soul-Centered Healing*. Grand Rapids: Union Street Press.

Chapter Eight

- BBC, 2015. *History: Good Friday Agreement*. BBC News Online. Available from: http://www.bbc.co.uk/history/events/good_friday_agreement [Accessed 21 October 2015].
- Beech, H, 2013. Straying From the Middle Way: Extremist Buddhist Monks Target Religious Minorities. New York: *Time*. Available from: http://world.time.com/2013/06/20/extremist-buddhist-monks-fight-oppression-with-violence/ [Accessed 21 October 2015].
- Blair, A, 1994. *Leader's Speech, Blackpool 1994*. British Political Speech. Available from: http://www.britishpoliticalspeech.org/speech-archive.htm?speech=200 [Accessed 25 November 2014].
- Crooke, A, 2014. *You Can't Understand ISIS If You Don't Know the History of Wahhabism*. The World Post. Available from: http://www.huffingtonpost.com/alastair-crooke/isis-wahhabism-saudi-arabia_b_5717157.html?utm_hp_ref=world [Accessed 13 July 2015].
- DrugScope, 2015. *How Many People Die from Drugs?* DrugScope. Available from: http://drugscope.org.uk/how-many-people-die-from-drugs/ [Accessed 19 October 2015].
- Estrin, D, 2010. The King's Torah: a rabbinic text or a call to terror? *Haaretz*. Available from: http://www.haaretz.com/jewish-world/2.209/the-king-s-torah-a-rabbinic-text-or-a-call-to-terror-1.261930 [Accessed 23 November 2014].
- *Exposure: Jihad – A British Story*, 2015. TV. Created by Deeyah Khan, ITV.
- GOV.UK, 2015. *Annual Road Fatalities*. London: Government Digital Service. Available from: https://www.gov.uk/government/publications/annual-road-fatalities. [Accessed 19 October 2015].
- Holocaust Encyclopedia, 2015. *Victims of the Nazi Era: Nazi Racial Ideology*. Washington: United States Holocaust Memorial

- Museum. Available from: http://www.ushmm.org/wlc/en/article.php?ModuleId=10007457 [Accessed 13 July 2015].
- Huey, D, 2014. The US War on Drugs and Its Legacy in Latin America. London: *The Guardian*. Available from: http://www.theguardian.com/global-development-professionals-network/2014/feb/03/us-war-on-drugs-impact-in-latin-american [Accessed 1 December 2014].
- Jacobs, R, 2015. *On Prostitution*. Soul Destruction. Available from: http://soul-destruction.com/on-prostitution/ [Accessed 12 July 2015].
- Jones, O, 2014. David Cameron Warns of Appeasing 'Putin as we did Hitler'. London: *The Guardian*. Available from: http://www.theguardian.com/politics/2014/sep/02/david-cameron-warns-appeasing-putin-ukraine-hitler [Accessed 1 December 2014].
- Krishnamurti, J, 1996. *Commentaries on Living*. Wheaton: Quest Books.
- Mills, K, 2014. Effects of Internet Use on the Adolescent Brain: Despite Popular Claims, Experimental Evidence Remains Scarce. *Trends in Cognitive Sciences*, Vol. 18:8 pp. 385-7.
- Muslims for Progressive Values, 2015. Available from: http://www.mpvusa.org [Accessed 10 September 2015].
- Office for National Statistics, 2012. *Deaths Related to Drug Poisoning in England and Wales, 2011*. Newport: Office for National Statistics. Available from: http://www.ons.gov.uk/ons/dcp171778_276681.pdf [Accessed 19 October 2015].
- Palmer, T, 2014. *The Science of Spirit Possession*. Cambridge Scholars Publishing.
- Pickthall, M, 1938. *The Meaning of the Glorious Quran*. Hyderabad-Deccan: Government Central Press. Available from http://www.sacred-texts.com/isl/pick/008.htm [Accessed 12 October 2015].
- Redmount, CA, 2001. Bitter lives: Israel in and out of Egypt. In: Coogan, M, *The Oxford History of the Biblical World*. Oxford: Oxford University Press.
- Roberts, G, 2014. *What Does the Religion of Peace Teach about Violence?*

- TheReligionofPeace.com. Available from: http://www.thereligionofpeace.com/quran/023-violence.htm [Accessed 25 November-2014].
- Roberts, J, 1995. *History of the World*. London: Penguin.
- SB, 2013. *What is the Difference Between Common and Civil Law?* London: *The Economist*. Available from: http://www.economist.com/blogs/economist-explains/2013/07/economist-explains-10 [Accessed 1 December 2014].
- Spector, T. 2013. *Identically Different: Why You Can Change Your Genes*. London: Weidenfeld & Nicolson.
- Tett, G, 2015. *The Silo Effect: Why Putting Everything in its Place Isn't Such a Bright Idea*. Kindle Edition.
- Wallis, L, 2013. *Is 25 the New Cut-off Point for Adulthood?* BBC News Online. Available from: http://www.bbc.co.uk/news/magazine-24173194 [Accessed 8 November 2014].
- Wikipedia, 2015. *Shadow Banking System*. Wikipedia. Available from: https://en.wikipedia.org/wiki/Shadow_banking_system [Accessed 27 October 2015].
- Zarembo, A, 2013. Many Researchers Taking a Different View of Pedophilia. Los Angeles: *Los Angeles Times*. Available from: http://articles.latimes.com/2013/jan/14/local/la-me-pedophiles-201301115 [Accessed 1 December 2014].
- Zonneveld, A, 2014. *Progressive Muslims in a World of ISIS and Islamophobes*. Open Democracy. Available from: https://www.opendemocracy.net/5050/ani-zonneveld/progressive-muslims-in-world-of-isis-and-islamophobes [Accessed 13 July 2014].

Chapter Nine

- Allison, R, 1974. A New Treatment Approach for Multiple Personalities. American Journal of Clinical Hypnosis, 17:15-32. Available from: http://www.dissociation.com/2007/docReader.asp?url=/index/published/NEWRXMP.TXT [Accessed 16 December 2014].
- Allison, R, 2014. *Dual Personality, Multiple Personality, Dissociative Identity Disorder – What's in a Name?* Dissociation.com. Available from: http://www.dissociation.com/2007/docreader.asp?url=/index/definition/index.html [Accessed 16 December 2014].
- Blavatsky, H, 1889. *The Key to Theosophy*. London: The Theosophical Publishing Society. Available from: http://blavatsyarchives.com/theosophypdfs/blavatsky_the_key_to_theosophy_1889.pdf [Accessed 16 December 2014].
- Furlong, D, 2008. *Develop Your Intuition and Psychic Powers*. Malvern: Atlanta.
- H-A, 1975. *Life Outside the Physical Body, Colour and Reincarnation*. Atlanteans Association Ltd.
- HeartMath, 2014. *Expanding Heart Connections*. HeartMath Institute. Available from: http://www.heartmath.org [Accessed 26 December 2014].
- Jowett, B, 1871, *Apology by Plato*. New York: C. Scribner's Sons. Available from: http://www.sacred-texts.com/cla/plato/apology.htm [Accessed 13 October 2015].
- Khatri, V, 2008. *Dreams and Premonitions*. Mahal.
- Newton, M, 1994. *Journey of Souls*. St Paul: Llewellyn.
- Stein, M, 2006. Individuation. In Papadoulos, R. ed *The Handbook of Jungian Psychology,* 196-214. London: Routledge.
- Zinser, T, 2011. *Soul-Centered Healing*. Grand Rapids: Union Street Press.

Chapter Ten

- Allison, R, 2014) *Dual Personality, Multiple Personality, Dissociative Identity Disorder – What's in a Name?* Dissociation.com. Available from: http://www.dissociation.com/2007/docreader.asp?url=/index/definition/index.html [Accessed 16 December 2014].
- Blavatsky, H, 1889. *The Key to Theosophy*. London: The Theosophical Publishing Society. Available from: http://blavatsyarchives.com/theosophypdfs/blavatsky_the_key_to_theosophy_1889.pdf [Accessed 16 December 2014].
- Ford, D, 2001. *The Dark Side of the Light Chasers*. London: Hodder & Stoughton.
- Furlong, D, 2008. *Develop Your Intuition and Psychic Powers*. Malvern: Atlanta.
- Geoghegan, T, 2009. *What's the ideal number of friends?* BBC News Online. Available from: http://news.bbc.co.uk/1/hi/7920434.stm [Accessed 13 October 2015].
- H-A, 1975. *Life Outside the Physical Body, Colour and Reincarnation*. Atlanteans Association Ltd.
- HeartMath, 2014. *Expanding Heart Connections*. HeartMath Institute. Available from: http://www.heartmath.org [Accessed 26 December 2014].
- Khatri, V, 2008. *Dreams and Premonitions*. Mahal.
- Newton, M, 2002. *Destiny of Souls*. St Paul: Llewellyn.
- Zinser, T, 2011. *Soul-Centered Healing*. Grand Rapids: Union Street Press.

Chapter Eleven

- Blonigen, D et al, 2008. *Psychopathic Personality Traits: Heritability and Genetic Overlap with Internalizing and Externalizing Psychopathology.* PMC. Available from: http://www.ncbi.nlm.nih.gov/pmc/articles/PMC2242349 [Accessed 19 March 2015].
- *Dead Poet's Society*, 1989. Film. Directed by Peter Weir. US: Buena Vista.
- Emmons, RA, 2007. *Thanks!: How the New Science of Gratitude Can Make You Happier*. Boston: Houghton Mifflin Harcourt.
- Emmons, RA and McCullough, ME, 2003. Counting Blessings Versus Burdens: an Experimental Investigation of Gratitude and Subjective Well-being in Daily Life. *Journal of Personality and Social Psychology*, 84(2), 377-389. Available from: http://www.psy.miami.edu/faculty/mmccullough/gratitude/Emmons_McCullough_2003_JPSP.pdf [Accessed 23 March 2015].
- Laville, S, 2015. Professionals Blamed Oxfordshire Girls for their Sexual Abuse, Report Finds. London: *The Guardian*. Available from: http://www.theguardian.com/society/2015/mar/03/professionals-blamed-oxfordshire-girls-for-their-sexual-abuse-report-finds [Accessed 23 October 2015].
- Moeller, P, 2012. *Why Helping Others Makes Us Happier*. US News – Money. Available from: http://money.usnews.com/money/personal-finance/articles/2012/04/04/why-helping-others-makes-us-happy [Accessed 23 March 2015].
- Wilson, A, 1979. *The Wise Virgin*. London: Turnstone.
- Williams, M, and Penman, D, 2011. *Mindfulness*. London: Piatkus.

Abuse

- Crosson-Tower, C, 2009. *Understanding Child Abuse and Neglect*. London: Pearson.
- Herman, J, 1994. *Trauma and Recovery: From Domestic Abuse to Political Terror*. Rivers Oram Press.
- Jones, D and Ramchandani, P, 1999. *Child Sexual Abuse: Informing Practice from Research*. Radcliffe Publishing.
- Levine, P, 1997. *Waking the Tiger: Healing Trauma*. Berkeley: North Atlantic Books.

Rejection

- Pritchard, C, 1995. *Suicide – the Ultimate Rejection?* Open University Press.
- Savage, E, 2002. *Don't Take It Personally!: The Art of Dealing with Rejection*. Lincoln: iUniverse.
- Winch, G, 2013. *Emotional First Aid*. Hudson Press.

Betrayal

- Manette, D, 2005. *Ultimate Betrayal: Recognizing, Uncovering and Dealing with Infidelity*. Square One Publishers.
- Schlessinger, L, 2011. *Surviving A Shark Attack (on Land): Overcoming Betrayal And Dealing with Revenge*. New York: HarperLuxe.
- Yager, J, 2002. *When Friendship Hurts: How to Deal with Friends Who Betray, Abandon, Or Wound You*. New York: Touchstone.

Abandonment

- Anderson, S, 1999. *Black Swan: The Twelve Lessons of Abandonment Recovery*. Partners Publishing Group.
- Anderson, S, 2014. *The Journey from Abandonment to Healing*. New York: Berkley Books.
- Black, C, 2008. *Changing Course: Healing from Loss, Abandonment and Fear*. Hazelden.
- Lynne, C, 2009. *When Daddy Went Away ... A Child's Story of Abandonment*. Createspace.
- Skeen, M, 2015. *Love Me, Don't Leave Me: Overcoming Fear of Abandonment & Building Lasting, Loving Relationships*. Oakland: New Harbinger.

Denial

- Cohen, S, 2000. *States of Denial: Knowing about Atrocities and Suffering*. Cambridge: Polity Press.
- Zerubavel, E, 2007. *The Elephant in the Room: Silence and Denial in Everyday Life*. Oxford: Oxford University Press.

Chapter Twelve

- Adams, D, 1995. *The Hitchhiker's Guide to the Galaxy*. London: Pan.
- Cairns, J, et al, 1988. The Origin of Mutants. *Nature*. 335: 142-145.
- ESNM, 2015, *Everything You Always Wanted to Know About the Gut Microbiota*. ESNM. Available from: http://www.gutmicrobiotawatch.org/en/gut-microbiota-info/ [Accessed 19 October 2015].
- Gagliano, M, et al, 2014. Experience Teaches Plants to Learn Faster and Forget Slower in Environments Where it Matters. *Oecologia*. doi: 10.1007/s00442-013-2873-7
- Gans, J, et al, 2005. Computational Improvements Reveal Great Bacterial Diversity and High Metal Toxicity in Soil. *Science*. 309,1387. Available from: http://www.webpages.uidaho.edu/newton/math501/Fa2007/Dunbar_Science.pdf [Accessed 25 March 2015].
- Goswami, A and Todd, D, 1997. Is There Conscious Choice in Directed Mutation, Phenocopies, and Related Phenomena? An Answer Based on Quantum Measurement Theory. *Integrative Physiological and Behavioral Science*, April-June 1997, Vol. 32, No. 2, 132-142.
- Lovelock, J, 1979. *Gaia: A New Look at Life on Earth*. Oxford: Oxford University Press.
- MacLeod, N, 2015. *The Great Extinctions: What Causes Them and How They Shape Life*. Richmond Hill: Firefly.
- Rettner, R, 2009. How Dinosaurs Got So Big. Live Science. Available from: http://www.livescience.com/5527-dinosaurs-big.html [Accessed 28 March 2015].
- Spangler, B, 2003. Competitive and Cooperative Approaches to Conflict. Boulder: *Beyond Intractability*. Available from: http://www.beyondintractability.org/essay/competitive-cooperative-frames [Accessed 28 March 2015].
- Thackeray, W, 1992. *Vanity Fair*. Ware: Wordsworth.

Chapter Head Quotations

All chapter head quotations have been accessed through BrainyQuote online using the keywords *shadow or shadows*. Available at: http://www.brainyquote.com

Useful Addresses

David Furlong
Email: atlanta@dial.pipex.com
Web: www.davidfurlong.co.uk

Dr Terence Palmer
Email: palmert55@gmail.com
Web: www.tjpalmer.org

Dr Tom Zinser
Web: www.soulcenteredhealing.net

College of Healing
Tel: 01684 577558
Email: info@collegeofhealing.org
Web: www.collegeofhealing.org

Spirit Release Forum
Tel: 07779 789047
Email: spiritrelease@dsl.pipex.com
Web: www.spiritrelease.org

Endnotes

1. The eight characters are as follows: Jesus of Nazareth. Akhenaten who was an Egyptian king who ruled in Egypt from 1353–1336 bce. The white winged horse Pegasus who was born from the head of the Gorgon Medusa and represents transformation. Thoth is one of the teaching gods from ancient Egypt and equates with the ancient Greek god Hermes and the Archangel Raphael. The White Owl, who can travel in the underworld, is a messenger of the gods and has access to all that is hidden. The Lady of the Lake comes from Arthurian mythology and relates to inner reflection and psychic wisdom. Kwan Yin is the goddess of mercy from ancient China and equates with all Divine Mother goddesses. Hathor is the ancient Egyptian goddess of joy, happiness and healing.

Index

abandonment 141, 157, 243, 250, 253, 260, 254-6, 263, 264, 266, 274, 283, 311
Aborigine 27
Abrahamic 174, 189, 276
abuse 6, 18, 141, 151, 157, 166, 168, 213, 216, 250-1, 254-6, 264-6, 269, 274, 283, 302, 310
  sexual 134, 137, 151, 165, 309
  drug 168
  self 265
abusers 6
Adam 3, 63, 74
Adams, Douglas 113, 278, 300, 312
Admetus 78-79, 21
adoption 254
Aesir 63-4
afterlife 3-4, 61, 108, 121, 181-2
Ahriman 64-5, 67
Akhenaten 233, 314
Alcestis 77, 78-80
Alcoholics Anonymous (AA) 168, 201
Alexander, Dr Eben 118, 119, 121, 300
Allah 110, 186, 187
Allison, Dr Ralph 195-6, 307
alters 9
al-Wahhab, Muhammad Ibn Abd 185-6
Amritsar 189
Ancient Mariner 50, 296
Andersen, Hans Christian ix, 95, 299
anger xvii, xviii, xx, 4, 5, 10, 13, 16, 24, 29, 37, 54, 60, 65, 90, 129, 142, 144, 153, 177, 201, 229, 231, 237, 238, 284
anima xvi, 28
animus xvi, 28
anorexia 255
Antigone 80-2, 297

Anubis 90
Apache 34
Aphrodite 99
Apollo 78, 80, 213
Apophis 60-2
Aquarius 90
  Age of 75
Arabs 177
Aragon 43
Arc, Joan of 72, 220
Arcana 89
archetype 102, 225, 247
Ares (Greek god) 82
Arwen 43
Aryan race 30, 176
Assad, President 181
asuras (Hindu) 67
Atheism 83
atheist xxii, 115-6, 183, 280
Athene 65, 73, 74, 76
Athos, Mt. 184
Atlas 75, 76
Aurora, Princess 28, 29
Avatar 26-8, 67, 294
bacteria 277, 279, 312
Bailey, George 33
Balder (Teutonic god) 64
Balrog 43
Barad-dûr 42
Beowulf 72
betray (ing) 6, 28, 29, 63, 157, 257, 266, 269, 276
betrayal 53, 64, 141-2, 157, 250, 256, 266, 267, 269, 274, 274, 283, 310
betrayers 6, 268
bigotry 112
Baggins, Bilbo 42
  Frodo 42, 43
bipolar 12, 86

Blake, William 107
Blavatsky, Madame Helena 122, 197, 300
Bond, James 25
Botticelli 52
Bradshaw, John 148, 302
Brown, Dan 52, 296
Brutus 53
Buddha, Gautama 21, 67, 73, 74
Buddhism 67, 183, 189
bulimia 255
Bylebog 67
Byron, Lord 46
Caesar, Julius 53
Capra, Frank 33, 294
Cassius 53
Catholic 183, 188
Celestial Sisters 99
Chardin, Pierre Teillard de 120, 300
Chernobog 67
Christ, Jesus xx, xxiv, 53, 61, 62, 73, 79, 99, 286
Christendom 4
Christian 3, 4, 54, 61-4, 67, 87, 153, 175, 176, 182, 189
Christianity 61, 65, 67, 112, 183, 188, 189, 277
Church, Roman Catholic 183
Churchill, Winston 220, 221
Cold War 172
Coleridge, Samuel, Taylor 50, 296
collective ix, x, xviii, xx, xxi, 19, 27, 47, 54, 61, 107, 109, 110, 125, 129, 132, 137, 159, 160 -1, 165, 167, 169, 170, 173, 175, 179, 182, 189, 191, 215, 252, 269, 284, 285, 287
human 159
psyche xx, xxii, 8, 20, 45, 269
scientific 83
social 165, 167
shadow see Shadow, collective
world 162, 235
Comanche 34
Commission, Truth and Reconciliation 154

complementary 11, 17, 131, 168, 181, 183, 266, 282
Cornick, Will 151, 152, 302
Cosgrove, Toby 171
cosmology 58, 103, 124
cosmos xvi, xxii, 10, 11, 19, 132, 284
countertransference 6
Creation xxi, 3, 222, 276, 282, 284, 287
Creative Intelligence 109, 125, 187, 196,
Creator 124, 125, 198, 200, 222, 281
Creon 80-2
criminal 148, 166, 167, 189, 190, 285
criminal fraternity xiv, 165
Croft, Lara 25
Crombie, Robert Ogilvie vi, 119, 120, 300
Crusades 175, 188
Cuchulainn (Celtic hero) 72
Cyrano de Bergerac 48-50, 296
Dahka, Azhi (demon) 65
damnation 4, 41, 54, 130, 184
Dante 52-4, 266, 296
dark xvi, 4, 15, 19, 45-6, 70, 93, 134, 184, 283, 288, 292
angel 4,
Lord 23, 24, 42-5
matter xiii, 110
night of the soul 19, 293
side xiii, xxii, 10, 15, 23-4, 42, 188, 194, 230, 308
spot 70, 129
darkness ix, x, xiii, xxii, 3, 7, 11, 15, 17, 42, 60, 62, 67, 124, 128-9, 282, 284, 289, 291
Prince of, 61
Darth Vader 23-4, 30, 213
Darwin, Charles 109, 112, 116, 122, 131, 288
Darwinism 109, 112, 115, 131, 278
Neo 289
Davison, Annie 141, 249
Dawkins, Richard ix, 83, 110, 112-6, 122, 128, 130, 183, 300
death xiv, xix, 4, 20, 24, 28, 29, 40, 42, 46, 47, 49, 50, 54, 64, 71-3, 80-3,

90, 108, 109, 113-8, 121, 180, 189, 242, 244, 253, 259, 277-8, 292, 296, 301-2, 305
fear of 83, 155, 185
near death experience see NDE
penalty 80, 153
deity 60-1, 64-5, 82, 107-8, 110, 112, 267, 276, 280
Demeter 68-70
demons xx, 41, 56, 61, 63, 65, 74, 213, 271-2
denial x, xi,
soul-wound 141, 157, 250, 257-8, 269-71, 274, 283, 311
depression 12, 86, 231
Descartes, Rene 114
devas (Hindu deities) 67
Devil 15, 41, 56, 61, 63, 89 -91, 258, 286
Dickens, Charles 48, 272
dimension
spiritual 107, 109, 111, 198, 266, 277
Divine, The xxiii, 19, 90, 112, 119, 125-6, 129, 131-2, 184, 187, 196, 203, 222, 281, 298, 314
divorce 253, 256
DNA 138, 183
dream world 8, 211, 235
drugs xi, 153, 166-8, 185, 190, 265, 304-5
abuse 168
addiction 168
dualism 114-5
Ea, (Assyro- Babylonian god) 66
Eden, Garden of 3
ego xix, 5, 7, 8, 9, 25, 30, 44, 48, 93, 127, 130, 177, 217-8, 220-1, 223, 241, 254-6, 265, 286
state 9, 139, 157, 248, 254
Egypt (ian) 3, 57-64, 87, 90, 103, 108, 124, 129, 174-5, 223, 232, 292, 297-8, 301, 305, 314
Einstein, Albert 110
Eleusis 69
embryo 9
enmity xviii, 47, 64

envy 215
Éowyn 43,
epigenetic 126, 138, 183, 266
Ereshkigal 70, 71
E.T. 25-6, 294
Eve 3, 61, 74
evil xiv, xxii, 3, 4, 7, 8, 12, 19, 24-5, 42, 44, 48, 56, 58, 60-7, 74, 82, 88-9, 129, 137, 151-2, 189, 258, 284
evolution xxii, 46, 109-113, 115-6, 121-2, 125- 7, 131, 132, 137, 139, 153, 161, 172, 182-3, 185, 216, 277-9, 282, 300
Darwinian 109, 115
Exercise
Body Consciousness 204-5, 208, 210, 219, 223, 235, 237, 239, 241, 245, 247, 260, 267
Experience
Near Death see NDE
Extremism 108
Eywa 27
Falkland Islands 178, 179
Faustus, Doctor 4, 40, 41, 292, 296
fear xv, xxii, 4, 7, 10, 16-9, 23-4, 27, 30, 31-3, 42, 44-5, 48, 54, 61-3, 69, 71-2, 74-5, 77, 83, 93, 95, 129, 130, 140, 142, 147, 148, 155, 157, 159, 164, 165, 167, 176-7, 184-6, 191, 201, 211-6, 223, 230-1, 244-5, 247, 254, 257-8, 265, 270-1, 283-90, 311
Findhorn vi, 119, 120, 300
force
benign 109
guardian 31
life 109, 127, 138, 216-7
malign 25, 74
military xviii
spiritual 55, 57, 62
supernatural 56
Ford, Debbie vi, 10, 236, 292, 308
forgiveness 17, 72, 95, 103, 112, 140, 154, 188, 190, 197, 241, 260, 266-9, 281
Forster, E.M. 195
Frankenstein 46-7, 296

free will xix, xxi, 9, 63, 109, 122-5, 128-9, 132, 153-4, 156-8, 161, 163-4, 166, 173, 176, 179, 188, 198, 200, 201, 217, 222, 228, 252, 277-8, 281-2, 284-5, 288
Freud, Sigmund 4, 5, 15, 80
Frog Prince (Fairy Tale) 95-6,
fundamentalism x, 185, 188-9
Gaddafi, Colonel 181
Gagliano, Dr Monica 279-80, 312
Gaia 65, 75-6
hypothesis 279, 312
Galadriel 43,
Gandalf 30, 43-4
Geb 58
Gerod – spiritual guide 124-6, 129, 197
Ghandi. Mahatma 220
Ghetto. Warsaw 30
Gibraltar 178-9
Gilgamesh 72
Gimli 43
God xxii, xxiv, 7, 15, 50, 52-3, 61-2, 90, 107, 108, 110, 112-3, 121, 125-6, 174, 176, 184, 199, 200, 222, 267-8, 285-6, 288-9, 300
Goeth, Amon 32
Gollum 42, 43
Good Friday Agreement 190, 304
Gothic , Victorian 46
Granger, Hermione 45
Great War 155
greed 5, 23, 27, 32, 45, 53, 92-3, 167
Grendel 72
groups, tribal 161
guidance xix, xxiii, 24,125, 198-9, 216, 220-1, 223, 283
guilt xxii, 19, 82,148,155,197
H-A, Spiritual guide, 124-6, 216, 300, 307-8
Hades 68, 69,73,79
Hall of Judgement 3
Hanged Man, Tarot card 14-5, 90
Hanuman (Hindu diety) 67
Harry Potter 44, 296
hate 12, 135, 146, 163, 169, 186, 284
Hathor (Egyptian goddess) 90, 233, 314
hatred xx, 5, 13, 23-4, 29, 37, 47, 54, 62, 64-6, 129, 142, 152-3, 159, 177, 184, 187, 196, 228, 231, 284
religious 180, 187-8, 191, 285, 287
self 95
tribal 180-1
healing xix, xx, xxii, 6,19, 20, 70, 140, 143,156, 184, 195-7, 201-2, 204, 206, 211-6, 221, 225, 230, 232, 237-8, 240-4, 246, 248, 252, 256, 258, 259-67, 269, 271, 281, 283, 302, 310-1, 313-4
self xx, 141, 216
soul-centred 123, 140, 293, 298, 301, 303, 307-8
spiritual 189
health 40, 124, 134, 139, 172, 177, 200, 222, 232
mental xi
National H Service 147
psychological 18, 169
HeartMath, institute 223, 307-8
Heliopolitan 58, 68, 90,103
Helios (Greek god) 69
Henry, Richard Conn 111, 300
Hera (Greek goddess) 65, 75, 76
Heracles (Greek hero) 65-6, 72,75-7, 79, 80
Hercules See Heracles
heresy 53
Hermes (Greek god) 73, 314
hero (es) xxiii, 17, 23-5, 27, 30, 48, 50, 56-7, 65, 71-9, 81-2, 92, 148, 232-3
anti 25, 48
heroine (s) 17, 23, 56, 77, 82, 97, 232-3, 297
Journey 17, 92
super 24-5, 37,225, 232-4, 239-40, 245-8
worship 5, 6
higher power xix,xxii, 135, 202,220, 241
Higher-Self. See H-S
Hill, Napoleon 150, 302
Hillsborough, Accord xviii, 190, 304
Hindu 65, 67, 121, 189

Hinduism 183
Hitler 148, 180,185, 284, 305
Holocaust 32, 176, 304
Holy Trinity 87, 284
homeostasis xvi
homophobia 163
Horus (Egyptian god) 59, 60, 87, 90
Hosenfeld, Wilm 31
H-S (Higher-Self) xxiii, 135,137-8, 140,154, 156-8, 195-224, 230, 233, 235-42, 244-7, 256, 260-4, 267, 269
humanity x, xx, xxii, 31-2, 36, 38, 47, 54, 69, 76, 107, 111, 124, 163, 175, 178, 215-6, 286, 288
Human Rights, declaration of 161,163
Hunt, William Morris 159
Hussein, Saddam 181
Huxley, Aldous 48, 296
Hyde, Mr 45-6, 296
Hydra 76, 77, 184
hypnotherapist, 122-3
hypnotherapy 121, 301
Iblis (Islam) 63
I Ching 11, 83, 84, 85-90, 102, 299
Inanna (Sumerian goddess) 70-2, 298
Inferno, Dante 52-4, 296
inner
characters 8, 213, 216 227, 232, 234-8, 248
child 26, 212, 228, 243
monsters xx, 213, 229, 290
intolerance 112, 130, 181, 187, 191, 285, 287
Iraq War 181
Ireland, Northern xviii, 188, 190
Iron Man 25
Iscariot, Judas 53
ISH (inner self-helper) 196
Isil (Caliphate) 181, 186, 285, 304, 306
Isis (Egyptian goddess) 58, 59, 68, 87, 90, 300
Islam 63,112, 175-6, 178,183, 185-9, 277, 284, 297, 306
Islamic 3, 177, 182, 185, 186,
Islamists 185
Israel 33, 174,177, 305

Israelis xviii, 174, 176-8
James, William 4
Janet, Pierre 139, 302
jealousy 5, 142, 231
Jeans, Sir James 111, 300
Jeddah 186
Jedi Knight 23, 24, 294
Jekyll, Dr 45-6, 296
Jesus 46, 61-2, 122, 233, 314
Jewish 30, 32, 174-6, 178, 304
Jews 20, 32, 47, 175,177
Jihad(ist) 155, 185, 187-8, 304
jinn 63
Job (bible) 62
Jonestown, massacre 176
Judaism 65, 112, 183,189, 276
Judas see Iscariot
Judgement
Day of 182
Halls of 223
Jung, Carl vi, xiii, xiv, xvi, xxi, 3, 4-6, 18, 220, 292, 300, 307
Kalevala 56, 298
K'an, (Chinese trigram) 88
Kardec, Allan 122, 300
Katie, Byron 13-4, 136, 146, 292
Keneally, Thomas 31, 294
Kenobi, Obi-Wan 24
Khan, Deeyah 187, 304
Kore see Persephone
Kosovo 180, 181
Kun (Chinese trigram) 88
Kwan Yin (Chinese goddess) 233, 314
Lady, of the Lake (Arthurian) 233, 314
Lascaux, Caves of 21
Legolas 43
Leia, Princes 23
light ix, x, xiii, xiv, xvi, xix, 4, 7, 10-1, 15, 17, 19, 24, 34, 36, 39, 42, 46, 48, 55, 57, 61, 62, 67, 71, 74,77, 107, 110, 112, 114, 117, 124-5, 129, 132-4, 140, 149, 153,159, 165, 167-8, 177, 184, 190,195, 201, 202-3, 205-7, 212-5, 219, 220, 225, 231, 237, 239, 241, 244, 247, 260, 263, 267, 276, 280-4, 286-9, 291

Loki (Teutonic god) 25, 63-4
Lonnrot, Elias 56
love xix, xx, 3, 12, 16-7, 18, 20, 26, 28, 29, 30, 37, 43, 47-52, 65, 68, 70, 72, 76-7, 79-80, 82, 83, 92, 95-101, 103, 109, 112, 116, 120, 121,125,129, 132, 140, 148-9, 155, 184, 187-8, 190, 196, 212, 215, 222, 239, 241, 244, 246, 252, 260-1, 272, 281, 284, 287, 290, 293, 298, 311
Lovelock, James 278, 312
Lucifer vi, xxii, 4, 41, 53, 61-2
Lugh (Celtic god) 72
Luke see Skywalker
Maat (Egyptian goddess) 60
Madonna (Mother of Jesus) 233
Major, John 147
Maleficent 28-30, 92, 294
Mandela, Nelson 154
Marduk (Assyrian god) 66,
Marlowe, Christopher 4, 40, 292, 296
Mary, Virgin 184
Master Race 176
Mazdah, Ahura (Zoroastrian) 64, 67
Mecca 186
Medina 186
Medusa, Gorgon (Greek) 73-75, 97, 314
mental illness xi,
Mephistophilis (Dark angel) 4, 41
Middle East x, 16, 175,
Milosevic, Slobodan 180, 181
mindlessness, sin of 74
Mohammed (Islamic prophet) 186, 187
monsters see inner monsters
Moody, Raymond 117, 118, 301
Myers, Frederic 4, 117, 122, 152, 301
Nations, United 161, 179, 180, 285
Na'vi 27, 28
Nazi regime xviii, 32-3, 46
Nazi Germany 20, 30, 47, 175-6, 185, 284, 304
NDE (near death experience) 117, 118, 121, 218, 300, 301
Neate, Tony (Channeller) 124
necromantic 41
Nephys 58, 90
Newton, Dr Michael 122-4, 139, 154, 217, 244, 301, 307-8
Neytiri 28
Nightingale, Florence 233
NLP (neuro-linguistic programming) 244
Norwich, Julian of 56
Nuremberg rallies 287
Nut (Egyptian goddess) 58
OCD (obsessive compulsive disorder) 7, 133
Oedipus 80
O'Malley, Austin 55
opposites 12, 19, 35, 44, 82, 99, 102,110, 132, 146-7, 161,163, 269-70, 289, 290-1
balance of xvi, 54, 60
Orwell, George 48, 296
Osiris (Egyptian god) 3, 58, 60, 68, 87, 90
paedophile 165, 215, 306
paedophilia 166, 306
Palestine 174, 177-9
Palestinian xviii, 174, 177, 178
Palmer, Dr Terence vi, ix-xi, 117, 152, 166, 301, 305, 313
Pan (Greek god) 119
Pandora 27-8, 74
paradigm xiv, 280
mechanistic 57, 107, 278
scientific 11
paradox xiv, 10-11, 23, 61, 110, 112, 114, 126, 137
past-life 128, 138, 154-5, 242, 249, 266, 274
Paul, St. 56
Pegasus (Greek) 74-5, 232-3, 314
pendulum 6, 19
persecutor 6, 169, 176-7, 238, 253, 269, 274
Persephone 69-70
Perseus (Greek hero) 73-4
Psychical Research, Society for 117, 122

physical
body xxi, 9, 90, 109, 114, 116, 122, 132, 137, 200, 204-5, 218-9, 221-2, 278, 281, 307-8
life xxii, 102, 200, 277
science ix, x, 23, 107, 116
world 57, 60, 82, 90, 99, 119, 132, 264
physics, Newtonian 11, 107, 111
Pirates, of the Caribbean 25, 294
Pisces, Age of 75
Plato 121, 220, 292, 307
Plutarch 84
polarity xvii, 10-12, 20, 30, 44, 54, 57-8, 67, 71, 82, 87, 92, 97, 110, 142, 144, 159, 163, 175-6, 183-4, 226, 234, 237, 261, 282-4
Poseidon (Greek god) 73
possession 120, 138-9
spirit xi, 152, 255, 301-2, 305,
Prodigal Son 46
projection xvii, xx, 5-6, 13-4, 20, 47, 74, 110, 163, 165, 176, 179, 181, 229, 282-3
Prometheus 75, 76
prostitution 164-5, 190, 305
Protestant 207
psi x
psyche xiii, xv, xvi, xix, xx, xxii, 4-10, 12-3, 19-20, 24-6, 30, 36, 43-6, 48, 50, 53-4, 61-2, 68-71, 74, 77, 82, 84-5, 87-9, 91, 93-5, 99, 102-3, 131, 133-5, 138-44, 148, 156, 176, 182, 191, 195-7, 201, 210-2, 214-7, 223-5, 227-9, 232, 234-5, 240, 243, 246, 250-1, 253-7, 259, 261, 263-7, 269-71, 272, 282-3
psychiatry xi, 266, 300
psychic x, xix, 9-10, 56, 89 90, 140, 201, 221, 226, 299, 307-8, 314
psychology xi, 4, 82, 117, 197, 266, 292, 300, 307, 309
transpersonal 249
Pythagoras 121, 133, 151, 233
quantum mechanics x, 11, 110-1, 114, 202, 279, 292, 312
Quran 185-8, 305-6

Ra see Ra-Atum
Ra-Atum 58, 124,129
Race see Master Race
Rajneesh 176
Rakshasas 67
Rama (Hindu deity) 67
Ravana (Hindu deity) 67
realm, spiritual 90, 102, 108, 122, 125, 128, 131-2, 156, 197-8, 200, 217-8, 221, 281
rebirth 121-2
referendum, Scottish 173
reincarnation 121-2, 307-8
rejection 5, 47, 116, 122, 129
soul wound see soul wound
religion (s) 23-4, 58, 107-8, 110, 112, 115-6, 128, 130, 153, 174, 176, 181-4, 187, 189, 191, 276, 281, 285, 294, 297, 305-6
Revolution. French 154
revulsion 142, 147, 157-8, 164, 212, 215
Rider-Waite 15, 84
Ringwraiths 42
roller coaster 12
Rostand, Edmond 48, 296
Rowling, JK 44-5, 296
Rwanda 180
sadnes 12-3, 16, 37, 231, 234
Sahasrara, chakra 202
Salafism 186
Sarajevo 180, 181
Sartori, Dr Penny 118, 301
Saruman 43-4,
Satan 61-2, 65, 67, 286
Saudi Arabia 186
Sauron 42
Savile, Jimmy 137,165, 215, 310
Schindler, Oskar 30-3, 294
science
physical ix, x, xi, xiii, 23, 25, 30, 34, 44, 48, 57, 107, 112, 114, 116-7, 121, 127, 131, 138, 152, 175, 182-3, 277, 280, 301-2, 305, 312
spiritual 127, 156, 309
Scully, Jake 27, 28

War, Second World 20, 30, 150, 180
self-abuse 255, 265
Self Helper see ISH
Seth 58-60, 62, 90, 102
sexual abuse 134, 151, 165, 309-10
shadow
  collective xxii, 48, 137, 159-60, 181, 189, 190
  cosmic xxi, 20, 42, 83, 91, 103, 107-10, 132, 137
  dark 46
  malign xviii, 7-8, 19, 25, 30-2, 44, 88, 129-30, 132, 151, 157-8, 160, 167, 175, 177, 181, 184, 189-90, 284-7
  negative xiv, xv, xx, 16, 19, 23, 36, 45, 54, 67, 71, 129, 133, 135, 137, 140, 142, 150, 157, 164, 167, 169, 191, 195, 206-9, 210, 212, 216, 228, 235, 238, 276, 286, 287
  personal xv, 4, 16-7, 20, 133, 157, 232
  positive xiii, xv, 5, 6-7, 16, 19, 54, 71, 129, 134, 147, 150, 157, 207-8, 286
  projected xv, 5, 11,19, 25, 82, 136,146, 150,157,159,163,167,170,177,
  rejected 7, 95, 99
  reviled 215
Shakespeare, William 38, 48, 118, 147, 303
shame xi, xxii, 18-9, 148-9, 155, 231, 249, 289
Shaytan 63
Shelley, Mary 46, 296

Shia, (Islamic sect) 181, 187
Shu (Egyptian god) 58,124
Sikh 189
Sinnet, AP 197
Sith 23
Skywalker
  Anakin 24 (see also Darth Vader)
  Luke 23-4
sloth 53, 215
Sméagol 42
Smiles, Samuel 276
Snow Queen (Fairy Tale) 95, 97-8
sociopath 82

Socrates 151, 220
soul xiv, 3-4, 9, 19, 41-2, 50-1, 53-4, 57, 60, 64, 66, 69-70, 74, 77, 81-3, 90, 92, 95, 122-9, 131-2, 137-40, 152-4, 156-8, 182, 195-7, 199, 200, 201, 205, 213, 214, 216, 218, 220, 223-4, 228, 241, 244, 249-50, 260, 263, 265, 274, 293, 298, 301-3, 305, 307-8, 313
  fragment 9, 214, 218, 248
  wound 141-2, 249-52, 254, 257-9, 262, 263-75
Sparrow, Jack 25
Spider-Man 24, 25, 294
spirit (s) xi, xiv, xiii, 3, 27, 64, 66, 82-3, 90, 109, 115, 120, 122, 124-5, 129, 132, 152-3, 158, 183, 199-201, 203, 217, 222, 224, 228, 240, 273, 300
  attachment 152, 266
  evil (malevolent) 42, 166
  guide 129, 249
  realm 83, 153
  release 267, 313
  possession xi, 152, 255, 271, 301-2, 305
Spiritist (Movement) 122
spiritual
  belief 113
  challenge 253, 255-8
  community 120
  component 121, 131, 152, 172, 182, 276
  concept 197
  dimension 107, 109, 111, 198, 266, 277
  evolution 46, 127, 131, 153
  experience 111, 113, 119, 120, 126-7, 280
  force 55, 57, 62
  growth 201
  guide (ance) xix, 123, 125, 197
  healing 189
  hierarchy 57, 153
  initiation 79
  journey 46, 53, 59
  knowledge xxiii, 68
  mentor 48
  mindset 178
  nature 77, 128

part 98
perspective 28, 138, 153
plane 109, 197, 200, 244
quest 93, 98, 100
realm 90, 102, 108, 122, 125, 128, 131-2, 156, 197-8, 200, 217-8, 221, 281
sage 111
science 127, 156
self xiv, 76, 80, 92, 95, 98, 100
shadow 73
soul 90
spirituality 77, 113, 121, 176, 182
Star Wars 23-4, 30, 294
Stevenson, Robert Louis 45, 46, 296
St. Francis 14, 72, 233
subconscious x, xiv, 4, 15, 36, 70, 84-5, 93, 133, 144
mind 7, 8
sub-personality (s) xix, xx, 8, 9-10, 18-9, 85, 139-40, 142-3, 156-7, 196, 201, 211, 213-6, 225, 228-30, 235-7, 238-9, 240-4, 248, 250, 254, 256, 259, 260, 260-1, 263, 265, 284
suicide 33, 53, 128, 153, 155, 196, 217, 244, 257, 264, 310
Sunni (Islamic Sect) 181, 187
superhero (es) 24-5, 37, 225, 232-4, 239-40, 245, 246-8
Superman 24
Superwoman 24
Syria 70, 181, 285
Szpilman, Wladyslaw 30, 31, 33
Taliban 167, 181
Tao, Te Ching xvi, 12, 292
Taoism xvi
tarot 14-5, 83-5, 89-91, 102, 299
Tefnut (Egyptian goddess) 58, 124
terrorist xviii, 215, 290
Tett, Gillian 169-72, 306
The Avengers 24, 25, 295
The Force 23
The Lord of the Rings 30, 42, 44, 296
The Madonna (Mother Mary) 233
The Pianist 30, 295
Theosophical Society 122, 197, 307-8
Thor (Teutonic god) 63

Tiamat (Assyrian goddess) 66
Tito, Josip 180
Tolkien, JRR 42, 43, 296
Torah (the King's) 177, 304
trance states xix, 21, 55-6, 121
transference 6
trauma (s) xiv, xix, xx, xxii, 7, 9-10, 17-8, 37, 123, 133-6, 138, 139-43, 153-5, 157, 166, 195, 212-4, 216-7, 225-7, 228-31, 238, 240-46, 248, 250, 253-5, 259, 263-5, 271-4, 283, 310
past-life 128, 244
treachery 32, 53, 63, 266
Treblinka 31
triangular relationships 86-7
trinity (s) 25, 41, 86-7, 92, 94, 284
trolls 169
twin(s) 23, 64, 124, 126-7, 132, 138, 164, 195, 216, 234
Twins Studies 126
Typhon (Greek monster) 68
Ukraine 173-4, 305
underworld 68-71, 79, 166, 314
Victorian 45
god of the 68, 70
Vedic tradition 202
Venus planet 61
victim 6, 30, 33, 65, 142, 148, 154, 155, 176, 238, 252, 258-9, 269, 271, 274, 284, 286, 302, 304
Vinci, Leonardo da xiii, 115
Virgil 53
virus xxi, 185
Vishnu (Hindu god) 67
Voldemort 45
Waco Siege 176
Waite
A.E. 84
Rider 14-5, 84
War on Terror 162
Weasley, Ron 45
Wen, (Chinese legendary king) 85
Wife Swap 34, 46, 295
Williams, Robin 257
Williamson, Marianne vi, 6, 249, 293
Winston, Robert ix

worlds, inner xix, 4, 9, 14, 23, 94, 99, 144, 206, 208, 210, 213, 216, 225-6, 236-7, 242, 246, 248, 252, 274
wrath 53
Yahweh (Hebrew god) 62, 65
yang (tao) xvi, 5, 11, 85-88, 282
yin (tao) xvi, 5, 11, 85-88, 282
Young, Thomas double slit experiments 11, 114, 292
Zeus (greek god) 65, 68-9, 72-6, 99
Zinser, Dr Tom vi, 9-10, 70, 123-4, 129, 139, 197, 293, 298, 301, 303, 307-8, 313
zodiac 75, 89, 297
Zonneveld, Ani 187-8, 306
Zoroastrianism 64